THE ABUNDANT LIFE
BIBLE
AMPLIFIER

ROMANS

JOHN C. BRUNT

THE ABUNDANT LIFE
BIBLE
AMPLIFIER

ROMANS

Mercy for All

GEORGE R. KNIGHT
General Editor

Pacific Press Publishing Association
Boise, Idaho
Oshawa, Ontario, Canada

Edited by Kenneth R. Wade
Designed by Tim Larson
Typeset in 11/14 Janson Text

Unless otherwise mentioned, all Bible quotations in this book are from the New International Version, and all emphasis in Bible quotations is supplied by the author.

Library of Congress Cataloging-in-Publication Data:

Brunt, John, 1943—
      Romans / John C. Brunt.
           p.   cm. — (Abundant life Bible amplifier)
      Includes bibliographical references.
      ISBN 0-8163-1296-6 (alk. paper). — ISBN 0-8163-1295-8
(pbk. : alk. paper)
      1. Bible. N.T. Romans—Study and teaching. I. Title.
II. Series.
BS2665.5.B78   1996
227'.107—dc20   95-42653
                                                              CIP

96 97 98 99 00 • 5 4 3 2 1

CONTENTS

DEDICATION

This book is dedicated to those with whom I have taught in the School of Theology at Walla Walla College over the past twenty-four years.
Through conversation they have stimulated my thinking,
Through friendship they have nurtured heart and soul,
Through fellowship they have brought me closer to God.
The following list includes those who have held tenure-track faculty positions in the School between 1971 and 1995.

Gordon Balharrie*
Darold Bigger
Ernest Bursey
Douglas Clark
J. Melvyn Clemons
Jon Dybdahl
Glen Greenwalt
J. Paul Grove
Bruce Johanson
Ron Jolliffe

Lucile Knapp
Sakae Kubo
Henry Lamberton
Larry Lewis
Gordon Mattison
D. Malcom Maxwell
Pedrito Maynard-Reid
Charles Scriven
Alden Thompson
Larry Veverka
Gerald Winslow

*Deceased

GENERAL PREFACE

The Abundant Life Bible Amplifier series is aimed at helping readers understand the Bible better. Rather than merely offering comments on or about the Bible, each volume seeks to enable people to study their Bibles with fuller understanding.

To accomplish that task, scholars who are also proven communicators have been selected to author each volume. The basic idea underlying this combination is that scholarship and the ability to communicate on a popular level are compatible skills.

While the Bible Amplifier is written with the needs and abilities of laypeople in mind, it will also prove helpful to pastors and teachers. Beyond individual readers, the series will be useful in church study groups and as guides to enrich participation in the weekly prayer meeting.

Rather than focusing on the details of each verse, the Bible Amplifier series seeks to give readers an understanding of the themes and patterns of each biblical book as a whole and how each passage fits into that context. As a result, the series does not seek to solve all the problems or answer all the questions that may be related to a given text. In the process of accomplishing the goal for the series, both inductive and explanatory methodologies are used.

Each volume in this series presents its author's understanding of the biblical book being studied. As such, it does not necessarily represent the "official" position of the Seventh-day Adventist Church.

It should be noted that the Bible Amplifier series utilizes the New International Version of the Bible as its basic text. *Every reader should read the "How to Use This Book" section to get the fullest benefit from the Bible Amplifier study volumes.*

Dr. John Brunt is vice-president for academic administration and a professor of biblical studies at Walla Walla College in Washington State. Prior to his present position, Dr. Brunt served as the dean of

the Walla Walla School of Theology and as a pastor in southern
California. He holds a doctorate in New Testament from Emory
University. He has authored *Good News for Troubled Times*, *Now and
Not Yet*, *A Day for Healing*, and *Decisions*. Having taught Romans to
college students for over two decades, Dr. Brunt brings to the writ-
ing of this commentary a wealth of insight into one of the New
Testament's most important books.

George R. Knight
Berrien Springs, Michigan

AUTHOR'S PREFACE

For several years I had the privilege of teaching two classes each year in Romans, one in English for general students and one in Greek for theology students. I have missed that opportunity during the last five years, while my primary work has been administrative. Getting back into Romans for this volume has been invigorating. It is impossible to take up this book without noticing new aspects of Paul's message and asking, "How did I miss that before?" It is also impossible to contemplate Paul's message of good news without being changed by the experience.

My prayer is that through the Spirit your study of Romans will lead you to new insights and to the transforming power of God's good news of grace.

I wish to thank George Knight and Pacific Press for giving me this wonderful opportunity, my Romans students over the years for asking questions that have motivated continuing study, and most of all, my wife, Ione, whose daily love and support nurture my life and my work.

How to Use This Book

The Abundant Life Amplifier series treats each major portion of each Bible book in five main sections.

The first section is called "Getting Into the Word." The purpose of this section is to encourage readers to study their own Bibles. For that reason, the text of the Bible has not been printed in the volumes in this series.

You will get the most out of your study if you work through the exercises in each of the "Getting Into the Word" sections. This will not only aid you in learning more about the Bible but will also increase your skill in using Bible tools and in asking (and answering) meaningful questions about the Bible.

It will be helpful if you write out the answers and keep them in a notebook or file folder for each biblical book. Writing out your thoughts will enhance your understanding. The benefit derived from such study, of course, will be proportionate to the amount of effort expended.

The "Getting Into the Word" sections assume that the reader has certain minimal tools available. Among these are a concordance and a Bible with maps and marginal cross-references. If you don't have a New International Version of the Bible, we recommend that you obtain one for use with this series, since all the Bible Amplifier authors are using the NIV as their basic text. For the same reason, your best choice of a concordance is the *NIV Exhaustive Concordance*, edited by E. W. Goodrick and J. R. Kohlenberger. Strong's *Exhaustive Concordance of the Bible* and Young's *Analytical Concordance to the Bible* are also useful. However, even if all you have is Cruden's *Concordance*, you will be able to do all of the "Getting Into the Word" exercises and most of the "Researching the Word" exercises.

The "Getting Into the Word" sections also assume that the reader has a Bible dictionary. The *Seventh-day Adventist Bible Dictionary* is quite helpful, but those interested in greater depth may want to acquire the four-volume *International Standard Bible Encyclopedia* (1974–1988 edition) or the six-volume *Anchor Bible Dictionary*.

The second section in the treatment of the biblical passages is called "Exploring the Word." The purpose of this section is to discuss the major themes in each biblical book. Thus the comments will typically deal with fairly large portions of Scripture (often an entire chapter) rather than providing a verse-by-verse treatment, such as is found in the *Seventh-day Adventist Bible Commentary*. In fact, many verses and perhaps whole passages in some biblical books may be treated minimally or passed over altogether.

Another thing that should be noted is that the purpose of the "Exploring the Word" sections is not to respond to all the problems or answer all the questions that might arise in each passage. Rather, as stated above, the "Exploring the Word" sections are to develop the Bible writers' major themes. In the process, the author of each volume will bring the best of modern scholarship into the discussion and thus enrich the reader's understanding of the biblical passage at hand. The "Exploring the Word" sections will also develop and provide insight into many of the issues first raised in the "Getting Into the Word" exercises.

The third section in the treatment of the biblical passage is "Applying the Word." This section is aimed at bringing the lessons of each passage into daily life. Once again, you may want to write out a response to these questions and keep them in your notebook or file folder on the biblical book being studied.

The fourth section, "Researching the Word," is for those students who want to delve more deeply into the Bible passage under study or into the history behind it. It is recognized that not everyone will have the research tools for this section. Those expecting to use the research sections should have an exhaustive Bible concordance, the *Seventh-day Adventist Bible Commentary*, a good Bible dictionary, and a Bible atlas. It will also be helpful to have several versions of the Bible.

The final component in each chapter of this book will be a list of recommendations for "Further Study of the Word." While most readers will not have all of these works, many of them may be available in local libraries. Others can be purchased through your local book dealer. It is assumed that many users of this series will already own the seven-volume *Seventh-day Adventist Bible Commentary* and the one-volume *Seventh-day Adventist Bible Dictionary*.

In closing, it should be noted that while a reader will learn much about the Bible from a *reading* of the books in the Bible Amplifier series, he or she will gain infinitely more by *studying* the Bible in connection with that reading.

The Book of Romans

■ Getting Into the Word

Begin by reading the book of Romans through in one sitting, preferably in a modern-speech translation.

If you have a tape library of the New Testament, listen to the letter in one sitting. (Remember that most of the original recipients heard, rather than read, the letter.)

After you have read and heard the letter, write out answers to the following questions.

1. Why do you think Paul wrote this letter? Was there a driving force or purpose behind the letter? What clues do you find in the letter?
2. What are the major themes and terms that you find in the letter?
3. What part of this letter best sums up Paul's overall purpose? Is there any part that could be singled out as the central core? (Suggestions have included chapters 3 to 8, 9 to 11, and 14 and 15.)
4. What do you learn about the church at Rome and about Paul's relationship to the church from this letter?

■ Exploring the Word

No scholar seriously doubts that Paul is the author of the letter to the Romans. Beyond this universal agreement, however, there are few elements about the letter that find such unanimity. Scholars have diverse views on the purpose of the book, its themes, and on the way that the various sections of the book fit together.

We can only answer such questions by reading the letter itself, yet the way we read is influenced by our understanding of these questions! That's why it is important to begin by reading the letter and thinking about some of the questions that are asked above. This exercise will help set the tone for the way we listen to the letter by giving us some overarching perspective. And yet that perspective must always be open to modification as we prayerfully and carefully study each section of the letter with the aid of God's Spirit.

We begin by looking at three questions that have occupied students of this letter. First, what drives this letter? What is Paul's purpose? Is he, for example, writing primarily as a theologian to share his perspective on the gospel or as a pastor to help solve some actual problems in Rome? Second, what is Paul's relationship to the Roman church? What is it that he hopes for this church, and how does the church fit with his plans for ministry? Third, what is the relationship between the different parts of the letter?

Paul's Driving Force and Purpose

Romans is different from most of Paul's letters. Usually Paul writes to a church that he knows well, often one that he has personally founded, in order to address specific problems that have arisen in the church. Sometimes these problems come from within (such as the divisions Paul addresses in 1 Corinthians), and sometimes they come from without (such as the Judaizers who afflicted the churches of Galatia). But Paul had never been to Rome (Rom. 1:13). He was not the founder of this church. So why did he write to them?

One fact is clear. Paul wanted to visit Rome (see 1:11-13 and 15:23, 24) on his way to Spain. Some have concluded from this that Romans is basically an introductory letter to let the church at Rome get to know Paul. They reason that the best way for Paul to get acquainted would be to share his basic theology with the church members. Thus they see Romans as more of a theological treatise introducing Paul's basic thought than as the kind of letter he usually writes.

Others argue that Paul needed the support of the church at Rome if he was to carry out a successful mission to Spain. Paul knew there were problems in the church that needed to be addressed if this church was to be the kind of church that could support his mission to Spain, and more broadly, be the kind of witness that early Christianity needed in the influential city of Rome. It was true; in the first century, all roads really did lead to Rome.

According to the first view, Paul writes primarily as a theologian, and Romans is to be understood as a powerful theological statement. The second view sees Paul as pastor and missionary, concerned about real problems in a church he had never visited but knew enough about to address, even to address "boldly," as he says in 15:15.

Paul and the Romans

What was Paul's relationship to the Roman church? This question is closely related to the last one. Some hold that Paul knew very little about the Roman congregation. They even doubt that Romans 16, which greets a number of people by name, was originally a part of the letter sent to Rome. They think it might have been a separate letter or a conclusion Paul added when he shared his Roman letter with another congregation, such as the one at Ephesus. This goes along with the notion that Romans is a letter of general theology.

Others, however, notice that there is a good bit of specificity in the advice that Paul gives the Romans toward the end of the book, especially in chapters 14 and 15. Paul is also quite specific about his travel plans in the fifteenth chapter. Paul must have had a purpose for this specificity. This might support the idea that Paul had an agenda that grew out of his knowledge of both the people and the situation at Rome.

Could Paul, however, have known so many people in the church at Rome, which, by his own admission, he had never visited? This is not at all unreasonable to assume. As we have said, all roads really did lead to Rome in the first century. Paul's own travels show how mobile people were at that time. People Paul had met in other places could easily have moved to Rome, and in Paul's travels he probably came across Roman Christians as well.

In fact, there is historical evidence that would make this even more probable. The Roman historian Suetonius (c. A.D. 100) tells us that around the year 49 Emperor Claudius expelled Jews from Rome. He says, "Because the Jews at Rome caused continuous disturbances at the instigation of Chrestus, he expelled them from the City" (*The Twelve Caesars*, "Claudius" 25). Chrestus is the Roman spelling for Christ, and this statement may well mean that the disturbances were between Christian Jews and opposing non-Christian Jews. If so, Jewish Christians in Rome may have had to flee to other parts of the empire, where Paul could have met them.

This would fit with what we find in Acts 18:2, 3, where Luke tells us that when Paul met Aquila and Priscilla in Corinth, they had recently come from Italy, because Claudius had commanded all Jews to leave Rome. Since Romans was written after Nero took the throne in 54 and allowed Jews to return, the presence of these two fellow tentmakers in Rome, according to Romans 16:3, would make sense. This return of Jews to Rome might also explain some of the tensions in the Roman church (or churches) when Paul wrote. First, Jewish Christians left, leaving the church entirely in the hands of Gentile Christians. Several years later, when these Jewish Christians, who probably founded the church, returned, the two groups might not have seen eye to eye on everything.

Thus it is quite possible that Paul would have known Christians who now lived at Rome and would have kept in touch with them. Just because Paul is writing to a church he had not visited doesn't mean he was writing blindly to a church he did not know. This brings us to the third question about the various parts of Romans.

The Different Sections of the Roman Letter

I once took a class in Romans that was one of my all-time favorite classes. Indeed, it was a life-changing experience. But the class only got as far as Romans 8. The teacher suggested that we had finished the meat of Romans and that we could read the appendices that followed on our own. But the letter doesn't end with chapter 8. That is only the halfway mark! Should we really view half of this letter as appendices that aren't part of the main argument?

It is true that the heaviest theological exposition is in chapters 1 to 8. It is also true that this section seems to stand alone with its own conceptual coherence. It is here that we find Paul's most extensive exposition of salvation by God's grace. These facts have led theologians not only to concentrate on that section but also to see it as the most important section of the letter. But there is good evidence that this initial section prepares the way for the practical, pastoral advice that follows.

For example, in Romans 14 and 15 Paul addresses a problem between weak and strong Christians. The weak are more strict in observing certain days and eating only vegetables, whereas the strong have less strict practices on these matters (14:2, 5). (We will explore the nature of this debate when we study these chapters.) But already in chapter 4, Paul begins using the language of weak and strong when he speaks of Abraham, who was not "weak in faith" (4:19).

Another example is seen in the latter chapters of Romans (14:1–15:14), where Paul emphasizes not judging other Christians. Paul had already introduced the subject of judging in chapter 2 (vss. 1-3). In fact, this is an important part of Paul's argument in the first section of the letter.

As we work our way through the letter, we will find many more links between the various sections of Romans. These links are sufficiently numerous to suggest that the various parts form a coherent whole. In other words, the main argument doesn't end in chapter 8!

How might this work? Maybe we can understand it best by working backward. In Romans 14 and 15, Paul speaks to the lack of unity in the Roman church and tries to bring them together into unity in

Christ in preparation for his visit to them and his hoped-for participation with them in ministry to new worlds such as Spain.

Probably at least part of this disunity involved suspicions and debates between Jew and Gentile. Therefore, it was important for Paul
to discuss God's purpose for both within His plan of salvation. Romans 9 to 11 does just that. Here Paul shows that God's ultimate
purpose is to save both Jew and Gentile. He also advises each as to
how they should treat each other. This helps prepare the way for
Paul's final advice about unity.

Paul knew, however, that the only real basis for unity in Christ is
the realization that we are all sinners and that we all share the same
basis for the hope of salvation—the grace revealed in Jesus Christ.
Therefore, he spent the first eight chapters laying the vital foundation of salvation in Christ.

This view holds that the whole letter of Romans forms a coherent
argument. The letter is not a theological treatise with some attached
appendices of generalized advice, as some hold. Nor is it three separate sections, virtually independent of each other, as others suggest.
Rather, it is a truly pastoral letter written to speak to the actual circumstances of the church at Rome.

At the same time, the letter certainly is theological. Paul was the
kind of pastor who believed that good theology is relevant to how
we live. The theological and the practical went together for him.
Many pastors today have forgotten this.

Recently I heard a pastor tell a group of students studying for
ministry that once they got out of school, they wouldn't spend time
reading and thinking about theology anymore, because they would
be occupied fully with practical matters and would devote all their
time to these everyday concerns.

The driving force behind Paul's letter to the Romans was practical and pastoral. But Paul, unlike many pastors today, knew that good
theology is necessary for good practice. So he begins by laying the
foundation in the first eight chapters. Here he shows that we are all
saved only by faith in God's gracious action on our behalf. That
includes both Jew and Gentile.

Next, Paul goes on to elaborate on God's saving purpose for both

Jew and Gentile in chapters 9 to 11. In chapter 12 he begins show-ing how we should respond to what God has done for us. God's free gift of salvation for all makes us debtors, not only to God, but to each other. Finally, in chapters 14 and the first part of 15, Paul ap-plies all this to the specific problems facing the Roman church. Then he goes on to share his plans with them and to greet as many as he possibly can in the final chapter.

Take some time to look over the outline that follows this intro-duction, and then read or listen to the whole letter once more. See if you can't see this line running through the letter from beginning to end.

At this point, we should take a brief overview of some of the most important themes that emerge from our reading of Romans.

Major Themes in Romans

Unity in Christ and salvation for all

One of the most important theological terms in Romans is the simple term *all*. With this term, Paul obliterates the distinctions that build barriers between human beings and keep them from enjoying unity in Christ. With this term, Paul puts all Christians in the same boat. *All* have sinned (3:23). *All* will stand before the judgment of Christ (14:10). *All* human beings stand under the wrath of sin with no claim to salvation and nothing they could ever do to save them-selves. Paul makes this universal condition of sin absolutely clear in the first three chapters of the letter.

But he does this only to pave the way for what follows. The universal need of humans leads to God's universal solution. Through Jesus Christ, God provides for the salvation of *all*. The good news of the gospel is the power for salvation to *all* who believe (1:16). God gave Jesus up for us *all* (8:32). Abraham is the father of *all* (4:11). God's goal is to have mercy on *all* (11:32). It doesn't matter whether a person is Jew or Gentile, God's saving action is for *all*. This theme accounts for Paul's emphasis on Jew and Gentile throughout the letter.

Yet for Paul the pastor, this message is hardly an abstract, theo-retical matter. It has all kinds of implications for life. If we are all in the same boat, sinners saved by God's grace, then we ought to be able to live in unity. So Paul advises that Christians, who have heard this universal message, should live at peace with *all* (12:18). They should be able to welcome each other (15:1).

This theme provides the basis for much practical advice in Romans, such as the counsel that Gentile Christians should not get bigheaded and think themselves superior to Jewish Christians (11:17-34); that the strict should not judge those who are more free, and vice versa; that those who are more free should not scorn the strict (14:1-5).

Thus we see that with this theme, as with so many others that he emphasizes, theological conviction and pastoral concern go hand in hand for Paul. The universality of God's provision for salvation calls us to recognize and act on our unity with all other Christians.

When you read Romans through again, notice how often this word *all* occurs, weaving a thread throughout the entire letter, binding the various parts together into a beautiful pattern of Christian unity.

The free gift of grace

This theme is closely connected with the former. The universal provision for salvation comes to humans through God's initiative of grace. Paul uses the term *grace* twenty-two times in this letter. It refers to God's free acceptance of human beings apart from any human achievement.

Paul proclaims that God's grace is a gift (3:24) that brings believers justification or righteousness (5:16) and eternal life (5:21). Although it rules out all works or achievements as the basis for human salvation (11:6), it is not a license for irresponsible action (6:1, 15). It becomes the atmosphere in which Christians now stand (5:2) that allows them to live in peace with God and to have hope. No other term does a better job of capturing Paul's core conviction that Christians' only hope and grounds for salvation is God's loving initiative to save them apart from any achievement of their own.

The obedience of faith

For Paul, the appropriate human response to God's initiative of grace is faith. Although the verbal form of this term Paul uses is often translated "believe," the term is much richer than that. Faith is a trusting commitment to God, a willingness to take Him at His word and trust Him for salvation.

Paul brackets the entire message of Romans with the interesting phrase "the obedience of faith." Right at the beginning, in 1:5, Paul says that through Jesus Christ he has received grace and apostleship to bring about the "obedience of faith" among all the Gentiles (or nations). He uses the phrase again at the end of the letter in the final benediction at 16:26. There he speaks of a mystery that was hidden but now has been made known, i.e., that all the nations or Gentiles should be brought to the obedience of faith.

By juxtaposing these two terms, Paul is identifying them. The obedience that God wants is precisely faith. This obedience is not merely adherence to a set of rules. It is the total, personal commitment to God. The obedience God is looking for is faith. Paul feels so strongly about this that he dares to assert that whatever does not spring from faith, this total, trusting commitment to God, is sin (14:23). It is the only appropriate human attitude, and it is this attitude of faith that motivates responsible human action. This faith excludes all human boasting and pride (3:27). It leads Christians to lives of appreciative, appropriate service to God (12:3).

Righteousness in Christ

When Paul sets forth the thesis of his letter in 1:16, 17, he quotes from Habakkuk 2:4 to introduce one of the most important analogies for salvation in Romans. When he says that the *righteous* will live by faith, Paul is using language of the lawcourt. The terms translated "just," "justification," "justify," "righteous," and "righteousness" all come from the same root in Greek and have the scene of a judge in their background. Yet this background can be misleading, since the judge played a very different role in Paul's day than today, as we shall see in more detail in a subsequent chapter. We think of judges as detached, objective deliberators who pass judgment. But in the first century, the judge was one who became actively involved in working for the vindication of the oppressed. So to be righteous before God is not merely to be acquitted or declared not guilty; it is to be vindicated and set free.

According to Paul, we are vindicated by our trust in God's grace, and therefore we enter into a new relationship with God. This new relationship changes our status, our outlook, and our direction. This is the experience of "righteousness." It is by faith from beginning to end (1:17).

In association with this theme, Paul addresses the issue of law in Romans. This emphasis comes to a head in chapter 7, where Paul shows that the law is holy, just, and good, even though it is powerless to save (7:11, 12). It cannot provide righteousness, but that doesn't mean it is dispensable.

Paul's use of Scripture

This is not so much a theme as it is a part of Paul's method in writing this letter, but it is a method with great theological significance. Unless the reader makes continual reference to marginal notes (or has virtually memorized the Old Testament), it is easy to miss the fact that Paul is constantly quoting from the Old Testament. (The Old Testament, of course, was his Scripture. When Paul wrote Romans, the Gospels and most of the other New Testament works had not yet been written.)

Paul's use of the Old Testament is neither an accident nor a rhetorical device. He firmly believed that Christ was the fulfillment of the law and the prophets. The Scripture played an important part in an understanding of the gospel (see Romans 1:2, 3:21, and 10:4, for example).

Paul especially goes to the Old Testament when he presents a point of view that might seem controversial to his Jewish readers. Over and over again, he shows that the Old Testament, if correctly understood, supports his message. It might seem strange that the Old Testament would permeate this letter so strongly when the majority of Paul's original readers were probably Gentile Christians. But Paul apparently believed that it was important that they also have a firm grounding in Scripture as a foundation for the gospel.

There are many other themes in Romans on which we could elaborate here, but it is time to get on with studying the letter itself to see how these themes play themselves out in the rich fabric of Paul's message. Following is an outline of the letter that we will follow throughout the exposition.

Outline of Romans

I. The Gospel Introduced (1:1-16)
   A. Letter Opening—the Obedience of Faith (1:1-7)
   B. Thanksgiving (1:8-15)
   C. The Revelation of Righteousness Through the Gospel (1:16, 17)
II. God's Wrath Revealed in Universal Human Sin (1:17–3:20)
   A. God's Wrath Revealed in the Idolatry and Immorality of the Nations (1:18-32)
   B. God's Wrath Revealed in the Judging and Disobedience of the Circumcised (2:1-29)
   C. The Universality of Sin (3:1-20)
III. God's Righteousness Revealed in Salvation by Grace Through Faith for All (3:21–8:39)
   A. God's Free Gift for All (3:21-31)
   B. Abraham as a Model of Salvation by Grace Through Faith for All (4:1-25)
   C. Death for All in Adam and Life for All in Christ (5:1-21)
   D. The Free Gift Is Not a License for Sin (6:1-23)
   E. The Role of Law—Holy and Good, but Powerless to Save (7:1-25)
   F. The Role of the Spirit (8:1-39)
IV. God's Continuing Purpose for the Jews (9:1–11:36)
   A. Paul's Concern for His People (9:1-5)
   B. Examples Showing That God's Promise Has Not Failed (9:6-32)
   C. Why Israel Failed (10:1-21)
   D. God Has Not Rejected His People (11:1-10)
   E. God's Surprising Plan to Save All (11:11-36)
V. The Christian Life of Love and Unity (12:1–15:13)
   A. Love in the Community (12:1-21)
   B. Christian Responsibility to the Authorities (13:1-7)
   C. The Law Fulfilled in Love (13:8-14)
   D. Unity When Christians Don't Agree—the Weak and Strong (14:1–15:13)

VI. Conclusion (15:14–16:27)
   A. Paul's Plans for Ministry (15:14-33)
   B. Personal Greetings (16:1-23)
   C. Concluding Doxology—the Obedience of Faith (16:25-27)

Time and Place of Writing

In the course of what we call his third missionary journey, Paul decided that when he left Ephesus he would go to Macedonia, then on to Achaia (Greece), on to Jerusalem, and finally on to Rome (Acts 19:21). In Acts 20:1-3 we read that he went to Macedonia and then spent three months in Greece.

According to Romans 15:25, 26, Paul had been to Macedonia and Achaia by the time he wrote to the Romans. Believers in both places had made contributions, and now he planned on leaving for Jerusalem and then going to Rome (15:23, 24). When we put these plans together with Acts, it seems logical that Paul was in Greece on his third missionary journey when he wrote Romans. The presence of several names in Romans 16 that are associated with Corinth or its suburb Cenchrea suggest Paul was probably there. Though scholars do not agree on the precise dating, most would place this letter in the late 50s of the Christian era.

We do not know when or how Christianity first arrived in Rome, although the reference in Suetonius suggests that it was before A.D. 49. Perhaps Jews who traveled to Jerusalem for feasts brought back news about Christ's life and message. Chapter 16 shows us that the church in Rome still met in homes in Paul's day (16:5).

■ Applying the Word

1. If Paul were to address my church, what specific problems would he tackle?
2. Are the major themes outlined above relevant to the spiritual situation I find myself in today? Which one is most relevant? How does it apply to my life?
3. If I were to write a short letter to my local church that I

think would convey the basic message of Romans in a way applicable to my church's circumstances, what would I say? (Write out a response.)

■ Further Study of the Word

1. For a technical commentary on Romans that includes details on the history of interpretation, see E. Kasemann's *Commentary on Romans*.
2. For a commentary that focuses on the theological and practical message of Romans in a thorough but readable way, see P. Achtemeier's *Romans*.
3. Two works that are lay-oriented, easy to read, and helpful are B. H. Throckmorton, *Adopted in Love*, and C. K. Barrett, *Reading Through Romans*.
4. A recent commentary that is both thorough and easy reading for a layperson has been published in the New International Biblical Commentary series by J. R. Edwards, *Romans*.
5. A useful German commentary that stresses the Old Testament and postbiblical Jewish traditions as the primary backdrop to Paul's thought has recently been translated into English. It is P. Stuhlmacher's, *Paul's Letter to the Romans: A Commentary*.
6. The most thorough recent scholarly American commentary is J. D. G. Dunn, *Romans 1–8* and *Romans 9–16*.
7. For a collection of essays on various issues relating to the purpose and background of Romans, see K. P. Donfried, ed., *The Romans Debate*, revised and expanded edition.

LIST OF WORKS CITED*

Achtemeier, Paul. *Romans.* Interpretation Commentaries. Atlanta: John Knox, 1985.

Barrett, C. K. *The Epistle of Paul to the Romans.* Harper's New Testament Commentaries. New York: Harper and Row, 1957.

_____. *The New Testament Background: Selected Documents.* New York: Harper and Row, 1961.

_____. *Reading Through Romans.* Philadelphia: Fortress Press, 1977.

Barth, Karl. *A Shorter Commentary on Romans.* London: S. C. M. Press, 1959.

_____. *The Teaching of the Church Regarding Baptism.* London: S. C. M. Press, 1948.

Beasley-Murray, G. R. *Baptism in the New Testament.* Grand Rapids, Mich.: Eerdmans, 1962.

Beker, J. Christiaan. *Paul's Apocalyptic Gospel: The Coming Triumph of God.* Philadelphia: Fortress Press, 1982.

Best, Ernest. *The Letter of Paul to the Romans.* Cambridge Bible Commentaries. Cambridge: University Press, 1967.

Borg, M. "A New Context for Romans 13." *New Testament Studies* 19 (1972): 205-218.

Brunt, John. *Now and Not Yet.* Hagerstown, Md.: Review and Herald, 1987.

_____. "Unclean or Unhealthful: An Adventist Perspective." *Spectrum* 11:3 (1980): 17-23.

Campbell, Douglas A. "Romans 1:17—A *Crux Interpretum* for the *Pistou Christou* Debate." *Journal of Biblical Literature* 113:2 (1994): 265-285.

Cervin, Richard S. "A Note Regarding the Name 'Junia(s)' in Ro-

---

*This list does not include classical works that utilize standard referencing systems across various editions.

mans 16:7." *New Testament Studies* 40 (July 1994): 464-470.

Clarke, A. D. "The Good and the Just in Romans 5:7." *Tyndale Bulletin* 41 (Jan. 1990): 128-142.

Cullmann, Oscar. *The State in the New Testament*. New York: Scribner's, 1956.

Dahl, Nils A. *Studies in Paul*. Minneapolis: Augsburg Press, 1977.

Davies, W. D. *Paul and Rabbinic Judaism: Some Rabbinic Elements in Pauline Theology*. London: S. P. C. K., 1962.

Derrett, J. Duncan M. "You Abominate False Gods; but Do You Rob Shrines?" *New Testament Studies* 40 (Oct. 1994): 558-571.

Dodd, C. H. *The Epistle of Paul to the Romans*. New Haven: Yale University Press, 1989.

Donfried, Karl P., ed. *The Romans Debate*. Revised and expanded edition. Peabody, Mass.: Hendrickson, 1991.

Dunn, James D. G. *Romans 1–8*. Waco: Word, 1988.

_____. *Romans 9–16*. Waco: Word, 1989.

Dybdahl, Jon L. *Exodus: God Creates a People*. Abundant Life Bible Amplifier. Boise, Idaho: Pacific Press Publishing Association, 1994.

Edwards, James R. *Romans*. New International Biblical Commentaries. Peabody, Mass.: Hendrickson, 1992.

Enslin, Morton Scott. *The Ethics of Paul*. Nashville: Abingdon Press, 1968.

Fee, Gordon D. *God's Empowering Presence: The Holy Spirit in the Letters of Paul*. Peabody, Mass.: Hendrickson, 1994.

Fitzmeyer, J. A. "The Consecutive Meaning of *eph' ho* in Romans 5:12." *New Testament Studies* 39 (Mar. 1993): 321-339.

Furnish, Victor Paul. *Theology and Ethics in Paul*. Nashville: Abingdon Press, 1968.

Greene, M. D. "A Note on Romans 8:3." *Biblische Zeitschrift* 35 (1991): 103-106.

Hanson, Anthony T. *Studies in Paul's Technique and Theology*. Grand Rapids, Mich.: Eerdmans, 1974.

Harrisville, Roy A. III. *The Figure of Abraham in the Epistles of St. Paul: In the Footsteps of Abraham*. Lewiston, N.Y.: Edwin Mellen Press, 1992.

Hasel, Gerhard. *The Remnant: The History and Theology of the Remnant Idea From Genesis to Isaiah*. Berrien Springs, Mich.: Andrews University Press, 1974.

Hays, Richard B. *Echoes of Scripture in the Letters of Paul*. New Haven, Conn.: Yale University Press, 1989.

_____. *The Faith of Jesus Christ: An Investigation of the Narrative Substructure of Galatians 3:1–4:11*. Society of Biblical Literature Dissertation Series. Chico, Calif.: Scholars Press, 1983.

Hills, J. V. "Christ Was the Goal of the Law." *Journal of Theological Studies* 44 (1993): 585-592.

Horn, Siegfried H., et. al. *Seventh-day Adventist Bible Dictionary*. Rev. ed, Edited by Raymond H. Woolsey. Hagerstown, Md.: Review and Herald, 1979.

Huggins, R. V. "Alleged Classical Parallels to Paul's 'What I Want to Do I Do Not Do, but What I Hate, That I Do. *Westminster Theological Journal* 54 (1992): 153-161.

Hvalik, R. "A *Sonderweg* for Israel: A Critical Examination of a Current Interpretation of Romans 11:25-27." *Journal for the Study of the New Testament* 38 (1990): 87-107.

Johnsson, William G. *Clean: The Meaning of Christian Baptism*. Nashville: Southern Publishing Association, 1980.

Kasemann, Ernst. *Commentary on Romans*. Translated and edited by Geoffrey Bromiley. Grand Rapids, Mich.: Eerdmans, 1980.

_____. *New Testament Questions of Today*. Philadelphia: Fortress Press, 1969.

Kaylor, R. David. *Paul's Covenant Community: Jew and Gentile in Romans*. Atlanta: John Knox Press, 1988.

Keck, Leander E. *Paul and His Letters*. Proclamation Commentaries. Philadelphia: Fortress Press, 1979.

Koester, Helmut. *Introduction to the New Testament. Vol. 1: History, Culture, and Religion of the Hellenistic Age*. Hermeneia: Foundations and Facets. Philadelphia: Fortress Press, 1982.

Linss, W. C. "Exegesis of *telos* in Romans 10:4." *Biblical Research* 33 (1988): 5-12.

Longenecker, Bruce W. "*PISTIS* in Romans 3:25: Neglected Evidence for the Faithfulness of Christ." *New Testament Studies* 39

(July 1993): 478-480.

Malherbe, Abraham J. *Moral Exhortation: A Greco-Roman Sourcebook.* Library of Early Christianity. Philadelphia: Westminster Press, 1983.

_____. *Paul and the Popular Philosophers.* Minneapolis: Fortress Press, 1989.

Martens, John W. "Romans 2:14-16: A Stoic Reading." *New Testament Studies* 40 (Jan. 1994): 55-67.

Martin, B. L. "Some Reflections on the Identity of *ego* in Romans 7:14-25." *Scottish Journal of Theology* 34 (1981): 39-47.

Osborne, W. L. "The Old Testament Background of Paul's 'All Israel' in Romans 11:26a." *Asia Journal of Theology* 2 (Feb. 1988): 282-293.

Peterson, D. "Worship and Ethics in Romans 12." *Tyndale Bulletin* 44 (Feb. 1993): 271-288.

Rauer, Max. *Die "Schwachen" in Korinth und Rom nach dem Paulusbriefen. Biblische Studien.* Freiburg: Herder, 1923.

Richardson, Peter. *Paul's Ethic of Freedom.* Philadelphia: Westminster Press, 1979.

Smiga, G. "Romans 12:1-2 and 15:30-32 and the Occasion of the Letter to the Romans." *Catholic Biblical Quarterly* 53 (Feb. 1991): 257-273.

Sanders, E. P. *Paul and Palestinian Judaism.* Minneapolis: Fortress Press, 1977.

Stein, Robert H. "The Argument of Romans 13:1-7." *Novum Testamentum* 31 (1989): 325-343.

Stendahl, Krister. *Paul Among Jews and Gentiles.* Philadelphia: Fortress Press, 1976.

Stowers, Stanley Kent. *The Diatribe and Paul's Letter to the Romans.* Chico, Calif.: Scholars Press, 1981.

Stuhlmacher, Peter. *Paul's Letter to the Romans: A Commentary.* Translated by Scott J. Hafemann. Louisville, Ky.: Westminster/John Knox, 1994.

Throckmorton, Burton H. *Adopted in Love.* New York: Seabury Press, 1978.

Trobisch, David. *Paul's Letter Collection: Tracing the Origins.* Minneapolis: Fortress Press, 1994.

Weiss, Herold. *Paul of Tarsus: His Gospel and Life*. Berrien Springs, Mich.: Andrews University Press, 1986.

White, Ellen G. *The Acts of the Apostles*. Boise, Idaho: Pacific Press, 1911.

PART ONE

Romans 1:1-17

The Gospel Introduced

CHAPTER ONE

Good News

Romans 1:1-17

In this chapter we see Paul begin his letter and introduce his message. We don't have to get very far into the letter to discover that the gospel, the good news of salvation through Jesus Christ, will take center stage. This beginning section of the letter not only introduces the gospel but also describes it and sets it forward as the power of God for salvation.

This beginning section of the letter will also let us see how Paul both uses and changes the standard forms and conventions of letter writing in his day to communicate his message.

■ Getting Into the Word

Romans 1:1-17

Read these verses carefully in at least two different versions of the Bible, and write out answers to the following questions.

1. How does the material in these verses anticipate the topics and themes that will follow in the rest of the letter?
2. What elements do you find in these verses that make Paul's writing sound like an actual letter? How is his letter writing the same and different from our own?
3. How would you evaluate Paul's attitude to the Roman congregation in these verses? How would you feel toward him if you were a member of the Roman church who did not

know him and were getting to know him by listening to this letter?

4. Make a list of everything Paul says about the gospel in these verses. From this list, write a one- or two-sentence definition of what the gospel is.

5. Use your Bible's marginal references to discover the Old Testament passage Paul quotes in verse 17. How does the Old Testament text use these words, and why do you think they are so important to Paul?

6. Why is the gospel first for the Jew, and then for the Gentile? What do you learn from these verses about Paul's understanding of Jew and Gentile?

■ Exploring the Word

Beginning the Letter

Letter writing was a common activity in the first century. There were different kinds of letters. At one end of the spectrum, philosophers wrote letter essays that took the form of a letter but were really intended for publication to a wide, general audience. At the other end were personal letters. These were usually short, often one page of papyrus, since street-corner scribes charged by the page. Also, since there was no public mail service and the letter would be carried by a friend or messenger, much of the information could be filled in by the person who carried the letter.

As is the case in most cultures, including ours, letters contained conventions that were standard and were given little thought. For example, we begin letters with "Dear" even when writing to strangers who are not dear to us at all. And where else other than in letter writing do we end conversations by saying "sincerely"? In most personal letters in Paul's day, letters began with the name of the writer of the letter, then the word *to*, followed by the name of the recipient, and then the word *greetings*. Thus if I were to write a letter to my son, I would begin, "John, to Larry, greetings." After this, the writer usually gave thanks to the gods for the recipient and wished him or her good health.

Paul appears to be sufficiently unconventional that he utilizes but modifies and adapts these standard conventions. He begins with his own name, but he even expands this usually simple beginning by emphasizing his role and authority. Paul's letter is not an open letter-essay; it is for a specific group of people. But neither is it a simple personal letter. It is much longer, and Paul writes with a sense of authority. Even though he certainly didn't know that he was writing what would eventually become part of the New Testament, he did write with a clear sense of apostolic authority as one who spoke for God (1:1).

He begins with the simple designation "servant of Christ Jesus." This is not typical for Paul. He uses it in the opening of letters elsewhere only in Philippians and Titus. After calling himself a servant of Jesus Christ, Paul goes on to point out that he was called to be an apostle, set apart for the gospel. Only in 1 and 2 Thessalonians and in Philippians does Paul fail to mention his apostleship at the beginning of his letters. This is Paul's source of authority and the reason that he can be bold enough to write to churches, teaching them and giving them direction.

In Acts 2:21, 22 we discover that apostles were those who had seen the risen Lord and been commissioned to witness for Him. Paul, of course, was not yet a follower of Jesus during those forty days when Jesus appeared to and commissioned the apostles. But in 1 Corinthians 9:1-2 and 15:8 Paul presents the basis for his apostleship. He had seen the Lord. Even though the timing was different from the other apostles, his encounter with Jesus on the road to Damascus was just as real as theirs. Paul's experience on that road was not merely a conversion; it was a commissioning. The risen Christ met him and called him to be an apostle, specifically, an apostle to the Gentiles (Rom. 1:5; Gal. 2:8). Paul's letters, including Romans, were a part of that apostolic ministry and were written with a sense of apostolic authority. Therefore, Paul begins by reminding the Romans that he was called to be an apostle.

Normally we would expect the name of the recipient at this point and then the word *greetings*. But Paul's mention of the word *gospel* sets him off on what appears to be a digression, but is actually part of the way he goes about introducing his important topic. It is as if he can't even wait to get through the "Dear ____" at the beginning of the letter before he gets into his message! We will come back to the content of this apparent digression later, but for now, skip down to verse 7, where Paul continues with the standard letter convention and tells us to whom he is writing: "To all in Rome who are loved by God and called to be saints."

For Paul, the term *saint* had none of the stained-glass window connotations that it has for us. A saint was not some ancient, larger-than-life, perfect Christian, but anyone called and set apart by God who became part of the community of faith. He uses the term frequently, even when he is speaking to Christians like those in Corinth who demonstrated some serious problems. Paul sees the Christian community in Rome as those God both loves and sets apart. And he makes it clear right at the beginning that this includes "all" the Christians in Rome.

Finally, in the latter half of verse 7, Paul comes to the point where he would be expected to say "greetings." But he doesn't. In all of Paul's letters, he adapts the standard convention for his theological purpose. Instead of saying "greetings," he says, "Grace to you and peace from God our Father and from the Lord Jesus Christ." The terms *greetings* and *grace* sound very much alike in Greek. Paul only has to alter a couple letters to substitute his most important theological term for the standard greeting, and this is what he consistently does. To this he adds the standard Hebrew greeting, "peace," translated into Greek. When we study Romans 3, we will see how important the term *grace* is for Paul and why he uses it for his standard greeting.

Next, Paul moves to the typical thanksgiving section of the letter, but as we would expect by now, he expands and modifies it. Paul is grateful to the church at Rome because of its faith and the witness that their faith gives all over the world. He remembers them in prayer and wants to come and see them (1:8-10). Paul will give more detail to this desire later in Romans 15.

As Paul briefly expresses his plans here, however, we gain insight into his sense of diplomacy. We can almost see Paul's mind working as he dictates this letter to his scribe Tertius (see 16:22). First, he says that he wants to see the Romans so that he may impart some spiritual gift to them to make them strong (1:11). Then he interrupts the flow of the sentence to correct himself. His visit with the Romans will be for mutual encouragement! He will benefit from them too. But it is clear, nevertheless, that Paul's goal is to have harvest among them as he has had among the other Gentiles (verse 13).

Now that we have seen how Paul begins his letter by using and modifying the standard forms that made up the typical letter, we turn to the most important content of these verses, Paul's teaching about the gospel, or good news.

The Good News

Already in verse 2 Paul introduced the term *gospel*. In verse 16 he repeats it again in a statement that serves as the thesis statement of this letter. This is such an important concept for Paul that we need to examine carefully what he says about it, both in the thesis statement and in his earlier apparent digression.

The term *gospel* originally could mean the messenger who carried good news or the good news itself. In Paul's day the term was used for official pronouncements declaring such events as the birthday of the emperor or an imperial victory. But Paul's good news is much more profound and all-encompassing. Notice what we learn about the good news from these few verses.

The roots of the gospel

In verse 2 Paul shows that this good news is not an innovation that he or other Christians made up. It had a history. It had already been promised through Israel's prophets in the Holy Scriptures, which for Paul was what we call the Old Testament. (Remember that the Gospels and most of the rest of what we call the New Testament had not yet been written when Paul penned this letter.)

Paul teaches that there is a definite continuity between Israel and its Scripture on the one hand and the Christian gospel on the other.

In the second century, a church leader in Rome (Marcion), whom the church eventually rejected as a heretic, taught that the Old Testament God was a different God from the God of Jesus. The former was a God of judgment, while the latter is a God of mercy. But such a teaching could never come from Paul. The Old Testament for him was the book of promise. God had already revealed the gospel there through promise. The gospel had roots. In accepting the gospel, Paul never believed that he was rejecting Judaism. Rather, he was being faithful to true Judaism. Jesus was the fulfillment of all that God had revealed in the Hebrew Scriptures.

The content of the gospel

The center of the gospel is Jesus Christ. It is the "gospel of God . . . regarding his Son" (vss. 2, 3). Here at the beginning of the letter Paul affirms that in human terms Jesus was the descendant of David. But He was much more than that. He was not only Son of David but was also Son of God. This divine power was particularly demonstrated in His resurrection from the dead. Compare this with the central role Paul gives the resurrection in 1 Corinthians 15. It is the sign of Jesus Christ's authority as our Lord and role as our Saviour. Without the cross and resurrection of Jesus Christ, there would be no good news.

Gordon Fee (see the "Further Study" section at the end of the chapter) has shown how Paul carefully structures what he says about Christ in these opening verses (1:3, 4). Paul uses parallelism in a chiastic way. (The term *chiasm* refers to a structure that goes A, B, C, C, B, A.) Fee (p. 480) translates verses 3 and 4 in the following way to demonstrate the structure of the original:

A. Concerning *his* Son,
   B. *who* came
      C. from the seed of David
         D. according to the flesh
   B. *who* was declared Son of God with power
         D. according to the Spirit of holiness
      C. from the resurrection of the dead
A. Jesus Christ *our* Lord.

The movement in this statement goes from Christ as God's Son, through the incarnation and resurrection, to Christ as our Lord. We see here that Jesus Christ is both the bearer of good news and the content of the good news. The gospel is the good news of God's Son, Jesus Christ.

The appropriate response to the gospel

The only fitting response to the good news that Jesus Christ is our Lord and Saviour is trust. The same root stands behind the noun *faith* and the verb *to believe*. But *faith* so often connotes a set or system of beliefs (as when we say "the faith"), and *believe* has so much sense of mental assent to it that both can be misleading. As we shall see later, Paul uses the term to refer to a deep, personal commitment of trust and dependence upon God's grace revealed in Jesus Christ.

This commitment of trust and dependence is the obedience that God demands. Therefore, as we saw in the introductory chapter, Paul brackets the entire letter of Romans with the phrase "the obedience of faith" (1:5; 16:26). We could translate this phrase "the obedience that is faith." The gospel demands a response, and that response is faith.

In verse 17 Paul quotes a verse from one of the most interesting of Israel's minor prophets, Habakkuk. This prophet was willing to come to God and complain because the land was full of violence, evil, and injustice. God told him that there was a plan. Babylon would come and serve as the agent of punishment by taking Judah into captivity. But that answer was no help for Habakkuk! Babylon was even worse than Judah. Yet in spite of Habakkuk's complaints and incredulity, he expressed his trust in God. Paul takes one of these expressions of trust, found in Habakkuk 2:4, as his text to confirm that the righteous find life by their trust in God. Paul draws from this that true righteousness is a matter of faith from beginning to end.

We could easily spend several chapters on this rich thesis statement found in verses 16 and 17, but these terms and concepts will find greater explication throughout the letter, and we should be patient. Therefore, we will wait until we study Romans 3 to investigate the meaning of the term *righteousness* that Paul uses here. Suffice it to say that although it has a legal background, it is a much broader term than analogy with our current legal system might suggest.

The result of the gospel

For those who respond with trust, i.e., those who believe, the gospel is the power of God for salvation (1:16). The gospel has the power to transform (compare 12:2).

Christians are constantly tempted to rely on something besides Christ for salvation: their own achievements, the ritual and forms of religion, knowledge, power, or a host of other idols. Preachers of salvation are tempted, too, to rely on their own oratory or even their ability to denounce evil and call sin by its right name. But there is only one reality that has the power for salvation: the gospel.

That is because it is God's gospel. In the life, death, and resurrection of Jesus Christ, God's gracious desire to save is effected and demonstrated. This good news is the only power that can ever bring salvation.

The scope of the gospel

Paul leaves no doubt on this subject. The gospel is the power of God for the salvation of *everyone* who believes (1:16). No one is left outside the good news. The gospel is for everyone, the Jew first and then the Gentile.

In the next chapter, we will see that this priority of the Jew is not a matter of discrimination or favoritism. God doesn't show any partiality. It is simply a matter of fact that the good news was first given to the Jews. But this privilege was also a responsibility. Therefore, judgment will come to the Jew first as well (2:9). But we are getting ahead of ourselves. Here in these verses Paul is establishing the universal scope of the gospel. Jew and Gentile includes everyone.

Thus we see that right upfront Paul starts telling us about the gospel. It was promised in the Old Testament, it is about Jesus Christ, it is received by faith, it brings salvation, and it is for everyone.

This section of Paul's letter ends on such a high note—salvation for all through the good news about Jesus Christ—that it is hard to believe the very next note in verse 18 has to do with God's wrath, yet this is the case. In the next chapter, we will explore how Paul understands this puzzling expression.

■ Applying the Word

Romans 1:1-17

1. How is the gospel or good news the power of God for salvation in my life? When did I first grasp the concept of the gospel as good news? What difference did it make at that point? How does the good news continue to function for my salvation?

2. As I analyze my own Christian experience, what gospel substitute tempts me the most? On what do I tend to rely other than God's good news for salvation?

3. How successful is my particular church in embracing "everyone" into the sphere of the gospel? What group or groups does it and do I have the most difficult time embracing? What specific suggestions do I have for reaching out to these groups?

4. If I were to draw a picture to communicate what the term *gospel* means to me, what kind of picture would it be? What would it look like? (Try it!) Share it with a family member or friend, and discuss what the picture says.

■ Researching the Word

1. Use a good Bible concordance to look up the term *gospel*. Read each of the verses in Romans where the word is found. How does this increase your understanding of the term? Notice the percentage of New Testament usages of this word that occur in Paul's writings. Why do you think Paul uses the term so frequently? Read the article on "gospel" in a good Bible dictionary. How does Paul's usage relate to other

usages, such as the application of the term to the first four books of the New Testament?

2. Compare the beginning of Romans with the beginnings of Paul's other letters. What are the standard elements that occur in all of them? What elements in Romans are unique?

■ Further Study of the Word

1. For a discussion of how Paul's thesis statement in Romans 1:16, 17 echoes the Old Testament discussions of God's justice, see R. B. Hays, *Echoes of Scripture in the Letters of Paul*, 36-41.

2. On Paul's view of God's impartiality vis-à-vis Jew and Gentile, see P. Richardson, *Paul's Ethic of Freedom*, 28-33.

3. For an overview of Romans as it relates to salvation for the Jews, see E. G. White, *The Acts of the Apostles*, 372-382.

4. For a background on letter writing, especially letter essays, in Paul's day, see M. L. Stirewalt, Jr., "The Form and Function of the Greek Letter-Essay," in K. P. Donfried, ed., *The Romans Debate*, 147-171.

5. For a discussion of Paul's understanding of being an "apostle of Jesus Christ" and his use of the term *gospel,* see excursuses 1 and 2 in P. Stuhlmacher, *Paul's Letter to the Romans*, 20-25.

6. For a discussion of the role of the Holy Spirit in this section of Romans, see G. D. Fee, *God's Empowering Presence*, 476-489.

PART TWO

Romans 1:18–3:20

Sin and Wrath

CHAPTER TWO

God's Wrath Revealed

Romans 1:18-32

Paul's transition from Romans 1:17 to 1:18 seems abrupt, even jarring, at first glance. In one breath we move from salvation, gospel, faith, and righteousness to wrath. Wrath comes as an unwelcome intruder into this sublime scene. Yet we will not understand the message of Romans until we come to terms with wrath.

We begin that task in this chapter.

■ Getting Into the Word

Romans 1:18-32

Read Romans 1:18-32 carefully in at least two versions, and write out answers to the following questions.

1. What does Paul mean by the term *wrath* in Romans 1? How do these verses help you define the word?
2. In verses 24, 26, and 28 Paul speaks of God "handing people over." What does this mean? How does God hand them over? To what or to whom does He hand them over? Does this mean that God gives up on people? Explain your answer in a paragraph or two.
3. What group of people is Paul speaking about in these verses? Characterize them.
4. Why are these people without excuse (vs. 20)? List the

reasons Paul gives.

5. In what sense is God known by what He has made? Is such knowledge sufficient for salvation? Do these verses suggest natural law or a method of salvation other than Christ? Provide evidence for your answer.

6. Compare the list of vices in 1:29-31 with those in 1 Corinthians 6:9-10, 2 Corinthians 12:20, and Galatians 5:19-21. What similarities do you find? Why do you think Paul uses such lists?

7. Through a careful reading of 1:18-32, indicate what you find to be the purpose of this passage.

■ Exploring the Word

God's Wrath in Romans

In order to understand what God's wrath is, we must move beyond the last half of chapter 1 and notice how Romans 1:18 to 3:20 forms a single coherent argument. The focus of this argument is the universality of sin, which prepares the way for Paul's teaching about the universality of salvation.

To put it another way, the picture of God's wrath prepares for the revelation of His righteousness. We will not understand the nature of God's righteousness unless we understand His wrath.

Therefore, let's go a bit beyond chapter 1 and survey God's wrath from the latter part of chapter 1 to the first part of chapter 3 before our detailed look at these chapters. Our study of God's wrath will go forth under these headings: the revelation of God's wrath, the results of God's wrath, the reasons for God's wrath, and the impartiality of God's wrath.

The revelation of God's wrath

Paul presents two aspects of God's wrath, one present and the other future. In the present, wrath is revealed in the freedom that God allows His creatures. God's wrath in Romans is the giving over of the wicked to their evil (see especially 1:18, 24, 26, 28). God simply turns His creatures over to the consequences of their sin. God's wrath is His permissiveness. In His love and respect for human beings, He gives them freedom to do evil and leaves them to the consequences of their evil.

This term "to hand over" or "to give over," which Paul uses three times to describe God's wrath (vss. 24, 26, 28), is one that can be used in many contexts. It can refer to written or oral tradition that is handed over to another person, to the giving over of one's self in an act of surrender, to entrusting an object to another person, or to handing over another person to authorities for arrest or even death, and these are but a few of its meanings. We will only fully appreciate Paul's use of the term later in the letter when we discover that God not only hands over sinners to their wickedness (the meaning of God's wrath for Paul) but also "hands over" Jesus on their behalf because of their transgressions (8:32; 4:25).

There is also a future aspect to wrath as well. God cannot allow evil to go on forever, so there is a time in the future when He will bring judgment to all (2:5, 6). Here God not only turns away and lets sinners be sinners; here God judges. This judgment is for all and is based on the works of each. In fact, if God didn't take the initiative to break into this inevitable cycle of judgment and wrath, there would be no hope for anyone.

The results of God's wrath

When God turns away and leaves humans to their own devices, the result is sexual immorality and all kinds of evil. God's gift of sexuality is perverted by promiscuous licentiousness, and a host of other sins from murder to slander and covetousness to ruthlessness ensue (1:26-31).

This produces an irony. The result of God's wrath against evil is more evil! For when God turns away and leaves humans to their evil, that evil multiplies. Paul will show us later in the letter (ch. 7) how this creates a vicious cycle of sin and death from which no one can escape.

The final result of God's wrath is destruction. When God hands sinners over to their sin, they destroy themselves. Here is where the present and future aspects of wrath come together. God's final judgment on sinners is but the logical end of their own self-destruction.

The reason for God's wrath

God's wrath is a reaction to human sin, universal human sin that is seen in both the Jewish and Gentile world (3:23).

Gentiles show it when they refuse to honor God, even though they have known Him from the natural world (1:21). Paul doesn't enter into a discussion of natural revelation here. (Natural revelation is that revelation of God that comes through nature, human experience, and reason, as opposed to God's special revelation through Christ and the Bible. Theologians argue over whether God can be known and salvation experienced through natural revelation.) Nor does he discuss whether natural revelation is sufficient for salvation. He merely asserts that God's power and deity have been sufficient to leave humans who fail to honor Him without excuse.

In addition, Gentiles have refused to thank God (vs. 21). And perhaps most important of all, they have exchanged the true God for idols (vs. 23), so that they worship creatures rather than the Creator (vs. 25).

God's wrath, however, is not only a response to Gentile sin. Jews knew the will of God through the law, but they failed to keep it (2:17-24). They did the very same things that they condemned the Gentiles for doing. Not only that, they also sinned through their judgmental attitude (2:1).

Paul makes it clear that no one can point a finger of blame. God's wrath has not been stirred up by the sin of any one group. Rather, all have sinned and contributed to this wrath (3:23).

The impartiality of God's wrath

No one escapes God's wrath. Sin is universal. It is true that the Jews were God's special people. The good news came to them first (1:16). But wrath will come to them first as well (2:9). Their privilege was for a purpose and brought added responsibility. God has never been partial. He has no favorites (vs. 11). There is no discrimination in His wrath.

Paul presents a seemingly bleak picture. All are under sin (3:9). No one is righteous (vs. 10). All have sinned and are falling short of God's glory (vs. 23). Wrath is therefore universal. Even though there are glimpses of light in this section, it is only when we come to the last part of Romans 3 that the infinitely brilliant light will break fully through this bleak picture.

Other Issues

Natural revelation and natural law

This section of Romans, especially Romans 1:20, has raised questions about natural revelation, an issue that has been hotly debated by many theologians. Is Paul affirming that there is a revelation from God that comes through nature? If so, is this revelation sufficient for salvation? Does nature present a universal ethic that gives everyone the same view of right and wrong? Does Paul present two ways of salvation, nature and Jesus Christ?

This topic will come to view again in Romans 2, where we will discuss it in more detail. But neither here nor in the next chapter will we find a definitive discussion of the question of natural revelation and natural law. We must keep the context clearly in view. Paul is not here addressing the question of how a person is saved. Rather, he is establishing the universality of sin.

Paul does affirm three things: there is a revelation of God in His creation (1:20), this enabled even the Gentiles to know God (vs. 21), and this knowledge is sufficient to leave everyone without excuse before God (vs. 20). Yet even with these affirmations Paul doesn't see this revelation as mechanistic or impersonal, for in verse 19 he says that what may be known about God is plain to people precisely because *God made it plain to them*. The creation reveals God because God continues to be active in His creation and is working to make Himself known. Therefore, when humans worship the creation rather than the Creator, they are turning their backs on God and are without excuse.

Sexuality

When Paul gives evidence of the depravity of the world, he turns to two issues: idolatry (vss. 22, 23) and sexual immorality (vss. 26, 27). These were the two main sins for which the Jews denounced the Gentile world. Paul is consistently clear that to accept Christ is to accept God's law with regard to sexual purity (see Rom. 13:13, 14; 1 Cor. 5:1-13; 6:9-20; 10:8; 1 Thes. 4:3-8).

This passage is different from the others in that Paul is not giving advice about sexual behavior, but using sexual behavior as evidence of the depravity of society, which in turn is evidence of God's wrath. Paul does not state here whether those who carry out sexual acts with those of the same sex did so exclusively or whether they added this to heterosexual activity. In fact, there are obviously issues about homosexuality, such as distinctions between homosexual orientation and homosexual practice, which Paul does not address here. His point is that the homosexual practices that he sees in society are evidence of the universality of sin and the all-embracing need of a Saviour.

List of vices

In the world of Paul's day, teachers and philosophers had standard ways of presenting material. One of the typical items in their bag of tricks was a list of vices to be avoided or virtues to be sought. Such lists were common among both Jewish and Greco-Roman teachers.

Paul adopts this popular practice in his letters. We find such a list of vices in Romans 1:29-31. Other lists may be found in 1 Corinthians 5:10; 6:9-10; 2 Corinthians 12:20; and Galatians 5:19-21. As we might expect from the previous chapter, where we saw how Paul not only adopted but also adapted the standard letter conventions, Paul adapted these typical lists for his own purposes. He tends to emphasize vices that break community. These include sexual sins and other sins that show a lack of respect for others. For example, this list includes envy, strife, deceit, gossip, and slander among the vices.

Something of the literary character of the lists is lost once they

are translated into another language. These lists often use allit-
eration and words that sound alike. For example, the original
words for "envy" and "murder" in verse 29 are *phthonou* and
phonou. Also placed together in verse 29 are *adikia*, *ponēria*, and
pleonexia ("wickedness," "evil," and "greed"), and verse 31 couples
asunetous and *asunthetous* ("foolish" and "faithless"). Also included
are graphic words that sound like their meaning. For example,
the word for "gossips" literally means "whisperers" (*psithuristas*).
If you can pronounce the word, you will hear the whispering.
These literary features are part of the appeal of this traditional
way of teaching, which Paul adopts and adapts.

Conclusion

To this point, Paul's Jewish readers could only have said "amen."
The kinds of charges Paul had made against the sins of pagan soci-
ety were common among Jewish teachers. But when we move on to
Romans 2, we will find an abrupt surprise. It is not just the idolatry
and immorality of the Gentile world that fall under Paul's scrutiny.
Sin is seen in all, and everyone needs a Saviour.

■ Applying the Word

Romans 1:18-32

1. **If God's wrath is His permissiveness and the freedom He
   allows, what implications does this have for the way I treat
   others? Does it have implications for parenting, for instance?
   Is permissiveness a kind of "wrath"? How do I strike the
   balance between allowing freedom and not leaving others
   to the evil consequences of their choices?**
2. **As I study what Paul says about God's *wrath*, what synonyms
   can I suggest for the term *wrath*? Do any of them do a better
   job of conveying Paul's meaning than the word *wrath*, with
   all its connotations?**
3. **After Paul points out all the evils of Greco-Roman society,**

he closes Romans 1 by saying that people not only do these things, but they approve of others who practice them. What does this suggest for me? In an age of tolerance, to what extent and in what ways should I register my disapproval of those who do evil?

■ Researching the Word

1. Use a Bible concordance to look up the term *wrath*. Read the verses in Romans that include this word. Does Paul use the term consistently throughout Romans? Try looking up the use of the term in at least one other New Testament writer. How does that usage compare and contrast with Romans? Compare your findings with the article on *wrath* in a good Bible dictionary.
2. Read other passages where Paul discusses the issue of sexuality (1 Cor. 5:1-13; 6:9-20; 1 Thes. 4:3-8; Rom. 13:13, 14). How did Paul's advice on this subject speak to young Christians who had come from the kind of world Paul describes in the latter part of Romans 1?

■ Further Study of the Word

1. For background on the use of lists of vices, see V. P. Furnish, *Theology and Ethics in Paul*, 84-86.
2. For examples of lists of vices and virtues from the Greco-Roman world, see A. J. Malherbe, *Moral Exhortation*, 138-141.
3. For a discussion of God's wrath, see H. Weiss, *Paul of Tarsus*, 43-46.
4. For an example of conservative (ascetic) teachings with regard to sexuality in the Greco-Roman world, see the passage from Musonius Rufus, quoted in A. J. Malherbe, *Moral Exhortation*, 152-154.

CHAPTER THREE

Sin and the True Jew

Romans 2

In Romans 1 Paul spoke about God's wrath as it relates to obvious sinners. Throughout the discussion, one can almost hear the pious saints cheering in the background. They would delight in Paul's indictment and would
know just where to point the finger at precisely the kinds of sinners Paul
was talking about.

But now Paul's attention turns to those pious saints who would have said
"Amen" to all he has just said. In the early part of Romans 2, their identity
is left unstated. Anyone who claims to be among the pious could be included.
In the latter part of the chapter, however, Paul specifically points to God's
special people, the Jews.

This challenge to the Jews, however, is by no means anti-Semitic. Only
when we reach Romans 9 to 11 will we see the depths of Paul's identification
with and concern for the Jews, whom he considers his people. But in this chapter, Paul challenges the idea that being a Jew shields one from God's wrath or
eliminates the need for salvation. They, too, stand under God's wrath.

■ Getting Into the Word

Romans 2

Read Romans 2, and write out answers to the following questions.

1. Who is Paul speaking to in this chapter? Is he addressing the

same people in the first and second halves of the chapter?
Compare and contrast these people with those addressed in
chapter 1.

2. What does Paul say is for the Jew first in this section of Romans? How does this relate to what he said was for the Jews
first in Romans 1? How can this be, when Paul also says that
there is no distinction and that God shows no partiality?

3. Compare and contrast what Paul says about wrath in this
chapter with what he said about it in Romans 1. Do you find
any differences? If so, list them.

4. Did the pious people Paul addressed in this chapter really
do all the evils recounted in chapter 1? If not, why are they
guilty too? Does Romans 2:3 help with this question? Why
is judging someone else's sin evil? Read Romans 14 in light
of Romans 2:3. How might Paul already be preparing the
way here for what he will say in chapter 14?

5. Compare and contrast what Paul says about the literal Jew
and the true Jew. What are the characteristics of each? What
makes a person a true Jew?

6. Do verses 14 to 16 mean that non-Christians can be saved
by being good without hearing the gospel? What does it mean
to have the law "written on the heart" in this context?

7. How does Paul understand the role of circumcision? Is it
still valid for him? Why do you think circumcision did not
continue as a religious ritual for Christians?

■ Exploring the Word

The Problem of Judging (2:1-4)

The time has come for Paul to turn the tables. Throughout the
latter part of Romans 1, Paul has spoken in the third person ("they")
about the sinners who are subject to God's wrath. Now he turns to
the second person ("you") and speaks *to* those who pass judgment
upon these obvious sinners.

Immediately he puts them all in the same boat. In Romans 1 he had said that the Gentile sinners were "without excuse" (vs. 20). Now in Romans 2 he contends that those who pass judgment "have no excuse" because they do the very same things (vs. 1). This is a serious charge. Both groups are without excuse because both groups do the same things.

Did God's people really do the same things? Probably some of them did. No doubt among God's professed people there were those with secret sins that looked very much like the sins of the obvious sinners. The only difference was that God's people kept such sins under wraps rather than committing them in the open and cheering on those who practiced them (see 1:32).

On the other hand, certainly there were many who would never have thought of committing such sins as idolatry and sexual immorality. What can Paul possibly mean when he accuses these pious people of "doing the same things"? Perhaps there is a clue in verse 3. Paul speaks of the "mere man" (as NIV puts it) passing judgment. Is Paul implicitly pointing to the sin of judging as being the same as the other sins because it usurps God's role and thus becomes a form of idolatry?

The point is only implicit here, but Paul makes it more explicitly in Romans 14:4, where he chides those who judge as judging someone else's servant, and in 14:10-12, where he shows from the Old Testament (Isa. 49:18; 45:23) that God alone has the right to judge. In other words, to judge another person, one of God's children, is to take a role on oneself that belongs only to God. What could be more idolatrous than to usurp God's role and take over His prerogative?

In verse 4 Paul accuses his readers of showing contempt for God's kindness, since this very kindness is meant to lead to repentance. Apparently a judgmental attitude stands in the way of both a full appreciation of God's kindness and the need to come to God in a spirit of repentance.

God's Role as Judge (2:5-11)

In verse 5 Paul goes on to announce that those who judge are storing up wrath for the day of wrath. Here Paul introduces a new aspect of God's wrath. He has already pointed to the present aspect of God's wrath in which God turns away and lets the world experience the reality of sin throughout Romans 1. But now Paul speaks of a future aspect of God's wrath, a day when God will judge. Yet here we get of glimpse of what will become clearer later on in Romans 3: this "day of wrath" is closely tied to God's righteousness, for it is the day when "his [God's] righteous judgment will be revealed" (2:5).

According to Paul, when God judges, both righteousness and wrath are revealed. God gives to each according to what she or he has done (vs. 6). For those who do good, this means eternal life (vs. 7). But to those who do evil, it will mean trouble, distress, wrath, and anger (vss. 8, 9).

This sounds very much like salvation by works. How are we to reconcile this simple picture of judgment as the reward for either good or evil works with the concept that we are not saved on the basis of our good works? Isn't Paul saying precisely what we so often seem to see him refuting? Is God's final judgment really a matter of handing out eternal life to those who have done good and pouring out wrath on those who have done evil?

Some theologians have argued that faith is the means by which Christians enter salvation, but works is the way they stay in salvation. Thus when Paul speaks of the final culmination of Christian life rather than its beginning, works determine salvation. Works are the basis for the judgment. A reading of these verses could certainly support such a view.

This way of resolving the problem is not sufficiently sensitive, however, to the context and the flow of Paul's argument here. We will find over and over in our study of this carefully reasoned letter that if we look at individual passages without seeing how they fit into Paul's overall thesis, we will be led astray. It is especially important to look at the end of the particular argument Paul makes. Frequently it is the bottom line that provides the clue to explaining the individual pieces of the discussion. This is certainly true in Romans 1:18–3:20.

The bottom line of this argument is that *all* are sinners and stand under God's wrath (3:23). Paul boldly concludes by emphasizing that not one person will be declared righteous by observing the law. The best the law can do is make us aware of what sinners we are (3:20). Since Romans 1:18–3:20 forms a cohesive unit, Romans 2:5-9 must be seen within the context of Paul's bottom line. Yes, at the final judgment God will give eternal life to those who have done good. But who has done good? Not a single one (3:10)! Paul's whole point in this section is that when God's righteous judgments are revealed and God fairly rewards the good with eternal life, there will be an amazing dearth of candidates! We will have to wait until the end of Romans 3 to find the solution to this tragic dilemma. But here in Romans 2 we are not at the solution stage. We are still dealing with the problem. Therefore, we must not isolate Romans 2:5-8 from its context and conclude that the solution is salvation by good works.

Paul concludes these few verses on God's final judgment by affirming God's impartiality. In 1:16 Paul proclaimed that the gospel was for the Jew first and then for the Gentile. Now he reverses the coin and says that trouble and distress will come to all who do evil—first for the Jew and then for the Gentile (2:9). He then reiterates that glory, honor, and peace will come to all who do good—first for the Jew and then for the Gentile (vs. 10). The privilege of the gospel brings responsibility. God's selection of a special people was never intended as an act of favoritism on God's part. God doesn't show favoritism (vs. 11). Different groups may play different roles in God's plan for salvation, but the final goal of the plan is that God will have mercy on all (11:32). Future chapters will show us how God's mysterious plan to have mercy on all works. But that gets ahead of the story. Here Paul highlights God's impartiality and lack of favoritism to show that we are all in the same boat—the boat of sin tossed about in the angry waves of God's wrath.

Law and Judgment (2:12-16)

The basic thrust of these verses is clear, but Paul adds a parenthetical statement in verses 14 and 15 that is difficult to understand and has proven controversial for interpreters. Paul begins in verse 12 by following up on the affirmation that God shows no favoritism by emphasizing that both the Gentiles (who sin apart from the law) and the Jews (who sin under the law) face judgment. The former will perish apart from the law, and the latter will be judged by the law. For whether they sin *apart* from the law or *under* the law, they hold one factor in common—they both sin! It isn't enough to hear the law; one must *obey* it to be justified (vs. 13). Here again Paul's words could be interpreted to mean that salvation is based on keeping the law, but that such a view would be a violation of the flow of Paul's discussion is even more obvious here.

At this point (vss. 14, 15) Paul adds a parenthetical disclaimer whose meaning has been hotly disputed. He speaks of Gentiles who do not have the law, but who by nature do the things required by the law and thus become a law unto themselves. The law is "written on their hearts." Who are these Gentiles to whom Paul refers?

Some claim that they are those who have never heard of God or the law but naturally do what is right and therefore find salvation. Others claim that Paul's use of new-covenant language (see, for example, Jeremiah 31:33, where God promises to write the law on Israel's heart under a new covenant) gives evidence that Paul is talking about Gentile Christians who have come to Christ and now have the law written on their hearts. Some of those who hold this view argue that their case is strengthened by the fact that the phrase (or word in the original language) "by nature" may not go with the verb in verse 14 but with the noun "Gentiles." Thus the passage would read, "For when Gentiles, who do not by nature have the law, do the things the law requires . . ." Thus Paul is not talking about those who "naturally" follow the law, but about those who have the law written in their hearts because they follow Christ.

Paul simply didn't give us enough data here to allow us to answer this question with certainty. We should remember, however, that we are not yet in the section of this letter where Paul begins to talk about salvation. It seems that within the context Paul is showing that Jews cannot claim superiority because they have the law, since they, as well as Gentiles, are sinners. In these verses he points out that even Gentiles do good things. This was, of course, true. The sordid portrait of the Gentile world in Romans 1 was hardly the whole picture. There were moral teachers with high ideals and admirable lifestyles in the Greco-Roman world. Paul doesn't point this out to explain how they are saved, however. He simply shows that the Jews have no monopoly on virtue, even though when all is said and done both Jew and Gentile will be declared sinners.

The Insufficiency of the Law (2:17-24)

Now Paul returns to the second person (you) and addresses Jews specifically. His language is strong, satirical, and even sarcastic. Much of this language, as is the case throughout this chapter, comes from allusions to the Old Testament. It is as if Paul turns the Jews' own Scripture against them. His basic problems with them are that they rely on the law and brag or "boast" in their relationship with God (2:17, 23). Keep these specific charges in mind so you can recall them when we come to the latter part of Romans 3. There we will see that the righteousness God offers comes apart from the law (3:23) and excludes all boasting (vs. 27). Paul is already preparing the way for God's solution to the problem of sin and wrath.

Even more problematic for Paul is the fact that in spite of God's people's boasting and claims to be guides to the blind and lights in darkness, instructors to the foolish and teachers of infants, they are in fact sinners who are in the same boat as the Gentiles, either because of their own moral lapses and failure to live up to their ideals or because of their judgmental attitude (2:19-22). (Commentators have suggested many possibilities for the meaning of Paul's accusation that they also rob temples [vs. 22], but probably no one knows for sure what he is referring to.) Instead of being God's witnesses to the world, they, like the Israelites to whom Isaiah spoke (see Isa. 52:5), actually defame God's name among the Gentiles (2:24). Their hypocrisy is a negative witness.

It would be a terrible mistake to become judgmental against the Jews of Paul's day because of what Paul says here. (Indeed, it would be evidence of our own sinfulness.) Paul isn't singling them out as more sinful than anyone else. We can hardly remind ourselves often enough that Paul's focus is on all of us. We are all sinners. It is true, however, that religious people face the special temptation of relying on their practices of piety and taking pride in them. At this point, Paul moves to a specific example of this false reliance on externals, namely circumcision.

Outward and Inward Circumcision (2:25-29)

Circumcision was the rite that symbolized every Jewish male's identity as one of God's people. Paul audaciously proclaims that it is only of value if one keeps the law. In fact, when a person breaks the law, his circumcision becomes uncircumcision. Then Paul proceeds to the logical next step. If one who is not circumcised keeps the law, it is as if he were circumcised (vs. 26). What does this mean? It means that God's people are condemned by those whose lives are closer to the law even though they don't have it. Paul is making the same point again that he made earlier in the chapter. Since all are sinners, none can rely on their religious status or standing.

This leads Paul to the conclusion that real Judaism is not a matter of outward rites or genealogy; it is a matter of the heart (vss. 28, 29). This is an obvious allusion to the Old Testament, where God promised that He would "circumcise your hearts and the hearts of your descendants" (Deut. 30:6). Paul is not as audacious as he sounds. He is merely reiterating and expanding on what God had said all along. Notice, too, that Paul doesn't oppose circumcision here. In Galatians he opposes those who would impose circumcision on Gentile Christians (Gal. 5:2-12), but even there it is not circumcision itself that he opposes.

Paul nails this point down with a play on words, one that Jesus, according to John, had also used. Paul says that for the true Jew, whose circumcision is from the heart, his "praise" is not from men, but from God (2:29). In the Hebrew language, the word for "Judah" and "Judaism" was related to the word *praise*. Thus this sentence could be taken to mean that the person's "Judaism" was from God, not humans. In John 5:44 Jesus says: "How can you believe if you accept praise from one another, yet make no effort to obtain the praise that comes from the only God." True Judaism, or any true religion, for that matter, must be bestowed by God, not by any human source. Both Jesus and Paul seem to make this point by playing on the connection between the terms *Judah* and *praise* in Hebrew, even though in Greek there is no connection between the two.

By this point in Romans, any reader might wonder why anyone should bother to be part of God's people. Paul will ask and answer that question as he continues his argument about the wrath of God and the sinfulness of humans in the next chapter.

■ Applying the Word

Romans 2

1. Who are the people whom I am tempted to judge? People who are different because of nationality or race? Church members with whom I disagree? Church members who do things I think are wrong? Non-Christians whose practices I abhor? What does it say about me when I judge?
2. What am I tempted to boast about? If I put aside the fact that I know better than to boast and am honest with my deep feelings, what would be the top items on my brag list? How can I replace these items by boasting only in Christ?
3. Since I don't view circumcision as a religious ritual, what would be the functional equivalent of circumcision for me? Would Paul's teaching about inward and outward circumcision apply to this as well? What practical consequences does this have for my life?

■ Researching the Word

1. Use a concordance to find and look up passages in Genesis that have to do with circumcision. How did circumcision begin? Why do you think God chose it as a religious symbol? Now use your concordance to see how the New Testament deals with circumcision. Does the treatment differ with different New Testament writers? Compare your findings with the article on circumcision in a good Bible dictionary.

2. Look up the terms *judge*, *judging*, and *judgment* in a Bible concordance, and survey their use in Romans. Why do you think Paul's most frequent use of these terms clusters in Romans 2 and 3 and then again in Romans 14?

3. Look up all forms of the terms *boast* and *brag* in a Bible concordance, and survey their usage in Romans. (It will help if you have an analytical concordance that allows you to look up the same Greek word even when it is translated in different ways. This is especially important for this word, since it is also translated "rejoice" in some passages. If you do not have access to an analytical concordance, here are the passages where the Greek word for "boast" is used in Romans: 2:17, 23; 4:2; 5:2, 3, 11.)

■ Further Study of the Word

1. For a brief presentation of the view that Romans 2:14, 15 refers to Gentile Christians, see K. Barth, *A Shorter Commentary on Romans*, 35-37.

2. For strong opposition to Barth's view that Romans 2:14, 15 refers to Gentile Christians, see W. D. Davies, *Paul and Rabbinic Judaism*, 325-328.

3. For the view that Stoic backgrounds indicate that in Romans 2:14-16 Paul is referring to the hypothetical possibility that Gentiles might keep the law by nature, but with emphasis on the probability against it, see J. W. Martens, "Romans 2:14-16: A Stoic Reading."

4. For a survey of Paul's use of the Old Testament in this chapter, see R. B. Hays, *Echoes of Scripture in the Letters of Paul*, 41-46.

5. For a survey of rabbinic material on reward and punishment in the world to come, see E. P. Sanders, *Paul and Palestinian Judaism*, 125-147.

6. For a discussion of Paul's thought on judgment according to works against its Old Testament background, see excursus 5 in P. Stuhlmacher, *Paul's Letter to the Romans*, 45-47.

7. For a survey of possible meanings of "robbing temples" in Romans 2:22 and a presentation of the view that this reference points to any kind of profiting from the assets of heathen religious endowment, see J. D. M. Derrett, "You Abominate False Gods; but Do You Rob Shrines?" in *New Testament Studies* 40 (Oct. 94): 538-571.

CHAPTER FOUR

Sinners One
and All

Romans 3:1-20

College teachers are often criticized for raising too many questions. Paul would have made a good college teacher, because he liked to ask questions. In fact, this section of Romans consists primarily of questions and a conclusion. The questions arise as hypothetical objections to some of the issues Paul has been discussing. Although he doesn't answer any of them in detail at this point, they do set the agenda for several important discussions that will follow in Romans.

The conclusion brings the discussion of God's wrath, which began in 1:18, to a close. It not only nails down the reality that all, both Jew and Gentile, are under the power of sin, but it also prepares the way for God's gracious answer to this bleak dilemma.

■ Getting Into the Word

Romans 3:1-20

Read Romans 3:1-20 in at least two different translations, and write out answers to the following questions.

1. Divide a sheet of paper in your Romans notebook into two columns. In the first column, make a list of the questions that Paul asks in Romans 3:1-9. How do these questions relate to what Paul has said up to this point in Romans?

2. In the second column, make a list of Paul's answers to these questions. Do the answers all make sense to you?
3. Why doesn't Paul give more detailed answers to these questions? Doesn't he seem to leave the reader hanging in some of them?
4. From your reading of the whole letter of Romans assigned in the introductory chapter, see if you can recall sections of Romans where Paul does answer these questions in greater detail.
5. In verses 4 and 6, Paul answers questions with a strong negative. What stands behind the intensity of this response?
6. Is the picture of human nature as bleak as Paul presents it here? Aren't there many who live good lives of integrity and compassion in the world? Why is Paul so insistent that everyone is under the power of sin?
7. What triggers Paul's concern about God's faithfulness? What is it that might lead some to question God's faithfulness? What evidence does Paul give that God is faithful?
8. What is Paul's final conclusion in this section of the letter?

■ Exploring the Word

Paul's Questions

Romans 3 begins with a whole list of questions that seem to break into the flow of the discussion. These questions come just before the concluding summary to this lengthy discussion of God's wrath. It is as if Paul must take note of some potential objections to his remarks before he nails down the final point. This style of answering potential objections was so common among Greco-Roman writers of Paul's day that it had a name—the diatribe style.

Notice how many questions are included in these few verses (1-9) as translated by the NIV:

"What advantage, then, is there in being a Jew?" (vs. 1).

"What value is there in circumcision?" (vs. 1).

"What if some did not have faith?" (vs. 3).

"Will their lack of faith nullify God's faithfulness?" (vs. 3).

"If our unrighteousness brings out God's righteousness more clearly, what shall we say?" (vs. 5).

"That God is unjust in bringing his wrath on us?" (vs. 5).

"If that were so, how could God judge the world?" (vs. 6).

"If my falsehood enhances God's truthfulness and so increases his glory, why am I still condemned as a sinner?" (vs. 7).

"Why not say—as we are being slanderously reported as saying and as some claim that we say—'Let us do evil that good may result' ?" (vs. 8).

"What shall we conclude then?" (vs. 9).

"Are we any better?" (vs. 9).

What are we to make of all these questions? The series boils down to three basic issues: the advantage of being a Jew, God's faithfulness, and continuing in sin. Let's look at them in this order.

The advantage of being a Jew

The conclusion to which Paul comes at the end of Romans 2 leads directly to this question. He had concluded that true circumcision is a matter of the heart and true Judaism is inward. This naturally leads to the questions, "Why, then, be a Jew? What is the advantage?" (3:1) to which we might logically expect the answer, "There is no advantage at all!" But Paul's answer shatters our expectations. He claims there is much advantage in every way to being a Jew. Why? Because the Jews were entrusted with the oracles of God (vs. 2). By this he means the promises of faithfulness that God had made in Scripture to His people.

The privilege of knowing these promises is a great blessing. Although we have already heard hints (1:16, 17) and will discover later in detail (see 3:21-31; 9-11) that God's promise of faithfulness and mercy extends to all, it is the Jews who have had the blessing of knowing and sharing these promises. The inward nature of true religious faith doesn't mean that Judaism is useless. But this leads to another question.

God's faithfulness

If the advantage of being a Jew is knowing the promises of faithfulness that God made to Israel and that have been recorded in Scripture, aren't those promises called into question by the very argument Paul is making? Paul is saying that God's people, the very recipients of these promises, have failed as miserably as the Gentiles and stand under God's wrath just as much as they do. If this is true, what validity can the promises have? How can God be faithful and just when He brings wrath on His people (3:5)?

Thus we can see why someone might quite naturally ask the questions "What if some did not have faith? Will their lack of faith nullify God's faithfulness?" (vs. 3). Paul's answer is a very strong "Absolutely not!" (vs. 4). (Although the KJV translates "God forbid," the term *God* is not actually used in the original language.) This line of questioning continues through verse 6, where it receives another "Absolutely not!" Paul can't be more clear. Nothing less than the moral integrity of God is at stake here. If God can't be trusted, then all is lost.

Yet in spite of Paul's definite No, he doesn't really answer the question behind these questions. How can God be faithful to His promises and at the same time act in wrath and judgment? The fact that Paul doesn't answer that question doesn't mean it is unimportant for him. In fact, it is crucial for him. But more water needs to go under the bridge before he can answer it adequately. Here he is setting the agenda. It will only be in Romans 9 to 11 that we will see Paul's careful working out of the answer to this crucial question.

Continuing in sin

Even though it gets him quite a bit ahead of his story, Paul turns in verse 7 to a third potential objection that grows out of the previous one. If God's faithfulness is preserved, even enhanced, in spite of my failure, then why not go for failure, live it up, and sin as I please? Why not say "let us do evil that good may result" (3:8)?

Paul fails to work out an argument for the answer to this question here. Again he is setting the agenda for future discussion. But he doesn't leave any room for doubt as to what his answer will be. Not only does he make it clear that this is fallacious reasoning; he also points out that the people who accuse him of teaching this deserve condemnation! Obviously some people took Paul's doctrine of salvation by grace to mean a license for sinning. It is in Romans 6 that Paul will ask this question again and do more than reject it; he will work out a careful answer using the Christian practice of baptism and the analogy of slavery to show that Christians saved by grace will never use grace as an excuse for sinning.

Paul's Conclusion

Finally in Romans 3:9-20 and 23, we come to the official conclusion of this discussion of God's wrath. We would be quite dense if we were unable to anticipate that conclusion by now. Even though Jews have the advantage of God's promises, we discover in verse 9 that they are no better off because all, both Jew and Gentile, are under sin. As Romans 7 will show, Paul sees sin as more than wrong acts. It is actually a power that enslaves or imprisons humans and holds them under its spell, keeping them from living up to their ideals and doing what they really want to do (e.g. vs. 23).

In Paul's conclusion (3:9-20), he focuses more on the Jewish side of the picture because it is less obvious and more problematic. Declaring that Jews stand as guilty before God as Gentiles do seems audacious and shocking. Therefore, Paul shows that this conclusion is not merely *his*, but is also attested by the Jews' very own Scripture. Verses 10 through 18 are all quotes from the Old Testament that speak of the sinfulness of the people. Paul gleans these indictments from a variety of passages, mostly in the Psalms. The following chart shows the sources of each verse from 10 to 18:

Verses	Old Testament Passage
10	Eccl. 7:20
11, 12	Ps. 14:1-3
13a	Ps. 5:9

13b	Ps. 140:3
14	Ps. 10:7
15, 17	Isa. 59:7, 8; see also Prov. 1:16
18	Ps. 36:1

All of these passages show the sinfulness of the people, and when Paul puts them all together, the picture is bleak indeed. We find words like *worthless* and *misery*. Graphic metaphors such as open graves and viper's poison describe the guilt of every part of the body, including throat, tongue, lips, mouth, and feet.

Do you catch the irony here? These very oracles of God that proclaim God's faithfulness and promises (and the very Psalms from which Paul quotes also contain many expressions of God's faithfulness) condemn God's people by accusing them of horrible sins and evil. These passages speak to the people who are under the law, i.e., the Jews, and what they say silences everyone and makes the whole world accountable before God (3:19). This prepares the way for the conclusion in verse 20, "Therefore no one will be declared righteous in his sight by observing the law; rather, through the law we become conscious of sin."

In this passage, Paul uses the law in a broad sense. Law includes the whole Old Testament, indeed, the whole of Judaism, although the focus is on the commands of the law. Anyone who expects righteousness through the law better look at the law and see what it says! It says, "You aren't righteous!" It says, "You are a sinner." So Paul's conclusion makes sense. Far from making one righteous, the law simply makes the one who stands under it conscious of sin.

The dilemma is inescapable. The very oracles of God that promise His faithfulness also make us aware of our sin. There is no solution. Wrath seems to have the last word, not just for the other guys, but for me too. "There is no difference, for all have sinned and fall short of the glory of God" (vs. 23). This is the dire conclusion.

Now it is time for Paul to get back to the good news and show us the one and only true solution to this dilemma. True, he has pulled every rug of security out from under us, but in the rest of Romans 3, which we will study in our next chapter, he transports us to the only real solution, God's solution.

■ Applying the Word

Romans 3:1-20

1. What is the advantage of being a Christian of my particular persuasion? In what ways am I better off? In what ways am I no better off than anyone else?
2. Am I ever tempted to take sin lightly and feel that I don't need to be concerned about my actions since God is gracious? What do I learn from Paul's intense denunciation of such a stance?
3. How does Scripture make me conscious of sin? If I were to make a list of specific ways my life has been challenged by reading Romans so far, what would it look like?
4. Do I really feel that the Old Testament passages Paul quotes in 3:10-18 accurately describe my life either now or in the past? Am I, or have I ever been, so horrible that my throat could be described as an open grave or I could be seen to have the poison of vipers on my lips?
5. If I were to draw a picture of the human situation Paul describes in these verses, what would it look like?

■ Researching the Word

1. Read each of the Old Testament passages Paul quotes in 3:10-18 in its entirety. Divide a page in your Romans notebook into three columns. In the first, indicate the passage. In the second, make a list of the negative statements of judgment and wrath in each passage. In the third, list the positive, encouraging statements of salvation in each passage. What can you conclude from such a study?

2. Look up all the passages where Paul uses the strong negative statement "Absolutely not" (Greek *mē genoito*) in Romans. (Since these are often difficult to find in an English
concordance because they are translated in different ways,
here is the list: 3:4; 3:6; 3:31; 6:2; 6:15; 7:7; 7:13; 9:14; 11:1;
and 11:11.) In your Romans notebook, make a list of all the
statements Paul debunks with this expression. What do they
have in common? What does this contribute to your understanding of Paul's thinking and of his literary style?

■ Further Study of the Word

1. For a study of Paul's expression "God forbid" or "absolutely
not" (*mē genoito*), especially in comparison with Epictetus,
see A. Malherbe, "*Mē Genoito* in the Diatribe and Paul," in
Paul and the Popular Philosophers, 25-33.
2. For a theological exposition of Paul's use of the Old Testament in this passage, see R. B. Hays, *Echoes of Scripture in
the Letters of Paul*, 46-54.
3. For a discussion of the covenant concept in relationship to
Paul's discussion of wrath in 1:18 to 3:20, see R. D. Kaylor,
Paul's Covenant Community, 33-49.
4. For examples of teaching by various Greco-Roman philosophers (Musonius Rufus, Dio Chrysostom, Seneca, and
Pseudo-Diogenes) on the human condition, see A. J.
Malherbe, *Moral Exhortation*, 140-147.

PART THREE

Romans 3:21–8:39

The Experience
of Salvation

CHAPTER FIVE

Free Gift for All

Romans 3:21-31

It is hard to imagine eleven verses of Scripture that contain as much meat as this section of Romans. Nowhere else can we find such a full theological exposition of salvation in such a few words. Every word is packed full, and we will need to spend some time on these verses.

This section of Romans represents a major shift in focus. We move from God's wrath to God's righteousness. We move from sin to salvation. We move from the human dilemma to the divine drama of salvation. We move from problem to solution. We move from death to life.

These eleven verses tell the story. The rest of Romans will elaborate in one way or another on these verses.

■ Getting Into the Word

Romans 3:21-31

Read these verses carefully in at least three different English translations, and write out your answers to the following questions.

1. What is the function of these verses in Paul's overall argument, and how do they relate to the first part of Romans 3?
2. Make a list of words that appear to be important theological terms in these eleven verses. Try to write a synonym for each term that is an everyday word that you use regularly

around the house in a nontheological way. A standard dictionary may help you in this exercise. Now read the passage, substituting your synonyms. Does this help your understanding?

3. Go back and review the section on the gospel in chapter 1 of this book. List the basic points that Paul makes about the gospel in Romans 1 that are repeated (perhaps in somewhat different language) in these eleven verses.

4. In verses 24 and 25, Paul uses several terms to describe God's saving work in Jesus Christ: justified (freely by His grace), redemption, and sacrifice of atonement. What does each of these expressions contribute to your understanding of salvation?

5. What do you learn about the law in these verses? How is it related to faith? To salvation? Is the presentation of law basically negative or positive in these verses?

6. What does Paul mean in verse 25 when he says that God left former sins unpunished or God passed over them? Don't we have many examples of God punishing sin in the Old Testament? Does God deal with sin differently since Christ died than He did before Christ died?

7. What is the basis for salvation according to these verses? Are there false bases of salvation that Paul warns about as well?

8. Make a list of what you learn about the Gentiles in these verses. In a paragraph or two, summarize the significance of your findings.

■ Exploring the Word

The previous section of Romans, which we have explored in the last three chapters of this book, began with the words "The wrath of God is revealed" (1:18). This new section begins, "The righteousness of God is revealed" (3:21). In order to understand this section, we need to become familiar with the term *righteousness* and its meaning for Paul.

The Term Righteousness

We should hardly be surprised that the meaning of this term is often debated by interpreters, once we recognize the translation difficulties that present themselves. There are several words in Greek that share a common root (*dik*), and all of them are translated in various ways in English. The adjective (*dikaios*) is translated as "just" or "righteous." The noun (*dikaiosynē*) can be translated "justice," "justification," or "righteousness." The verb (*dikaioō*) is sometimes translated "justify," "declare righteous," "pronounce righteous," or "make righteous." Not only is there little consistency among translations, but even within a given version these terms are translated differently. For example, of the four occurrences of *dikaiosynē* in 3:21-31, the NIV translates "righteousness" in verses 21 and 22 and "justice" in verses 25 and 26. The choices that a translator makes often reflect his or her theological interpretation.

Many interpreters point to the fact that this term was used in the courts of the day as a legal term, and they therefore emphasize the forensic or legal nature of righteousness. To be justified was synonymous with being acquitted. Those who hold this view argue that on the basis of Jesus' death God acquits sinners. They often translate the verb form as "declare righteous" or "pronounce righteous" to show that this is a legal pronouncement God makes.

Others argue against this forensic emphasis on the basis that it seems to make God pronounce an untruth. If women and men are really sinners and God pronounces them righteous, isn't He making an untruthful declaration? They hold that God really changes people when He justifies them, and they prefer to translate the verb in question as "make righteous."

This debate between "make righteous" and "declare righteous" is somewhat misplaced, however. In a sense, both assume that righteousness is an ethical concept that is somewhat synonymous with goodness, so that the debate is over whether God legally declares sinners good (on the basis of Christ's substitution) or whether He actually makes them good. However, if the term is not primarily an ethical term but a relational one, with the Old Testament covenant as an important background, then perhaps neither "declare righteous" nor "make righteous" tells the whole story.

Two considerations are important here. First, even though there is no doubt that this whole cluster of terminology does have a legal background, we must remember that both the role of a judge and the nature of the legal system in biblical times were quite different than today. We think of a judge as an objective deliberator who hands down decisions. Our vision of justice is the blindfolded woman with the scales of justice. In biblical times, however, the judge was much more actively involved in the lives of people he or she served. The judge was responsible for setting things right and working to vindicate the oppressed.

This is what we see in the Gospels when Jesus tells a story about an unjust judge (Luke 18:1-8). Jesus' point has to do with the woman's persistence as a model for prayer, but the story tells us something about the expectations placed on judges too. In the story, the judge feared neither God nor humans. A woman who had been wronged kept coming to him to find vindication against her adversary. Since he didn't care about justice, he kept sending her away, but finally because of her persistence he said, "Even though I don't fear God or care about men, yet because this widow keeps bothering me, I will see that she gets justice, so that she won't eventually wear me out with her coming" (Luke 18:5). Here we see that judges were expected to take action, get their hands dirty, and act on behalf of the oppressed. They didn't just sit at a bench and make declarations.

A second important consideration for understanding this cluster of terms is the Old Testament background. There God's righteousness is not an abstract quality, but His covenant faithfulness to His people and His resulting action on their behalf. The psalmist, for example, can call on God's righteousness as a source of confidence that God will act to save: "Rescue me and deliver me in your righteousness; turn your ear to me and save me" (Ps. 71, 2). God judges on the basis of this righteousness (Ps. 96:13; 98:9). But passages such as Isaiah 11:4 show that God's role as judge is to act faithfully for the needy and the oppressed: "With righteousness he will judge the needy, with justice he will give decisions for the poor of the earth."

God's righteousness can be synonymous with His salvation (Isa. 51:5). In the covenant, God had promised to keep faith with Israel and be their God. His righteousness is that faithfulness that acts on behalf of His people and keeps them in relationship with Him.

The verses that ended Paul's long section on God's wrath (3:1-20; see the previous chapter) made it clear that whatever righteousness means with regard to humans must take its cue from God's own righteousness. When 3:3 and 3:5 are compared, it appears that God's faithfulness and His righteousness are the same. This fits with the Old Testament picture. God's righteousness is His faithfulness to the covenant and to the people. At its root, righteousness (as used in the Old Testament and in Paul) is a relational concept. God had promised that He would be Israel's God and they would be His people. His righteousness is that relational faithfulness to the covenant.

Obviously human righteousness cannot be identical to God's, for God and humans do not come to the covenant on equal terms. But human and divine righteousness are closely related. Both are relational. Human righteousness has to do with being in the proper covenant relationship with God. Because of the universal sin of both Jew and Gentile that Paul has clearly outlined in 1:18 to 3:20, the only possible solution is for God to take the initiative and set this relationship right. God's righteousness is His faithful action on behalf of His people. This action comes through Jesus Christ. In Christ God acts as the faithful judge who vindicates the oppressed.

God is not only righteous; He also justifies humans by His grace (3:24). This does not mean that He merely declares them to be something they are not. Nor does it mean that He instantaneously makes them righteous in the sense of making them sinless. It does mean that He sets them into right relationship with Him and restores the covenant that they had broken.

Righteousness, therefore, is not primarily an ethical concept, although we will see that it has significant ethical implications. Behavioral consequences follow from being in covenant with God. And although it is a forensic or legal term, its legal background must be seen in the context of the biblical concepts of judges and courts, especially as these concepts pertain to God in the Old Testament, rather than in twentieth-century legal terms.

Finally, we should notice that the concept has a social dimension. The covenant not only creates individual relationships with God; it creates a people in relationship with God. When God establishes righteousness through Christ, it is not merely to let individuals know how they can be saved; it is to create a new community in relationship to Himself that includes both Jew and Gentile (3:29). Righteousness by faith is not only a method for individual salvation; it is God's action to form a new covenant community.

Many of the debates about righteousness, both in the Adventist Church and in the wider Christian community, have completely missed this social dimension. Opponents argue over the mechanics of salvation (too often in ways that divide people and even destroy community) without grasping the important point that God's righteousness is a community-forming righteousness. It creates a people, God's people, who share in His blessings together. This people is an all-embracing people that excludes no one on the basis of race, gender, nation, or status. We don't really understand righteousness unless we see its social dimension, and we don't really understand Paul's message of righteousness unless we recognize that it is for *all*.

Before we conclude this overview of the term *righteousness*, we should say a bit more about a term we have used several times in this discussion: *covenant*. Even though Paul uses the term only twice in Romans (9:4 and 11:27), the concept underlies much of what he says. In Old Testament times, a covenant was a contract, agreement, or treaty between two parties. The parties could be equals, or one could be subservient, as in the case of a king making a covenant with vassals. As is the case with contracts today, covenants were generally sealed and witnessed with provisions spelled out.

According to Exodus 24, Moses recounted all the commands and laws that God had given, and Israel agreed to live by them. God promised to be Israel's God and give her the land of Canaan. Moses sealed the covenant by reading the book of the covenant to the people, eliciting their promise to obey, and then sprinkling the blood of sacrificed bulls on them (Exod. 24:7, 8). This promise, of course, was really a renewal of the covenant God had made with Abraham (see Gen. 15) to multiply his descendants and bless all nations through him. The covenant was repeated to David (2 Sam. 7) and was attested by the prophets (see Jer. 33).

The concept of covenant is closely connected with the term *right-eousness* because both have to do with God's faithfulness and His promises to His people. One of Paul's chief concerns in Romans is to affirm God's faithfulness to His people. Even though the message of the gospel to the Gentiles might be interpreted by some to mean that God was not faithful to the covenant, Paul will go right back to the beginning and show that in the covenant with Abraham God had included all nations. Romans 9 to 11 will focus specifically on how God remains faithful in spite of Jewish rejection.

To summarize, righteousness is first God's faithfulness to His people and His action on their behalf. When God justifies (there is no good English verb to correspond with the English adjective *right-eous*) He restores the covenant with humans, so that righteousness is a relational concept. To be righteous is to be restored to a covenant relationship with God and to become part of His covenant community. Before we are ready to look at the content of Paul's teaching about righteousness through faith in Romans 3:21-31, we must also take some time to explore the term *faith*.

The Term Faith

This root, in either its noun or verbal form, occurs almost sixty times in Romans and can have a fairly wide range of meaning. The verbal form, for instance, can have various kinds of objects. Paul can speak of "believing" or "having faith in" God (3:22; 4:17). He can also use the same term to refer to believing a truth that comes from God, as when Abraham believes that he will be the father of many nations (4:18) or when we believe that God raised Jesus from the dead (10:9) or that we will live with Christ (6:8). He can also speak of believing a message (10:16) or even believing an opinion about practice, as when some believe it is permissible to eat anything (14:2). There is also variance in the use of the noun form. It can refer to

God's faithfulness (3:3) or to the Roman believers' faith (1:8).

The most consistent use, however, is for the appropriate response to God's grace on behalf of humans. We see this throughout Romans 4, for example, where it is Abraham's faith that is reckoned to him as righteousness. This faith is a reliance on and commitment to God.

There are some occurrences of the term where the meaning is not altogether clear, however, and several of those are found in the verses we are studying in this chapter. Romans 3:22, for example, speaks of the "faith of Jesus Christ." (The NIV translates "faith in Jesus Christ," which is an interpretation.) The Greek construction used here could be understood in two ways: either faith in Jesus Christ (as the NIV translates) or Jesus Christ's own faith/faithfulness. Clearly the term *faith* can be used in both ways. In Romans 1:8, for example, faith is a human response, whereas in 3:3 it is a divine quality and/or action. When Romans speaks of the faith of Christ in 3:22, 25, 26, and where the term *faith* is used without specific reference to Christ (see 3:27, 28, 30, 31; 5:1; 9:30, 32; 10:6, 8, for example), is Paul referring to Christ's faith or to human faith?

Many of the arguments that scholars use to debate this issue are technical, linguistic ones that are too complex for our purposes here. Here are some of the less technical arguments used by those who hold that "faith" in these passages refers to human faith in Christ: (1) Romans 9:32 contrasts faith and works of law in a way that seems to make faith a human response. (2) Romans 10:14 clearly makes faith a human response to the message of the gospel. (3) Since Abraham's faith was reckoned to him as righteousness (4:3), the analogy with chapter 3 would suggest that human faith is in view. (4) Other Pauline passages outside of Romans, such as Philippians 1:29 and Galatians 2:16, unambiguously speak of having faith in Christ.

Those who argue that "faith of Christ" refers to Christ's faithfulness as the basis for our salvation use these arguments among others: (1) Throughout Romans, Paul only uses the verb "to have faith" to refer to faith in God, not in Christ (see Romans 4:3, 5, 17, 24; 10:11). (2) The analogy with God's faithfulness in 3:3 is the closest analogy to Paul's usage with reference to Christ in the latter part of the chapter. (3) Since the phrase "faith of God" in 3:3 refers to God's faithfulness and the phrase "faith of Abraham" in 4:12 and 4:16 refers to Abraham's faith, the phrase "faith of Christ" should refer to Christ's faith. (4) Paul emphasizes Christ's faithfulness as the basis for salvation to show that nothing human can serve as the basis for our salvation. When taken as a human response, faith becomes a human work that replaces God's action in Christ as the basis for salvation.

Because the Greek phrase "faith of Jesus Christ" could legitimately be taken either way, and because there are appropriate analogies for either usage in Paul, it is impossible to resolve this question with certainty. Some have even argued that Paul was purposely being ambiguous so that the phrase could be taken either way, but this is doubtful. How one interprets the phrase does make a difference in the way some specific passages are understood, and we will attempt to notice these different possibilities as we look at the individual texts. Ultimately, however, the reader will have to come to her or his own conclusion with a certain humility that recognizes that not all questions of interpretation have clear solutions. Whichever interpretation one takes, however, the unambiguous passages make the overall point that faith, or total reliance on, trust in, and commitment to God, is the only appropriate response to His grace and that the salvation freely offered to all is based, not even on this response, but solely on God's gracious action in Christ.

God's Gift of Righteousness

The main content in Romans 3:21-31 will be summarized under several subheadings. You will notice some repetition in comparison with what we saw about the gospel in Romans 1, but this repetition is an important part of Paul's presentation of his basic point. Our subheadings are: the basis for righteousness, the time for righteousness, the relationship of righteousness to the law, the scope of righteousness, metaphors for God's gift of righteousness, and the results of righteousness.

The basis for righteousness

Paul begins by saying that "now a righteousness from God, apart from law, has been make known. . . . This righteousness from God comes through faith in [or of] Jesus Christ" (vss. 21, 22). The phrase that the NIV translates "righteousness from God" in verses 21 and 22 is more ambiguous in the original language. The phrase could mean righteousness that comes from God, but it could also refer to God's own righteousness. Paul's primary focus is on the latter here. Just as God's wrath was revealed, now His righteousness is revealed. But the theological significance of this ambiguity is not great, since both meanings are true, as verse 26 clearly shows. Righteousness is something God is, and He justifies humans as well. God is righteous, but His righteousness comes to all who believe (vs. 22) as well. In fact, God shows His righteousness or faithfulness precisely in His action to restore humans or set them right so they can stand in covenant relationship with Him.

There is no doubt about the basis for the righteousness that comes to those who have faith: it is the free gift of God's grace (vs. 24). When Paul says men and women are justified "freely" by "grace," either of these terms would give the idea that the gift is completely free, but when they are coupled, the concept is underlined and printed in bold. Grace is one of Paul's most important theological terms. He uses it twenty-two times in Romans and over one hundred times throughout his letters. It refers to absolutely free acceptance. The other term Paul uses (translated "freely") is an adverb that means "completely without charge." The result is clear: righteousness comes apart from anything we have done, are doing, or ever could do to earn it. It comes at God's initiative and completely without cost. The basis is God's action in Jesus Christ.

Here Paul breaks with any purely forensic or legal concept of righteousness. Judges don't acquit people freely by grace. Even the broader Old Testament concept of judge affirms that the righteous judge is not to acquit the guilty. For example, Proverbs 17:15 reads: "Acquitting the guilty and condemning the innocent—the LORD detests them both." But remember, God is not merely acquitting the guilty. He is acting to restore them to a relationship with Him, to make them His people. And this initiative on His part is offered absolutely freely.

This righteousness is made effective for the individual by the "law" (or perhaps it would be better to translate "principle" or "system") of faith (3:27). Whether one understands the term *faith* here as Christ's faithfulness in giving His life for us or as the human response to God, this faith is not a work that Christians perform. The ultimate basis is God's grace. But even if this passage refers to Christ's faith, the chapter as a whole shows that the appropriate human response to this grace is faith, for righteousness comes to "all who believe" or "all who have faith" (vs. 22). This grace is both revealed in and made effective by Christ's sacrifice (vss. 24, 25). Paul doesn't explain how this works, although as we will see later, he uses several metaphors to help us understand what God accomplished in Christ. But the only appropriate response to this gift of God in Christ is trusting acceptance of the gift and reliance on God alone for identity, meaning, and salvation.

So we see that the basis of righteousness is God's free gift of grace in Christ, which is appropriated by a response of trusting reliance on Him.

The time for righteousness

The first word in the paragraph beginning in verse 21 is *now*. "Now" God's righteousness is revealed decisively in Christ. It is Christ's sacrifice of atonement that reveals God's righteousness (verse 25) and that makes it possible for God to be both the One who is righteous and the One who justifies on the basis of faith (verse 26). In verse 26 Paul emphasizes the *now* of all this again.

Paul leaves us with some questions about the past. He talks briefly about it but gives us very little detail. God passed over the sins of the past with a view to demonstrating His righteousness now (verse 26). Does this mean that God dealt with sin in different ways before and after the cross? Is there a kind of dispensationalism here? What is Paul trying to say? Probably not as much as we wish he would. He appears to be brushing the question of the past aside. God simply put the problem of sin on the table to wait for the solution that came in Christ. In Romans 5 Paul will say a little more along these lines. Right now, his real interest is in the *now* and the revelation of righteousness that it provides in Christ.

The relationship of righteousness to the law

Clearly the law is not the basis for this righteousness. Paul begins by claiming that it is revealed "apart from law" (3:21). In verse 28 he emphasizes that we are justified apart from works of law. This phrase can refer in a narrow sense to reliance upon Judaism and in a broad sense to reliance upon any human achievement or accomplishment. Neither one's achievements nor obedience to the law nor reliance on the whole system of Judaism can produce righteousness. Only reliance on God's gift of grace in Christ can save.

But even though righteousness is "apart from" law, it is by no means antithetical to law. Paul has already told us in 3:20 that the law cannot justify; rather, it brings the consciousness of sin. There is a role for law, and we see that again in this section of Romans. The law and the prophets bear witness to this righteousness (vs. 21). Here is another positive function of the law. It testifies about and points toward God's righteousness.

At the end of our verses, it seems that Paul realizes that some of the things he has said could be taken to mean that the law is negative and useless. Thus he asks, "Do we, then, nullify the law by this faith?" We could hardly be faulted for expecting a Yes answer in the light of what Paul has said. But in reality his answer is another one of those "absolutely not's." He concludes, "Rather, we uphold the law" (vs. 31). The role of the law will become clearer in Romans 7, but Paul wants us to be aware here that the law is not the problem. It still has a positive function. What he is saying doesn't nullify the law. But the function of the law is not to produce righteousness. Only God's grace can do that. Therefore, righteousness is revealed apart from law (vs. 21).

The scope of righteousness

After noticing Paul's emphasis on the word *all* in Romans 1:16 and 3:9, it should hardly surprise us to see the word stressed again here. *All* have sinned (vs. 23), but it is also true that God's righteousness is for *all* who believe (vs. 22). There is no distinction (vs. 22). All are in the same boat.

Although this seems self-evident to those of us who live in cultures that assume equality and freedom, we need to try to understand how hard this concept would have been for many of Paul's Jewish readers. Their identity was based on the fact that God did make distinctions. After all, hadn't God set them apart? When God prepared to lead them out of Egypt and make them a nation according to His covenant, He sent the plague of a swarm of flies on Egypt, but He spared Israel as He announced in the following words: "On that day I will deal differently with the land of Goshen, where my people live; no swarms of flies will be there, so that you will know that I, the LORD, am in this land. I will make a distinction between my people and your people" (Exod. 8:22, 23). It is audacious indeed for Paul to claim that God makes no distinctions. After all, in Exodus God Himself claimed that He did make distinctions.

But Paul draws on one of the pillars of Judaism to make his point. In verse 30 he draws on the truth that God is one. To this day, one of the important moments in Jewish synagogue worship is the recitation of the *Shema* (the Hebrew word "hear"), found in Deuteronomy 6:4: "Hear, O Israel: The LORD our God, the LORD is one." Paul argues that if a person takes this central affirmation of Judaism seriously, God cannot be the God of the Jews only; He must also be the God of the Gentiles (3:29). And if God is the God of both Jew and Gentile, and if both have sinned, and His restoring righteousness must be given freely at His own initiative by grace, then doesn't it make sense that God would deal the same with both Jew and Gentile? Paul will continue this theme in more detail in Romans 9 to 11, where he will show that God's inclusion of the Gentiles in no way nullifies His promise of faithfulness to the Jews.

Therefore, the scope of this gift is as wide as it can be. It embraces all. The free gift is for everyone who responds appropriately with faith.

Metaphors for God's gift of righteousness

For centuries, theologians have argued about various theories of the atonement, such as the substitutionary theory, the ransom theory, and the moral influence theory. Each is supposed to explain the inner workings of salvation. Obviously, Paul doesn't present any detailed theory of how the atonement works in these verses. He does, however, use several analogies that have given rise to theories of the atonement.

We understand Paul best when we avoid the temptation to press his metaphors into full-blown theories. We understand him worst when we ignore some of his metaphors and attempt to turn any one of them into the one and only explanation of the atonement. In this section, Paul uses several metaphors that are instructive for our understanding of salvation. We should learn from each of them and therefore increase our understanding of what God accomplished through Christ.

We have already studied the term *righteousness*. This, of course, is a metaphor that would have brought pictures of a court of law where a good judge acted to vindicate people and pictures of God the Covenant Maker, who was faithful to His people. Paul's message about God's righteousness goes beyond what any earthly judge could do. God justifies freely by His grace. He does this on the basis of Christ's death, as the following metaphors show.

God's free justification occurs through the "redemption" that is in Christ Jesus (3:24). This is also a picture word that would have brought familiar scenes to the minds of Paul's readers. The background of this term is the institution of slavery that prevailed in Paul's culture. A significant percentage of the population were slaves, and this term referred to the setting free of a slave. As God is the righteous judge who acts to vindicate us, He is also the liberator who breaks our bond and sets us free from slavery. (Paul will spell out the nature of this slavery to sin from which we are liberated in Romans 6 and 7.) This liberation from slavery comes through Christ Jesus. Paul clearly means that it is both revealed by and effected by Christ's sacrifice on the cross, but he doesn't provide detail on how this works. Theories of the atonement that press the details and posit a ransom paid to the devil to set us free go far beyond Paul's thought here.

Another analogy that follows in verse 25 is what the NIV calls a "sacrifice of atonement." This term is sometimes translated "propitiation" or "expiation," although neither of those terms means very much to us. In its most literal sense, this term refers to the mercy seat above the ark in the Most Holy Place of the sanctuary. (It is used in this way in the only other passage where it occurs in the New Testament, Hebrews 9:5.) The background picture that would probably have come to mind for Paul's readers was the Old Testament sanctuary service, in which the blood of animals was spilled to symbolize the removal of sin. As the sin problem was symbolically dealt with through sacrifice in the sanctuary, now the ultimate sacrifice of Christ, who shed His blood for us, becomes God's way of solving the dilemma of sin. (Paul may also have Abraham's near sacrifice of Isaac and God's provision of a sacrifice instead of Isaac in mind. See Genesis 22.) Our reliance on God's provision of Christ as our sacrifice accomplishes what the ancient sacrifices could only symbolize. Again, Paul hardly gives us a full-blown theory of the atonement, but he uses this picture from sacrificial temple worship as another window to help us understand what God has done for us in Christ.

Paul's metaphor of the sacrificial system in verse 25 provides another example of a passage where the verse is read differently depending on whether one understands "faith" here as Christ's faith or human faith. In the former case, the passage would mean that God set Christ forth as a sacrifice of atonement and that Christ accomplished this through His faithfulness to God in shedding His blood. If one holds the latter view, God set Christ forth as a sacrifice of atonement that we receive by faith. In either case, the sacrificial metaphor is intact.

What does all this mean for us? Each of these metaphors should be a personal picture of God's faithfulness to us. As we read this passage, we see ourselves as sinners whose sin problem is solved by Jesus Himself becoming our sacrifice, as slaves who are set free by Jesus, as guilty people, separated from God, acquitted and restored to a right relationship with Him as one of His covenant people. The more we can put ourselves in the picture, experience ourselves as the beneficiaries, and recognize God acting in Christ as the benefactor in each of these metaphors, the more we will appreciate Paul's message.

Here we see Paul's practical side. We have so often forced him into the mold of an abstract, hard-to-understand theologian, without noticing how he constantly uses analogies and symbols designed to let us experience the reality of his message.

The results of righteousness

So what are the results of this righteousness? What difference does it make? Let's first answer this question with regard to ourselves. The sin problem is decisively solved (vs. 25). We are put into a new standing before God through His salvation-creating righteousness, which He reveals and offers to us through Jesus. As a result, all of our boasting is excluded (vs. 27). This is a significant statement for Paul. For Paul, the opposite of faith is boasting. Faith is reliance upon God. Boasting reveals our reliance on ourselves and our achievements. The two are polar opposites (compare Eph. 2:8, 9). Through this process, God is seen to be both righteous Himself and the One who justifies on the basis of faith (3:26).

Let us try to summarize Paul's message up to this point in Romans. God's wrath has been revealed in the world's evil, which is seen in the idolatry and immorality of the Gentiles as well as in the moral lapses and judging of God's people. All have sinned and have failed to achieve a covenant relationship with God. Yet God remains faithful to His covenant, and through Jesus Christ, apart from the law, reveals His saving righteousness that freely, by His grace, restores all who put their reliance on God to a new covenant relationship with God. This excludes all boasting and reliance on human achievement. It is for all, without any distinctions, for God is one and is the God of everyone. This puts all of us on the same ground and gives us a basis for a new community of responsibility toward God and each other.

All that Paul says in the rest of the letter will either buttress this foundation or build on it in one way or another.

■ Applying the Word

Romans 3:21-31

1. Which of the metaphors Paul uses to help us understand salvation appeals to me most? If I use my imagination and picture this analogy applying to me personally, what do I learn?
2. What is the role of Christ's blood in my salvation? How do I

make this meaningful in an age when we no longer participate in sacrifices?
3. When faith excludes all my boasting, will I still have self-
confidence and positive self-esteem? If so, how?
4. How does the fact that God is "one" affect my daily life with
other people?
5. How do I avoid relying on the law, as Paul shows I should,
and at the same time "uphold" the law?
6. In what specific ways do I rely on God alone and accept His
absolutely free gift without letting my response become another "work" upon which I rely?
7. If I were to draw a picture portraying God's righteousness,
what would it look like?

■ Researching the Word

1. Do a word study of the term *righteousness* or *justification*.
(They are usually translations of the same Greek word,
dikaiosyne.) Begin with your concordance, and look up all
the verses in Romans where this word occurs (there are over
thirty). In an English concordance, you will need to look up
both terms, *righteousness* and *justification*. Next, look up these
terms in a Bible dictionary. Finally, write a paragraph indi-
cating your understanding of the meaning of this word.
2. Use your Bible concordance to find all the verses where the
term *grace* appears in Romans. Look up all of these verses,
and make a list in your Romans notebook of the ways grace
is used. Write a paragraph summarizing the meaning of
grace. Compare your findings with those in a Bible dictionary or other reference work.
3. Read 2 Corinthians 10 to 13, where Paul, by his own admission, plays the fool and does some boasting. How does Paul's
boasting fit with Romans 3:27? Is Paul consistent? If so, explain how.
4. Compare Romans 3:21-31 with Galatians 2:15-21. What similarities do you find? What differences?

■ Further Study of the Word

1. For an example of the argument that *justification* in Paul's writings has to do, not only with individual salvation, but also with Christian communal life, see N. A. Dahl, "The Doctrine of Justification: Its Social Function and Implications," in *Studies in Paul*, 95-120.
2. For a discussion of righteousness as the "rectification of the ungodly," see L. E. Keck, *Paul and His Letters*, 117-130.
3. For a discussion of the term *righteousness* as a relational term, see P. Achtemeier, *Romans*, 61-66.
4. For a discussion of various ways that "righteousness" has been understood in Paul, see E. Kasemann, "The Righteousness of God in Paul," in *New Testament Questions of Today*, 168-182.
5. For a discussion of the meaning of the metaphors Paul uses, see C. H. Dodd, *The Epistle of Paul to the Romans*, 75-80.
6. For a treatment of the phrase "the righteousness of God" in Paul's thought and in Judaism, see excursus 3 in P. Stuhlmacher, *Paul's Letter to the Romans*, 29-32. For a discussion of the meaning of "faith" according to Paul, see excursus 7 in the same work, 76-78.
7. For the view that Romans 3:21-31 is the key to understanding Romans, see W. S. Campbell, "Romans III as a Key to the Structure and Thought of the Letter," in K. P. Donfried, ed., *The Romans Debate*, 251-264.
8. For arguments that "faith of Christ" in Romans 3 refers to Christ's faithfulness, see B. W. Longenecker, "*PISTIS* in Romans 3:25: Neglected Evidence for the 'Faithfulness of Christ'?"; R. B. Hays, *The Faith of Jesus Christ: An Investigation of the Narrative Substructure of Galatians 3:1-4:11*; D. A. Campbell, "Romans 1:17—A *Crux Interpretum* for the *Pistis Christou* Debate." Campbell argues that in Romans 1:17, the first reference to faith is to Christ's faithfulness and the second is to human faith, with the resultant meaning "the eschatological saving righteousness of God is being revealed

in the gospel by means of faithfulness (namely, the faithfulness of Christ), with the goal of faith/fulness (in the Christian)" (see p. 281).

9. For an argument that "faith of Jesus Christ" refers to faith
   in Christ, see J. D. G. Dunn, *Romans*, 1:166, 167.

CHAPTER SIX

Father Abraham

Romans 4

In Romans 3 Paul claimed that salvation is based on God's free act of grace and that it is for all, both Jew and Gentile. It would have been easy for antagonists to claim that both of these points were innovations designed to subvert the historic faith of Israel and to nullify God's covenant promises to Israel. After all, Israel was God's chosen nation and had been called to obedience. Wouldn't grace subvert the latter, and wouldn't an inclusive community, where Jews and Gentiles were on an equal footing, subvert the former? (Many Jews, of course, believed that Gentiles would find salvation, but only by becoming Jews first. Paul, however, not only places proselytes, or converts to Judaism, within the sphere of salvation; he includes Gentiles as Gentiles on an equal basis with Jews.)

So where might we expect Paul to go to meet the antagonists' arguments? We have already seen him make free use of the Old Testament. Now he continues that line of defense and even finds the clincher to his claims. Paul finds in the father of the Jews, Abraham himself, the example par excellence of the truth of his claims. How can this be so? Paul will show us in Romans 4.

■ Getting Into the Word

Romans 4

Read Romans 4 in at least two different translations, and write out answers to the following questions.

1. What does this chapter teach you about the law and its function in the Christian life?
2. What does this chapter teach you about the way a person receives salvation? Make a list of as many specifics as you can.
3. Why do you think Paul spends so much time on Abraham? Are there other Old Testament figures that might have served Paul's purposes as well? Why or why not?
4. Make a list of all the ways that Abraham serves as an example in this chapter.
5. Why does Paul bring in David in verses 6 to 8? Use your marginal references to see what psalm Paul quotes here. Read the entire psalm. What does the example of David and the use of this psalm in particular contribute to Paul's discussion in Romans 4?
6. Explain the meaning of verse 15: "And where there is no law there is no transgression." Wouldn't sin be sin even if the law were not present? What does Paul mean earlier in the same verse when he says that the law brings wrath?
7. What does Paul mean in verse 18, where he says: "Against all hope, Abraham in hope believed"?
8. How does this chapter function in the flow of Paul's argument?

■ Exploring the Word

Abraham, Our Forefather (4:1)

In the latter part of Isaiah, the prophet offers hope to the exiles and addresses those who would pursue righteousness, saying, "Listen to me, you who pursue righteousness and who seek the LORD: Look to the rock from which you were cut and to the quarry from which you were hewn; look to Abraham, your father, and to Sarah, who gave you birth" (Isa. 51:1, 2a). Abraham was the father of the Jews. They were to look to him in order to pursue righteousness.

This status given to Abraham continued in intertestamental times, when Jews emphasized that Abraham had kept the law even before it was given. For example, in the intertestamental work Ecclesiasticus (also called the Wisdom of Ben Sirach; not to be confused with the Old Testament book Ecclesiastes) we read: "Abraham was the great father of a multitude of nations, and no one has been found like him in glory. He kept the law of the Most High, and entered into a covenant with him" (44:20, NRSV).

The New Testament carries on the tradition of Abraham's exalted status. It repeatedly testifies to the importance that was attached to having Abraham as one's father. Matthew traces the genealogy of Jesus back to Abraham and calls Jesus "the son of David, the son of Abraham (Matt. 1:1, 2). In the "faith chapter," Hebrews 11, which presents the Old Testament examples of faith, it is Abraham who receives the most attention (vss. 8-12, 17-19).

We also find, however, that often in the New Testament there is a critique of false reliance upon being a descendant of Abraham. For example, John the Baptist warns his hearers, "Produce fruit in keeping with repentance. And do not begin to say to yourselves, 'We have Abraham as our father.' For I tell you that out of these stones God can raise up children for Abraham" (Luke 3:8). In the Gospel of John, Jews object when Jesus teaches that the truth will set them free by saying, "We are Abraham's descendants, and have never been slaves of anyone. How can you say that we shall be set free?" (John 8:33), But Jesus replies, "If you were Abraham's children, then you would do the things Abraham did" (vs. 40).

Jesus also challenges the standard definition of what it means to be a son of Abraham. After He brought salvation to the house of the hated tax collector Zacchaeus, He reminded His hearers, "This man, too, is a son of Abraham" (Luke 19:9). He did the same when He called the stooped woman He healed on Sabbath a daughter of Abraham (Luke 13:16).

Paul finds Abraham, the undisputed forefather of the Jews, to be the perfect example to prove the two basic points he has made: that salvation is based on faith in God's *grace*, not works, and that salvation is for *all*. This proof comes from two texts in the Genesis story of Abraham. The first is Genesis 15:6, which reads, "Abram believed

the LORD, and he credited it to him as righteousness." The second is
Genesis 17:5, where God says to Abram, "No longer will you be
called Abram; your name will be Abraham, for I have made you a
father of many nations." These two verses, as well as some additional reflections by Paul, lead to a number of points of comparison
where Abraham becomes an important model for the faith that Paul
proclaims.

Here are some of the points about Abraham that Paul will make
in the course of Romans 4:

> Abraham trusted God, not works (vss. 3-5).
> Abraham received righteousness as a gift, not as wages
> (vs. 4).
> Abraham was uncircumcised when he was justified (vs. 10).
> Abraham became heir through promise, not law (vs. 13).
> Abraham became the father of *all* (vss. 12, 16).
> Abraham hoped against hope (vs. 18).
> Abraham was strong, not weak in faith (vss. 20, 21).
> Abraham is an example for us (vs. 23).

Throughout this chapter, we will see the significance of these
points for Paul's understanding of our Christian faith.

Abraham's Salvation (4:2-5)

In verse 2 Paul raises the question of Abraham's justification. If it
were by works, Abraham would have something to boast about. The
idea is so objectionable and unthinkable that Paul immediately adds,
"but not before God." If Abraham had something to boast about, it
would blow all that Paul said in Romans 3:21-31, for Paul believed
that as long as righteousness came by God's grace and was available
to all on an equal basis, boasting was excluded (vs. 27). So how will
Paul show that Abraham was not justified by works?

Paul's evidence comes in the first of his two important texts from
the Genesis account of the Abraham story, Genesis 15:6. The text,
after all, speaks of Abraham receiving righteousness. Paul finds two

extremely important concepts in this short verse. First, Abraham believed (or had faith or trusted, depending on how we translate the word) God. The basic truth Paul has been arguing for is right there in the Genesis story. Abraham believed! It was his faith or trust that led to his righteousness.

Paul finds even more good news in this verse, however. When Abraham believed or trusted, it was credited or reckoned to him as righteousness. The original Hebrew word can often mean "to be counted or considered." Paul concludes from this that righteousness is not wages paid for work done, but a gift credited to Abraham on the basis of his faith. He explains this in verses 4 and 5. In verse 4 Paul says, "Now when a man *works*, his wages are not credited to him as a gift [the actual words in Greek are "according to grace"], but as an obligation." On the other hand, in verse 5 Paul contrasts the one who believes and whose *faith* is credited as righteousness. So the word *credited* tells Paul that Abraham received righteousness on the basis of grace, not works. This grace is appropriated by Abraham's faith in "God who justifies the wicked" (vs. 5).

This phrase is a shocking one. We saw in the last chapter that no good judge would acquit the guilty. God detests such a practice (Prov. 17:15). We might add to this Proverbs 24:24: "Whoever says to the guilty, 'You are innocent'—peoples will curse him and nations denounce him." We certainly would find it offensive today. If a criminal commits a particularly grisly murder and is then acquitted on a technicality, our blood boils. But God is a God who acquits the guilty.

We won't really understand what this means unless we remember that Paul has already shown us we are all guilty (3:9, 10). If God only acquitted the good guys, the innocent, there would be no hope for anyone. Yet how does God keep integrity and acquit the guilty? At least two factors are important in providing an answer to this question. First, God's righteousness is not only made known but is also effected by the sacrifice of atonement, Jesus Christ. Even though Paul doesn't give us the details of how this works, he makes it clear that it is true (vss. 24, 25). Second, God's acquittal is more than a forensic declaration; it is an initiative that sets the situation right and actually makes a difference by bringing the wicked into a new relationship with Him.

Abraham trusted such a God, and it was credited to him as righteousness. This makes him a perfect example of righteousness by grace through faith. Boasting is excluded even for father Abraham. He, too, received his righteousness as a gift of God's grace.

The Example of David's Psalm (4:6-8)

Paul now turns very briefly and almost parenthetically to another example, again a central figure in Israel's history. This passage is related to verses 1 through 5 because Paul notes that the same word *credited* or *reckoned* that he was dealing with in the Abraham story also occurs in the passage penned by David in Psalm 32. Here the idea is converse. It is not a matter of crediting righteousness to a person but of *not* crediting sins against a person.

That Paul takes the two ideas as synonymous is seen in his introduction to the quotation in verse 6. He says that David speaks "of the blessedness of the man to whom God credits righteousness apart from works." This identification of the two concepts is actually helpful for understanding Paul's view of righteousness. At least in part, righteousness means not having our sins counted against us. In other words, righteousness includes forgiveness, although it is also more.

So Genesis, with its narrative statement about Abraham's righteousness, and Psalm 32, with its poetic statement about forgiveness, both make use of the same term, *credited* or *counted*, to testify about the same truth of God's grace.

Righteousness and Circumcision (4:9-12)

In verse 9 Paul asks a question that grows out of the psalm, but to answer it he turns back to Abraham. Is the blessedness the psalm pronounces only for the circumcised, or is it also for the uncircumcised? For Paul, this is the equivalent of asking whether it is for the Jews only or also for the Gentiles. The chronology of the Genesis account of Abraham provides an answer.

Paul's text about Abraham being reckoned righteous on the basis of his faith appears in Genesis 15:6. But it is some years later, in Genesis 17, that Abraham is circumcised. This proves to Paul that the righteousness credited to Abraham was in no way dependent on his circumcision. Abraham's circumcision, i.e., his Judaism, was not the basis for his righteousness. Rather, Paul sees circumcision as sign or seal of the righteousness credited to him by faith before he was circumcised (4:11).

This uniquely qualifies Abraham to be the father of both Jew and Gentile. He is the father of Gentiles, who, like him, receive right-eousness on the basis of their faith without being circumcised (vs. 11b). But he is also the father of those Jews who have the same kind of faith that he did (vs. 12). In other words, it is not merely on the basis of biological relationship that Abraham is the father of the Jews. His real descendants are those who share his faith. Paul already an-ticipates what he will argue more explicitly in verses 16 and 17. Abraham is the father of all, both Jew and Gentile, for he is the model of faith for both. The obvious implication is that faith, not circumcision, is the basis for righteousness.

Promise, Not Law (4:13-15)

Paul continues by showing that not only is circumcision ruled out as a basis for righteousness, but the law is also ruled out. Given the tradition that Abraham kept the law even before it was given, one might conclude that this obedience was the basis for righteousness. But Paul refutes such an idea by contrasting law with promise.

In the verse just before Genesis 15:6, which Paul has been treat-ing, we find a promise. God promised Abraham that his offspring would be as numerous as the stars of the heavens. The fact that these two verses are coupled together shows Paul that God's promise of grace is not dependent on law. This promise is worthless if one can be an heir on the basis of law. In verse 15 Paul summarizes again what he said in 1:18 to 3:20—the law brings wrath.

When Paul goes on to say that where there is no law there is no transgression of the law, his words must be understood within the context of that earlier discussion of God's wrath. Paul obviously doesn't mean that where there is no law there is no accountability before God, for he has shown in Romans 1 that even those who are outside of the law still stand under judgment. His point here is the same as in Romans 3:20. Law brings consciousness of sin, not right-eousness.

The Father of All (4:16, 17)

Now Paul comes to his second text from the Genesis story of Abraham. In Genesis 17:5 God tells Abraham, "I have made you a father of many nations." To understand the significance of this verse for Paul, we need to remember that in Greek the same word is used for "nation" and "Gentile." So the verse could be translated that Abraham would be the father of many Gentiles. Thus Paul sees clear Old Testament evidence for what he has already pointed to in verses 11 and 12. The promise is not only for the Jews. Abraham is the father of all. The promise is for all of Abraham's offspring, both Jew and Gentile. Abraham is the father of *all*.

We shouldn't pass over the significance of this verse. It provides an Old Testament basis for one of Paul's most important themes in this letter. No term is more important in Romans than the word *all*. God's grace is for all. Abraham embodies this truth, because the promise made to him, the father of the Jews and the father of "na-tions," brings Jew and Gentile together under God's one gracious promise.

Hope Against Hope (4:18-22)

In these verses, Paul first introduces the concept of hope into Romans. Even though we wouldn't realize it up to this point, we will see in Romans 5 and again in Romans 8 that it is an important part of Paul's understanding of the Christian life, and we find here that Abraham serves as a model for it as well. Even though the promise that he would be the father of many nations came when he was so old that the promise appeared ludicrous, Abraham trusted the prom-ise. After all, this was the God who could give life to the dead and

call things that were not into being (vs. 17). Even though his body
was old and as good as dead, and Sarah's womb was also as good as
dead, Abraham would trust this God and His promise. He trusted
that God would do what He promised, and this is why faith was
credited to him as righteousness (vs. 22).

From this we gain additional insight into the nature of faith. What
Abraham did is precisely what we are called to do—to trust God's
promise and rely on it completely. Whenever we rely on anything
else, we show a lack of faith.

In verses 20 and 21 Paul emphasizes Abraham's faith in a way that
seems to anticipate his major discussion of Christian life and practice in Romans 14 to 15. There Paul talks about divisions over certain dietary practices. He refers to the more strict Christians who
eat only vegetables as "weak in faith" (14:1). Paul, on the other hand,
identifies with the "strong" (15:1), although he gives advice that transcends either position and tries to bring both groups into unity. Paul
tells us that Abraham didn't weaken in faith, but was strengthened
in faith. Certainly Paul expects his readers to remember this when
they come to the end of the letter. In other words, Abraham serves
not only as a theological model, but also as a model for the practical
problems that faced the Romans. We will say more about this when
we study Romans 14.

A Model for Us (4:23-26)

Finally, at the end of this chapter, Paul tells us what any atten-
tive reader would already know! These words about Abraham
trusting God and it being credited to him as righteousness are
for us too. Paul hasn't just been presenting us with an interesting
story or a history lesson. As the father of all, Abraham models the
experience of salvation for all of us. We, too, will have righteousness credited to us if we trust God's promise and rely on Him
who raised Jesus from the dead. Jesus Christ is the living reality
of this promise.

Remember that in Romans 1 (verses 24, 26, and 28) we learned
how God in His wrath "gives over" sinners to their sin. Now Paul

reverses this picture of God's wrath by using the same word to announce that Jesus was "handed over" for our sin and raised for our righteousness so that we no longer need fear God's wrath. Thus Abraham's story becomes our story. We, too, trust God's promise and find righteousness credited to us as a gift of God's grace.

Summary

This radical good news of God's grace and salvation through trust in Christ didn't cut Paul off from his Jewish past. He saw it in continuity with his Judaism, even though the law of Judaism could not serve as its basis. The good news was already anticipated in the story of the father of the Jews, Abraham.

After all, Abraham trusted God and received righteousness. It was counted to him as a gift. He wasn't even circumcised yet. So Abraham is a fitting symbol of salvation by faith.

And beyond that, Paul also sees that God promised Abraham that all the nations of the earth would be blessed in him. So he is not only the father of the Jews, but also of the Gentiles who will receive God's righteousness by trusting God just like Abraham did.

Abraham's example affirms God's impartial generosity to all people, Jew and Gentile, and assures every one of us that God is our Saviour too.

■ Applying the Word

Romans 4

1. **How is Abraham my father? If I go through the list of points that Paul makes about Abraham in Romans 4, how does each one apply to my own walk with God?**
2. **Has the law brought "wrath" for me, as Paul says in 4:15? Isn't the law supposed to be a delight? How, then, does it bring wrath? What is the role of the law in my life? Can it bring wrath and still be a delight?**

3. Abraham hoped that God would fulfil His promise that Abraham would have vast descendants "against all hope" (4:18). What is it that I must hope "against all hope"? What is it that makes it most difficult for me to trust God's promise?

■ Researching the Word

1. Read Genesis 12:1 to 25:11. Make a list of all God's promises to Abraham. Although Paul only emphasizes Abraham's strong faith, do you find places where Abraham's trust in God seemed to waver? List all the evidence you find for the strength of Abraham's faith. Write a page characterizing the Abraham you meet in Genesis. How does this picture compare and contrast with Paul's picture of Abraham in Romans 4?

2. Read Hebrews 11. What role does Abraham play in this chapter? How does this picture of Abraham compare and contrast with your pictures from Genesis and Romans? How many of the same points are made in Hebrews and Romans?

3. Read Galatians 3:6-9. How many of the major points Paul makes about Abraham appear in this short paragraph? What Scripture texts does Paul use in the Galatians passage? Could you consider this passage to be a summary of Romans 4? Are there any new or different emphases in Galatians?

4. Read James 2:20-26. How do you harmonize James and Paul? Are they saying opposite things? Are they saying the same thing in different words? In order to support your answer, you will probably need to look beyond these few verses to see what role Christian behavior and ethical responsibility play in the whole of both Romans and James.

■ Further Study of the Word

1. For a brief discussion of Paul's use of the diatribe style in this section of Romans and its significance for an understanding of Paul's relationship to Jewish readers, see P.

Achtemeier, *Romans*, 73-76.

2. For a thorough study of Paul's diatribe style, see S. K. Stowers, *The Diatribe and Paul's Letter to the Romans*.

3. For Paul's use of the Old Testament in Romans 4, see R. B. Hays, *Echoes of Scripture in the Letters of Paul*, 54-57.

4. For a discussion of Romans 4 that is more helpful in including background material on Jewish understandings of Abraham than it is in some of its theological conclusions, see A. T. Hanson, *Studies in Paul's Technique and Theology*, 52-66.

5. For an in-depth, 314-page study of Paul's use of Abraham in his letters, see R. A. Harrisville, III, *The Figure of Abraham in the Epistles of St. Paul*.

CHAPTER SEVEN

Christ and Adam

Romans 5

In fifteenth-century Spain, a coin appeared that pictured the pillars Hercules, symbolizing the straits of Gibraltar. The inscription read "N more beyond." Thanks to Columbus and other explorers, the coin becam obsolete. Around 1537 another coin appeared with the same picture but a new inscription, "Much more beyond."

Romans 5 points us to much more beyond. The phrase "much more" is repeated four times in verses 9, 10, 15, and 17. Each time Paul either leads us from our present experience with Christ and the good news about what God has already done for us to even greater promises for the future, or he contrasts the negative results of Adam's legacy with the promises that come through Christ. Paul contrasts our relationship with Adam and with Christ. Open your Bible to Romans 5, and discover what good news God's promises of "much more" provide.

■ Getting Into the Word

Romans 5

Read Romans 5 in at least two different translations, and write out answers to the following questions after you have spent some time contemplating each one.

1. **Outline Paul's summary of the Christian life in verses 1 to 5. List all the benefits that Christians have in the present. How**

does suffering fit in with this experience? What is reserved for the future? How are present and future tied together in this passage?

2. Look at the four "much more" passages in this chapter (verses 9, 10, 15, and 17). List the present reality Paul mentions first and then the "much more" we can also expect in each passage. What does this suggest to you about the relationship between the present and the future for Paul? How do these "much more" promises speak to your own personal relationship with Christ?

3. Analyze Paul's contrast between Christ and Adam. Make two columns in your Romans notebook. In the first, list all that Adam did and how that affects us. Then in the second, list all that Christ did and how that affects us. What is Paul trying to show us through this analogy?

4. Explain the words "because all sinned" in 5:12. Do these words make sense as a conclusion for all that Paul has already said in this verse? What is the relationship between Adam's sin and my sin? For which am I condemned? What evidence supports your answer?

5. Do you see a conflict between Paul's words in 4:15 and 5:13? Is there sin or transgression where there is no law?

6. What does Paul mean to say by his use of the contrast between the "righteous" man and the "good" man in 5:7? What is the difference?

7. In what way does law increase the trespass (verse 20)? Is this really why God gave the law? How do you make sense out of these words?

■ Exploring the Word

New Life in God's Grace (5:1-5)

Paul has left no doubt about our justification through Christ. Romans 4 ended with these words about Christ: "He was delivered over to death for our sins and was raised to life for our justification."

So we have been justified. So what? What difference does it make? Paul takes up that question in the first few verses of Romans 5.

He begins with the words "Therefore since." What he is about to say obviously flows from what he has already said. In the first five verses of this chapter, Paul summarizes this new experience of justification through faith in Christ and points us to the realities that flow from it.

The first of the new realities that flow from justification is peace with God through our Lord Jesus Christ. The Hebrew concept of peace that Paul grew up with was much more holistic than our concept of the term usually is. Peace referred to well-being and wholeness in its broadest sense. Once we have been justified, there is no longer any thought of God's wrath. Once we have become acquainted with God's love and His action for us, we live at peace, secure in a new relationship of total well-being in harmony with God.

Yet that isn't all. We have also gained access into grace. What is more, we now stand in that grace (vs. 2). It is as if grace is a new air that we breathe or a new world on which we stand. We live in a new atmosphere, a new place. To be a Christian is to breathe the atmosphere of grace, secure in God's acceptance.

But there is even more. A new stance to the future flows from justification as well. This stance is characterized by hope. The NIV reads, "And we rejoice in the hope of the glory of God." But the Greek word that stands behind the word *rejoice* is really stronger than the translation "rejoice" suggests. In addition, the translation "rejoice" misses an important connection between these verses and things Paul has said in each of the last two chapters. What Paul really says is, "We *boast* in the hope of the glory of God" (vs. 2).

Now this poses something of a problem. Paul has already told us that faith excludes *all* boasting (3:27) and that even Abraham had nothing to boast about (4:5). And now he tells us that one of the characteristics of the Christian life is boasting, specifically, boasting in hope!

Obviously Paul isn't talking here about arrogance or pride, the kind of self-reliance that he speaks against in Romans 3. But now Paul shows what it is that replaces that other kind of boasting that he excludes. Boasting in hope is a confidence that faces the future unafraid. Paul actually repeats the term *boast* three times in this chapter. He tells us that we *boast in hope* (vs. 2), *we boast in our sufferings* (vs. 3), and *we boast in God* (vs. 11). These three together show the kind of confidence and assurance that define the Christian life. Because we have confidence in God, we also have confidence in the future and live in hope.

But what about boasting in our sufferings? Doesn't that seem negative and perhaps even a bit morbid? Paul's emphasis is on the way that hope transcends everything else in life, even suffering. Christians can boast in suffering because they boast in God and know that the future is in His hands. Not even suffering can deter such hope and confidence. In fact, Paul sees benefits to suffering, although he certainly wasn't the type who tried to bring on suffering in order to revel in it in a neurotic way. That isn't the kind of boasting in suffering he has in mind. Rather, he knows that suffering with the right spirit leads to perseverance and produces character, which in turn produces more hope (vss. 3, 4).

Paul adds that hope doesn't disappoint us (vs. 5). Again Paul's word is stronger than the English translation suggests. Paul says that hope doesn't put us to shame. Paul lived in a world where shame and honor were important concepts. In our individualistic society, we tend to do our own thing without worrying about what others think. But in the more community-oriented world of the first century, there was nothing worse than having the community look at you and see shame. It was almost as if shame were something real worn on the face for all to see (something like the expression we use about "having egg on one's face"). Paul says that hope doesn't bring shame. Rather, it brings confidence.

Paul ends this brief summary of Christian experience with a beautiful image. Through the Holy Spirit, God has poured out His love into our hearts (vs. 5). Grace, peace, faith, righteousness, redemption, and the other terms that Paul uses to communicate his message are all metaphors and picture words that open the window on the one reality. God loves us and pours out His love into our hearts. We can respond to this love and find a new kind of life in the present and hope for the future. This is Paul's good news.

The Basis Once Again (5:6-8)

It seems that Paul can't go very long without returning to the basis of his good news. In verses 6 to 8 Paul points us to the basis once again by reminding us that it is Christ's death that makes the good news possible. He affirms that at just the right time, when we were still weak, Christ died for the ungodly. Let us notice in turn the terms *time*, *weak*, and *ungodly*.

The Greek language has at least two different words for time. The first, from which we get our word *chronology*, refers to a period of time in a chronological or quantitative sense. Paul uses a different word here (and several other times in Romans). It refers to a welcome or favorable time in a qualitative sense. Sometimes Paul uses the term with the word *now* to refer to the present time (3:26; 8:18; 11:5). But here and in 9:9 (where he quotes from Genesis 18:10) he uses it with a preposition to refer to the appointed time or the right time. Christ's death wasn't an accident of history. It was part of God's plan. As such, it came at the appointed time, according to plan.

At this time, we were still "weak." In Romans 4 Paul used this term to show that Abraham didn't "weaken" in faith, and in Romans 14 he will use it to refer to those scrupulous in diet as the "weak" in faith. Here Paul uses it to emphasize our powerlessness. It was when we were absolutely powerless to do anything that Christ died for us, proving that our only basis for the hope of salvation is the death of Christ. This is true on a cosmic level. When humans were powerless, Christ died for us. But Paul also wants us to understand it at the personal level. I was powerless, and Christ died for me. Nothing I could have done would earn my salvation. But my weakness serves to show God's strength.

In Romans 4:5 Paul told us that Abraham trusted the God who justifies the ungodly. Now, in verse 6, Paul shows the basis for that justification: Christ died for the ungodly. Of course, we are all ungodly. Again Paul emphasizes that we bring no goodness to our salvation. He stresses it again at the end of verse 8. While we were still sinners, Christ died for us. By now the picture should be clear. We were weak. We were ungodly. We were sinners. Christ died for us. There is no doubt that Christ, not we ourselves, saves us. But it was not only Christ who was involved in this sacrifice on our behalf. God was active in Christ. God was demonstrating His own love for us in Christ's death.

In this short, three-verse section, Paul tells us several important truths about Christ's death. It was part of God's plan and came at the appointed time. It was a death on our behalf. However we understand the atonement, the indisputable fact is that Christ's death was efficacious for us. Because of Christ's death, we are freed from death. Paul may not explain all the details of precisely how the atonement works, but he leaves no question that Christ's death on our behalf makes salvation possible for us. Finally, Paul shows us that the death of Christ was also a demonstration of God's love. When we look at the cross, we see God's love poured out for us.

In the middle verse of this short section, verse 7, Paul makes an interesting contrast between Christ's death for us and typical human action. While Christ was willing to die for weak, ungodly sinners, humans aren't even willing to give their lives for a righteous person. This contrast between human and divine attitudes is clear enough, but then Paul goes on to add a caveat that seems confusing. Although humans won't die for a righteous person, they might die for a "good" person. What is the difference between the righteous person and the good person, and why would one be more willing to die for the latter?

Various answers have been suggested. Most interpreters believe that *good* refers to the person who is appealing, winsome, and charismatic. One might dare to die for such a person. Others see this against a more specific background in Paul's day and suggest that Paul is referring to the benefactor in the prevalent system of patronage. Thus one would not die for just anyone, even if righteous, but might die for one's patron or the master he/she was pledged to protect. We probably can't tell for sure, but the basic point is evident nevertheless. Christ did something that goes beyond the best of human altruism when He died on behalf of the ungodly.

Much More (5:9-11)

In verse 9 Paul begins a series of contrasts between the present and the "much more" that we can expect. In the first two, Paul contrasts the positive present experience we have with the even greater promise of the future. The second two contrast the past negative legacy of Adam with the positive promise of our expectations in Christ. The following chart shows these contrasts:

Verse 9
Now: Since we have now been justified by his blood,
Much More: How *much more* shall we be saved from God's wrath through him.

Verse 10
Now: For if, when we were God's enemies, we were reconciled to him through the death of his Son,
Much More: How *much more*, having been reconciled, shall we be saved through his life!

Verse 15
Adam: For if the many died by the trespass of the one man,
Much More: How *much more* did God's grace and the gift that came by the grace of the one man, Jesus Christ, overflow to the many!

Verse 17
Adam: For if, by the trespass of the one man, death reigned through that one man,
Much More: How *much more* will those who receive God's abundant provision of grace and of the gift of righteousness reign in life through the one man, Jesus Christ.

In this section we will concentrate on the first two of these "much more" contrasts. The last two will fit in the next section on the Christ-Adam typology.

The first two contrasts are especially important for understanding Paul's eschatology. We usually think of eschatology as the study of last-day events leading to the second coming of Christ. But for Paul, the death and resurrection of Christ was already an eschatological event. The decisive event in salvation had already occurred. In Christ, God had already won the decisive battle that assured the final outcome of earth's history. Paul saw a strong "already" aspect in Christian eschatology. And this "already" had to do, not just with the world as a whole, but with the individual Christian as well. Christians have already, *now* been justified by Christ's blood (vs. 9). They have already, *now* been reconciled with God through the death of God's Son (vs. 10). The Christian's present is already an experience so overwhelmingly new and decisive that it can be characterized as eschatological salvation.

Yet this present aspect of salvation and eschatology in no way detracts from Paul's emphasis on hope for the future. On the contrary, it is what we have already experienced in the present that gives shape and meaning to the future. Moreover, this present experience provides assurance for the future. Here is where the *much more* becomes most vivid. If we have already been justified and reconciled to God, think how much more we can expect! If our present experience of salvation is so powerfully overwhelming, think how much more we can trust God's promises for the future. For Paul, eschatological hope is not idle speculation. Our present experience gives us evidence for future hope (vss. 9, 10). By this pattern, Paul consistently ties the present and the future together in his eschatology.

We should say a word here about the concept of reconciliation (vss. 10, 11). This is the first time the concept appears in Romans (we will meet it once more in Romans 11:15), although Paul had already worked with it in more detail in 2 Corinthians 5:17-20 (which was probably written before Romans). This is yet another metaphor Paul uses to provide one more window on salvation. It fits well with Paul's earlier emphasis on the universality of God's wrath (Romans 1:18–3:20). Christ's death removed us from the atmosphere of God's wrath and brought us into harmony with God. We became reconciled to Him.

Again Paul makes no attempt to explain the inner workings of this dynamic; he simply declares that it happened. As is the case with most metaphors, this one can be misunderstood. Some theories of the atonement have pictured a hostile God who must be assuaged by Christ's death. That is far from Paul's perspective. When Paul speaks of us as "God's enemies" (vs. 10), that doesn't mean that God was ever hostile to us. Remember that even God's wrath has to do with His love and respect for humans and their freedom. We were the enemies, not God. We must remember what Paul says in 2 Corinthians 5:18, 19: "All this is from God, who reconciled us to himself through Christ and gave us the ministry of reconciliation: that God was reconciling the world to himself in Christ." God was not the hostile party whom Christ had to convince to accept us. God was active in the process of reconciliation from the beginning.

To find evidence that this is often misunderstood, one only need ask a group of college students to reflect on their childhood images of God and Christ. Inevitably they say they found Christ a much friendlier figure than God. But Paul leaves no room for such a difference. Through Christ, God reconciled us to Himself. The cross demonstrates God's love and grace.

Christ and Adam (5:12-21)

In Romans 5:12 Paul begins a sustained analogy that contrasts Christ and Adam. But this is not just a contrast of the two; it is a contrast of the results of each for us. Paul explores our relationship to Adam and the results of that relationship, and our relationship to Christ and its results. The following chart summarizes Paul's major points.

Adam	*Christ*
Sin entered through him (vs. 12).	
By his trespass the many died (vs. 15).	Through Him God's grace overflows (vs. 15).
He brings condemnation (vs. 16).	He brings justification (vs. 16).
Through him death	Through Him, we reign in

reigned (vs. 17).	life (vs. 17).
He brings condemnation to all (vs. 18).	He brings life to all (vs. 18).
Through his disobedience the many were made sinners (vs. 19).	Through His obedience, the many will be made righteous (vs. 19).

One doesn't need to spend long with this chart to get the idea that everything bad came from Adam and everything good came from Christ. But how did sin and death come from Adam? That has been debated since the days of the early church. Much of the discussion has centered around verse 12.

This is a strange verse that linguists call an "anacoluthon." That simply means that the sentence never ends the way it should. (Unfortunately, students often hear me do the same thing when I lecture. I start a sentence, but then go off on another thought before I complete the sentence correctly.) Paul begins by saying, "Therefore, just as sin entered the world through one man . . ." The grammar of this beginning demands some kind of contrast, but Paul never quite gets there, even though the sentence in Greek doesn't end until the end of verse 14. From the later contrasts that Paul makes in this chapter, it is obvious that Paul started out to say that just as sin entered through one man, so life or salvation entered through the one man Jesus Christ.

It is clear in verse 12 that sin and death came through Adam, but it is not clear *how* it came, and a translation ambiguity in verse 12 has helped to fuel the centuries-long debate. The last phrase of verse 12 begins with a preposition and a pronoun that literally mean "in which" or "in whom." Since the time of Augustine, some have taken this to mean "in whom all sinned" with reference to Adam. Thus they argue for an original sin passed on from Adam to all his posterity. We are all sinners because Adam sinned. Indeed, we sinned in him. We are born sinners because we receive sin as an inheritance from Adam. (This view is one of the reasons for infant baptism, which some see as a much-needed cleansing from this original sin with which one is born.)

Others (including almost all modern translators) take this preposition-pronoun combination to mean "because." With this reading we are sinners, not "in" Adam, but "because" we sinned. Paul uses this particular preposition-pronoun structure on at least three other occasions (2 Cor. 5:4; Phil. 3:12; 4:12), and in each case the meaning is "because," and that is probably the meaning here as well. But knowing that doesn't answer the question of how our sinning is related to Adam's first sin. The fact is that Paul doesn't really answer that question.

His concern is different. He accepts as fact that Adam's sin is what got the world and all of us into trouble. It introduced the deadly power of sin into the world. What Paul is really interested in doing, however, is contrasting two different kinds of life. Adam and Christ are the models for these two kinds of life, and all of us participate in one or the other. Adam represents sin-oriented life. Christ represents salvation-oriented life. Either Adam or Christ represents our particular orientation. We identify with and are in solidarity with one or the other. We may take comfort in blaming Adam for getting us into this mess, but if we live a sin-oriented life we simply repeat his kind of life and prove that we are in solidarity with him.

What Paul is most interested in showing us, however, is that no matter how big a mess Adam got us into, Christ's solution not only cleaned up the mess but went far beyond. Yes, Adam got everyone into a mess. (The term *many* which Paul uses several times in this section, should be taken as a synonym for *all*. The language comes from Isaiah 53, upon which Paul draws in recounting Christ's accomplishments for us.) But now Christ brings a solution for everyone as well. If Adam brought sin, death, and condemnation to all, Christ much more brought grace, justification, and life to all. Adam brings the problem, but Christ brings an even bigger solution, for grace is greater than sin. No matter how great the sin, God has grace to spare.

There is a historical element to the matters of law, sin, and death that seems somewhat confusing in this chapter. In the previous chapter (4:15), Paul said that where there is no law there is no transgression. This might lead us to conclude that there was not a sin problem until the law entered. Yet in 5:13 Paul says that sin was in the world before the law was given, although it wasn't "reckoned" or "counted." Then in 5:20 he tells us that the law was added so the trespass might increase. How are we to make sense out of all this?

Paul teaches us that the sin problem began with Adam. He transgressed a specific command of God. The result of sin is death, and so the fact that death reigned from the time of Adam to that of Moses (vs. 14) shows that sin was in the world. But when the law was given, it revealed the nature and scope of sin. Even though sin was in the world doing its damage, it wasn't plainly seen or understood until the law defined it. This is one way in which the law "increased" sin. (But it is not the only way. Paul will show us another in Romans 7.)

Paul's bottom line is that even when the law increased the sin that Adam had introduced, grace still increased all the more. There is no need for us to live a sin-oriented life in solidarity with Adam. God's grace, available to *all* in Christ, far exceeds the problem of sin.

If this is such good news, and if grace can really cover any amount of sin, why not go on sinning so that grace can increase all the more? There seems to be a certain logic about it. Paul will take up that question when we move to Romans 6 in the next chapter.

■ Applying the Word

Romans 5

1. **What is the role of peace, grace, and hope in my life? What kinds of pictures come to mind as I think about "gaining access" into grace and "standing" in it?**
2. **What comes to mind when I contemplate the meaning of Paul's declaration that Christ died for the ungodly, while we were still sinners? Is it easy or hard to think of myself as an ungodly sinner? Is it easy or hard to think of Christ's death being just for me? What feelings and insights come as I meditate on the cross as a picture of Christ dying for just me? How do the feelings and insights change when I meditate on the cross as a picture of Christ dying for my worst enemy?**

3. What specific things can I list that are part of my own personal experience with Christ that help build my hope and confidence that Christ also holds my future in His hands?
4. If I contemplate the picture of God pouring His love into my heart, what are some of the shapes and forms that come into view? Can I see this love? What does it look like? How have I experienced it today?
5. If I were to draw a picture of Adam and me on one side of a piece of paper and of Christ and me on the other side, what would the pictures look like?

■ Researching the Word

1. Think about Paul's words in 5:6 that Christ came at "just the right time." What does this mean to you? Then read chapter 3, "The Fullness of Time," in *The Desire of Ages*, by E. G. White. How does this chapter add meaning to Paul's words?
2. Read Genesis 3. Make a list of all that you can about Adam's sin and its results. Compare and contrast your findings with Paul's use of Adam in this chapter. How does Genesis 3 aid in your understanding of Romans 5?
3. Read Isaiah 53. What can you list that indicates that Paul had this chapter in mind when he wrote Romans 5? How does the chapter serve Paul's message?

■ Further Study of the Word

1. For a study of Paul's missionary theology in this chapter, see N. A. Dahl, "The Missionary Theology in the Epistle to the Romans," in *Studies in Paul*, 70-94.
2. For the view that Paul uses the term *good person* in Romans 5:7 to refer to benefactors in the patronage system of the first century, see A. D. Clarke, "The Good and the Just in Romans 5:7," 128-142.
3. For a discussion of the last phrase of Romans 5:12 ("because

all sinned"), including a survey of translation possibilities and an argument for translating "with the result that all have sinned," see J. A. Fitzmeyer, "The Consecutive Meaning of *eph' ho* in Romans 5:12," 321-339.

4. For a brief summary of Paul's eschatological thinking, see J. Brunt, *Now and Not Yet*, 29-35.

5. For a discussion of the relationship between justification and reconciliation, see excursus 8 in P. Stuhlmacher, *Paul's Letter to the Romans*, 82, 83.

CHAPTER EIGHT

The End of
Slavery to Sin

Romans 6

Paul's message of God's grace is overwhelmingly wonderful. But it is also subject to misunderstanding, or even corruption. If, as the hymn says (and Paul would certainly agree), God's grace is "greater than all our sin," why not just sin all the more? After all, doesn't more sin just mean more grace? If so, it would seem that humans can increase grace by sinning more. It all seems very logical.

For Paul, this "logical" understanding was probably a problem in two ways. From one side people falsely accused him of saying this, thus hurting his influence and detracting from his true teaching. On the other hand, Paul had to put up with others who did say this. Therefore, the topic is important for Paul, so much so that he devotes all of Romans 6 to it. He asks the question twice and answers it in two different ways with two different analogies (6:1, 15). Let's open chapter 6 and see how he goes about it.

■ Getting Into the Word

Romans 6

Read Romans 6 in at least two different Bible translations, and write out answers to the following questions.

1. **Paul asks significant questions in verses 1 and 15 of this chapter. Are these two different questions or the same ques-**

tion worded in two different ways? What evidence do you find for your answer?

2. How does Paul's use of baptism in verses 3 to 14 answer the question posed in verse 1? Why do you think Paul chose to use baptism as an analogy in answering this question?

3. Apart from the point that Paul makes about continuing in sin by using the example of baptism, do these verses teach anything about the manner and meaning of baptism? On a sheet in your Romans notebook, list everything that you learn about baptism from this chapter.

4. How does Paul's use of the analogy of slavery answer the question he poses in verse 15? Why do you think Paul chose to use slavery in answering this question?

5. On a sheet in your Romans notebook, make two columns. Title the columns "Slavery to Sin" and "Slavery to God." List everything that Paul says about each of these two kinds of slavery in the appropriate column. Then write a paragraph contrasting the two.

6. What does Paul mean by the term *not under law but under grace* (verses 14 and 15)? Does Paul mean that because we are not under the law but under grace we can break the law? Support your answer with evidence from this chapter.

7. In what way are the wages of sin death (verse 23)? What is the connection between sin and death?

8. Several times in this chapter Paul refers to the body or parts of the body. List these passages. What does Paul say about the body and its parts in each one? What do you conclude about the relationship between sin and the body from these passages?

9. Take another page from your Romans notebook, and divide it into two columns. Read through the chapter again, paying close attention to the tense of the verbs Paul uses. In the first column, list those things that Paul says about our present experience with Christ. In the second column, list those items for which Paul uses the future tense to talk about what our experience will be in the future. What do you conclude from this study?

■ Exploring the Word

The Question—Shall We Sin?

Already in Romans 3 Paul raised the issue that he treats in Romans 6. Remember the list of rhetorical questions that Paul asked in that chapter. To refresh our memories, verses 7 and 8 read as follows: "Someone might argue, If my falsehood enhances God's truthfulness and so increases his glory, why am I still condemned as a sinner? Why not say—as we are being slanderously reported as saying and as some claim that we say—Let us do evil that good may result? Their condemnation is deserved."

Although Paul doesn't really answer the question in these verses, his perspective on it is obvious. It is also obvious that he had a strong emotional response to it. These strong feelings undoubtedly flowed from the personal controversy he had endured over the issue. Opponents of his message of grace had slandered him by saying grace was just an excuse for sin. They probably accused Paul of making it easy for his Gentile converts by letting them go on sinning in the false confidence that grace would take care of everything. Even though Paul never took the position that these opponents charged him with, there were probably those who did, and they may even have pointed to Paul's teaching for support. Paul's personal involvement in controversy made it a highly charged question for him. In Romans 3 we see only Paul's emotional response to the question, however. In Romans 6 we see his carefully reasoned theological response.

Paul probably recognized that the words "But where sin increased, grace increased all the more" at the conclusion of Romans 5 (verse 20) would raise the question again in the minds of some readers. One could make a nice, neat, logical formula out of it. Where sin increases, God's grace increases all the more, so the more I sin the more of God's grace there will be. God's grace is good, so my sin, which brings more good, must be good too. Or, as one nineteenth-century satirist put it, "Free from the law, O happy condition; I can sin as I please and still have remission." Now the point comes in

Paul's argument where he must seriously answer this question that he only reacted to in Romans 3.

Although Romans 6 is divided into two separate halves that answer two questions, one in verse 1 and the other in verse 15, the two questions are essentially one and the same. The first, "Shall we go on sinning so that grace may increase?" focuses on the all-sufficiency of God's grace as an excuse for sinning. The second, "Shall we sin because we are not under the law but under grace?" focuses on the inability of the law to save as an excuse for sin. But both ask the question whether the experience of grace allows us to go on sinning.

Paul answers both questions with the same "Absolutely not" ("By no means," vss. 2, 15) phrase that we encountered several times in Romans 3. In each case, what follows the "absolutely not" is an analogy, but the analogies are different in each case. To the first question, "Shall we go on sinning so that grace may increase?" he answers, Absolutely not, because in baptism we were buried with Christ, dying to sin and crucifying our old way of life by identifying with Christ's death in the hope of also being raised with Him. To the second question, "Shall we sin because we are not under law but under grace?" he answers, Absolutely not, because you are a slave to whomever you obey, either to sin, which leads to death, or to God, who gives life.

Before we look at each of Paul's answers in more detail, we should look briefly at the term *sin* as it is used in this chapter. We often take our cue from 1 John 3:4, "Sin is the transgression of the law," and think of sin as a concrete, specific act of breaking one of the commandments. It is, of course, not wrong to use the term *sin* in that way, but to understand what Paul is saying in this chapter and the next, we must recognize that Paul uses the term in a broader sense in Romans, especially in chapters 6 and 7. For Paul, sin is much more than an occasional act. It is a way of life or an atmosphere in which one can live (6:2). But even beyond this, it is a power that can "exercise dominion" over a person (vs. 12), enslave a person (vs. 16), and take advantage of the law by "seizing the opportunity" and deceiving a person (7:11).

Once we understand this, it broadens our understanding of Paul's questions in verses 1 and 15. When Paul asks, "Shall we sin?" he is asking more than whether or not we will commit specific acts of transgression. He is asking whether or not we will continue in a way of life contrary to God's will and allow it to be our king (6:12) and slavemaster (vs. 16). With this in mind, let's look in more detail at Paul's answers to the first question.

The First Answer—No, Because of Our Baptism With Christ (6:1-14)

As Paul takes up the answer to the question of verse 1, he again returns to the diatribe style of argument with a hypothetical opponent who objects and to whom Paul responds. Paul's initial assertion after his "absolutely not" is "We died to sin; how can we live in it any longer?" (vs. 2). He assumes that Christians know they died to sin. To go on living in it is unthinkable. But what if someone doubts Paul's initial assertion? How do we know that we died to sin? Paul considers this possibility and answers almost sarcastically, "Don't you know that all of us who were baptized into Christ Jesus were baptized into his death?" (vs. 3). It is as if he were saying, "Didn't you understand what was going on when you were baptized? Were you ignorant of its meaning?" Then Paul goes on to show how an understanding of what happened in baptism should make the answer to this question obvious.

Perhaps we can best summarize Paul's response by focusing on three aspects of what he says: our past experience as symbolized by our baptism, our present experience and its responsibilities, and our future experience of resurrection with Christ.

The past

Paul says that when we were baptized we were baptized into Christ's death and buried with Him in His death (vss. 3, 4). This means that the old person whom we used to be was crucified with Christ (vs. 6). This crucifixion abolishes what Paul calls the "body of sin." Paul uses the term *body* to refer to the whole person. The body of sin is the whole person oriented to sin and ruled by it. It is that old orientation that is crucified in baptism so that the new Christian can instead be oriented to Christ and His values. This death frees the Christian from the domination of sin (vs. 7) and is possible because Christ died to sin once and for all and now lives to God (vs. 10). Since Christ died this death once and for all, our death or crucifixion is not a death separate from His, but is rather an identification with His death.

The present

The past crucifixion of our old selves with Christ has implications for the present, which Paul sums up in verse 4: "We were therefore buried with him through baptism into death in order that, just as Christ was raised from the dead through the glory of the Father, we too may live a new life." Our death to an old way of life and identification with Christ has a goal, a new way of life oriented to Christ. This new way of life frees us from slavery to sin (vs. 6).

Most of what Paul has said to this point has been in the indicative mode—in other words, Paul has made declarative statements about what God has done for us. But as he speaks to our present experience, he includes the imperative mode—in other words, commands for us. There are responsibilities that go with the Christian life. But for Paul these demands always grow out of what Christ has done for us. They are never the basis for our salvation, but are the appropriate way of responding to the gift of our salvation. Paul gives us several commands that grow out of our experience with Christ in baptism. They are:

> Count yourself dead to sin (vs. 11).
> Do not let sin reign in your mortal body (vs. 12).
> Do not offer the parts of your body to sin (vs. 13).
> Offer yourselves to God (vs. 13).
> Offer the parts of your body to God as instruments of righteousness (vs. 13).

What are we to make of these commands? First, we must remember the context of the commands. They follow the assurances of

God's grace. They show how to respond to a God of grace. First we respond by "reckoning" or counting (the same word Paul uses in 4:3 to speak of faith being reckoned to Abraham) ourselves dead to sin (6:11). Does this mean that we truly are dead to sin? Yes, because we trust God's word that says we died to sin in baptism. By trusting, we take on a new mind-set. We still live in a world of sin and death. Our self is still a mortal self (vs. 12), subject to death. We still are not sinless, so we make mistakes. But even in this world of sin and death, we can consider ourselves dead to sin through God's promise.

Paul next says that we should not let sin rule over our mortal selves (vs. 12). The word he uses for "rule" suggests the kind of rule a king exercises over his subjects. Don't let sin be your king. He adds that we should not hand over parts of ourselves to be instruments of sin (vs. 13). By this he probably means not only specific parts of our bodies, but aspects of our lives such as our feelings, temperaments, and talents. Obviously we have choices once we have discovered new life in Christ, and Paul wants us to exercise these choices responsibly.

The most important choices, however, are the positive choices, for it is these that make the first three commands possible. We are to offer ourselves to God and let the parts of ourselves be offered to God (vs. 13). In Romans 8 Paul will give us much more detail on how we offer ourselves to God and choose the right kind of mind-set. Notice Paul has not said that Christians will be free from temptation to sin or the consequences of sin in this life, nor has he promised Christians sinlessness in the present. But he has called us to a new orientation directed toward God, who frees us from the domination of sin. Through God's power, we don't have to let sin enslave us. We can live in newness of life. To reject God's gracious offer and simply go on sinning would totally miss the point of the cross. Christ died to free us from bondage. If we simply put the chains back on, we flout His sacrifice for us.

The future

Christ's resurrection demonstrates His power and ultimate victory over death. Death no longer has mastery over Christ (vs. 9). In hope, this victory is ours. We have not yet received it, but our death with Christ in baptism and our present union with Him make it certain that we will be united with Christ in His resurrection as well (vs. 5). This promise is in the future tense, but it is certain. Paul is careful consistently to use the future tense when he speaks of our resurrection in this chapter. But it is a future that grows out of and is guaranteed by the experience we already have with Christ. As Paul says, "Now if we died with Christ, we believe that we will also live with him" (vs. 8).

This promise of the future helps motivate us to accept the challenges that Paul gives for the present. After all, if our bodies are destined for resurrection with Christ, think how inappropriate it would be to hand them over as instruments of sin, which is in opposition to the God of life, who raised Jesus and promises to raise us with Him.

Let us summarize Paul's first answer to the question, Shall we sin? The answer is No, because our solidarity with Christ, symbolized in baptism, shows it is unthinkable. We died to the old, sinful way of life when we were baptized in union with Christ, we now live in a new atmosphere of union with Him, and we share in the certainty of being united with Him in resurrection as well. He has freed us from slavery to sin; therefore, we should now live by reckoning ourselves dead to sin and offering ourselves to God to let Him lead us according to His values and His will.

The Meaning of Baptism

Although Paul is not addressing the question of baptism per se, but is using baptism as a part of his argument against the position that we can continue sinning because of grace, what he says, nevertheless, sheds light on both the meaning and manner of baptism. If baptism is a symbol of burial and resurrection with Christ, then immersion, in which the person being baptized actually goes down into the water and is covered by it, is the only manner of baptism that appropriately symbolizes burial and resurrection (vs. 4). It is also clear from what Paul says that baptism is a symbol of the decision to identify with Christ's death and resurrection and choose solidarity with Christ. If baptism represents a decision or a choice, then one who participates in it must be of sufficient age and maturity to make a thoughtful decision.

These verses also have much to teach us about the meaning of baptism. Paul shows us that to be baptized is to make a decision and a statement of identification with Christ, His death, and His resurrection. In baptism we identify with Christ so fully that in a real sense it was not only Christ who died on the cross two thousand years ago; we died with Him. The person who we were, dominated by sin, no longer lives. In baptism we also unite ourselves with the hope of the resurrection, so that even though we live in a world of sin and death, we already live in the confidence of the end. This is why we can consider ourselves dead to sin and be confident that because Christ died for sin once and for all (vs. 10) and was raised never to die again (vs. 9) we will live with Him. This picture of union with Christ, symbolized in baptism, is perhaps the richest source of material for theological reflection on the meaning of baptism to be found anywhere in the New Testament.

The Second Answer—No, Because Sin Is Slavery (6:15-23)

Already in verse 6 of this chapter Paul has referred to sin as slavery. Now he fleshes out that notion in his second argument as to why grace does not give us an excuse to go on sinning.

Before we look at Paul's argument, we should say a word about slavery in Paul's day. In the first-century Greco-Roman world, wide disparities existed in economic conditions. In rural agrarian environments, there were wealthy absentee landlords who ruled over the modern equivalents of sharecroppers. In the cities, there were the extremely rich as well as those who were almost totally dependent on Roman welfare for their existence. In between were skilled tradespeople and government workers of various types who made up a middle class that varied in size in different parts of the empire.

Throughout the empire, but especially in Rome, the number of slaves was very high. It is estimated that in the city of Rome as much as a third of the population, between two hundred thousand and three hundred thousand, were slaves (see Koester, 1:60). People originally became slaves through debt, piracy, and, primarily, war. Generation after generation was born into slavery. Even the status of slaves varied greatly, however. Some were highly educated and trusted tutors who had considerable status and power in the household, while others were severely mistreated, exploited, and even abused sexually.

For the most part, the institution of slavery was simply accepted as part of the social order, although the philosophers of the day argued that slaves should be treated humanely, and some even went so far as to challenge the idea of slavery.

The following excerpts from the moral letters of one of those philosophers, Seneca, the brother of Gallio, the proconsul at Corinth before whom Paul once appeared (see Acts 18:12-17), show how philosophers argued that slaves should be treated with respect, but also demonstrate how slaves were often mistreated by the rich who lived in wanton luxury.

> I am glad to learn, through those who come from you, that you live on friendly terms with your slaves. This befits a sensible and well-educated man like yourself. "They are slaves," people declare. Nay, rather they are men. "Slaves!" No, comrades. "Slaves!" No, they are unpretentious friends. "Slaves!"No, they are our fellow-slaves, if one reflects that Fortune has equal rights over slaves and free men alike (Seneca, *Ad Lucilum Epistulae Morales*, Epistle XLVII, Loeb, 1:301-303).

> When we recline at a banquet, one slave mops up the disgorged food, another crouches beneath the table and gathers up the left-overs of the tipsy guests. Another carves the priceless game birds; with unerring strokes and skilled hand he cuts choice morsels along the breast or the rump. Hapless fellow, to live only for the purpose of cutting fat capons correctly—unless, indeed, the other man is still more unhappy than he, who teaches this art for pleasure's sake, rather than he who learns it because

he must. Another, who serves the wine, must dress like a woman and wrestle with his advancing years; he cannot get away from his boyhood; he is dragged back to it; and though he has already acquired a soldier's figure, he is kept beardless by having his hair smoothed away or plucked out by the roots, and he must remain awake throughout the night, dividing his time between his master's drunkenness and his lust; in the chamber he must be a man, at the feast a boy. . . . With slaves like these the master cannot bear to dine; he would think it beneath his dignity to associate with his slave at the same table! Heaven forfend! (ibid, 305.)

One large class of people in the first-century empire was that of freedmen, former slaves who had gained their freedom. This could be accomplished in a number of ways. Some were allowed to earn money and buy their freedom. Others were set free in their master's wills. The freed slave often participated in a service at the temple or shrine of one of the gods where the slave was symbolically sold to the god and received freedom. This class of former slaves became so large and powerful that the emperors felt the need to placate them by giving them official functions in the emperor cult.

All of this means that Paul's readers in first-century Rome would have been very familiar with the practice of slavery. In fact, in Romans 16, when Paul greets those of the household of a specific person (vss. 10, 11), he probably is referring to the person's slaves. In other words, not only were Paul's readers familiar with slavery; some of them were slaves. As noted above, some of these may have been trusted, well-treated, respected members of the household. But all of them were also familiar with the degrading abuse that slaves often had to suffer. Paul now uses this familiar institution as an example in his argument.

As he begins, the structure repeats what we have already seen in the first half of the chapter. First, he asks the question in verse 15 (Shall we sin because we are not under law but under grace?), followed by an "Absolutely not," and then the question "Don't you know?" This time, the "Don't you know?" has to do with slavery. In verse 13 Paul admonished the Roman Christians not to *offer* the parts of their body to sin but to *offer* themselves to God. Now he asks if they don't know that when they *offer* themselves to someone they become the slaves of that someone (vs. 16). Then he presents two alternatives, and only two. They can choose to be slaves to sin, which leads to death, or to obedience, which leads to righteousness. Paul doesn't present freedom from all slavery as an option, although he does speak of slavery to righteousness as having been set free from sin (vs. 18). But there is no place where humans can stand in total autonomy, unrelated to sin and to God. Every life is oriented in one direction or the other. We can choose either slavery to sin or slavery to God.

In verse 19 Paul reminds his readers that he is using a human analogy here, and naturally all human analogies have their limits. But in spite of those limits, this analogy is powerful in contrasting the life of sin and the life of obedience. Paul now turns to the results of these two different kinds of slavery.

In the past, slavery to sin had led Paul's readers to offer their bodies for sexual immorality and other wickedness, actions of which they were now ashamed (vs. 19). In addition, the final result of that life was death (vss. 20, 21). The result of slavery to God, on the other hand, is holiness and, ultimately, eternal life (vs. 22). The root idea of the word *holiness* is being set apart or consecrated for a special purpose. Priests, for example, were set apart for a different kind of life. Christians are set apart for a life of purity and obedience to God's will. In other words, Paul sees moral implications that flow from the Christian's committed response to God's grace. If we really understand what God has done for us, the only possible response is to offer ourselves to God and His will, which means living a different kind of life, no longer dominated by sin, immorality, and wickedness, but by purity and obedience. Paul will elaborate on this when we come to Romans 12.

In verse 23 Paul sums up the difference between these two kinds of slavery in one graphic contrast: "The wages of sin is death, but the gift of God is eternal life in Christ Jesus our Lord." Paul makes this summary graphic through the use of some interesting, vivid

words. The term translated "wages" was not the usual term for re-
muneration. It comes from a military context and refers to a soldier's
ration. Such wages were noted for being small, yet the soldier's work
was noted for being hard. Skimpy wages for grueling work. That is
the wages of sin. In fact, the wages turn out to be nothing but death.

On the other hand, Paul doesn't even talk about wages or salary
when he talks about the benefits of slavery to God. Rather, he says
that the free gift of God is eternal life. No one earns eternal life. But
when you offer yourself to God, He gives the gift of eternal life.
The term *gift* that Paul uses here means an absolutely free gift and
has the same root as the term he uses for "grace." The contrast
couldn't be more disparate. In one kind of slavery, you work hard
and get death. In the other, you receive the free gift of eternal life.

Not Under Law but Under Grace

Twice in this chapter (verses 14 and 15) Paul uses the phrase "not
under law but under grace." This phrase is often misunderstood, and
perhaps a brief look at what it means for Paul will serve as a summary
for the chapter. First, it is obvious from the context of the entire chapter
that the phrase doesn't mean we can use grace as an excuse to ignore the
law and simply live as we please without regard for God's will. That is
precisely what Paul says "No!" to throughout this chapter.

Second, Paul's reasoning in verse 14 is interesting. He claims that
sin will not have mastery over us because we are not under law but
under grace. How does this follow? To be "under the law" means to
be outside the atmosphere of grace to which God invites us. Outside
of that atmosphere, we are in the hopeless situation Paul addressed
in 1:18 to 3:20. Remember how the law functioned in that situation?
It did not save but instead brought awareness of sin (3:20). So to be
under law is to be aware of sin, indeed, ruled by sin, and in turn
condemned by the law. To be under grace, on the other hand, is to
be in the atmosphere of God's acceptance, with all the results that
we saw at the beginning of Romans 5, and with the promise of eternal life that we see at the end of chapter 6. Therefore, not being
under law but under grace doesn't mean sinning, as verse 15 ex-

plicitly makes clear, but rather means living for God, in an amazing, unique slavery that brings the gift of eternal life.

But what is the role of law in all this? Does this mean that the law is evil? Does freedom from the law mean freedom from something bad? In Romans 7 Paul will answer these questions for us.

■ Applying the Word

Romans 6

1. As I contemplate my own baptism, what did it mean for me at the time? What feelings were associated with it? What did I think about? How has my understanding grown since that time? How does Romans 6 help me understand the meaning of my baptism?
2. If I have died to sin with Christ, what actual differences has it made in my life, my attitudes, my actions, and my feelings? How are these differences gifts of God's grace?
3. What does the concept "slavery to God" mean to me? What are some of the tangible ways I might "offer" myself to God? How can this experience really be "slavery" if what I receive from it is a free gift?
4. Can I say at this point in my life that sin is no longer the king or slavemaster that rules me? If not, what can I do to change this? If so, how do I continue to live free from this slavery?
5. Do I have personal evidence that sin is slavery? Do I have personal evidence that slavery to God brings the benefits of holiness and the free gift of eternal life? If I were to draw two pictures contrasting these two kinds of slavery, what would I draw? (Try drawing the pictures.)

■ Researching the Word

1. Look up all the New Testament references to "baptize" and "baptism" in a Bible concordance. (There are many occurrences of these terms, but you will find that they come from

a much smaller list of passages.) What do you learn about the meaning and significance of baptism from the New Testament? Read a good Bible dictionary article on baptism, and compare what it says with your findings.

2. Study Galatians 5, where Paul talks about freedom in Christ. Compare and contrast the freedom in Christ to which Paul calls Christians in that chapter with the slavery to God to which he calls them in Romans 6. Are the two concepts compatible? What is Paul trying to say with each one?

■ Further Study of the Word

1. For a general discussion of the theme of dying and rising with Christ in Paul, see V. P. Furnish, *Theology and Ethics in Paul*, 171-176. For a specific discussion of 6:12 and following, see pages 194-203.

2. For an excellent discussion of the meaning of baptism from an Adventist perspective, see W. G. Johnsson, *Clean: The Meaning of Christian Baptism*. See pages 40-47 for a discussion of Romans 6.

3. For an in-depth treatment of baptism in the New Testament and the history of baptism in the early church, including the rise of infant baptism, from a Baptist perspective, see G. R. Beasley-Murray, *Baptism in the New Testament*. Romans 6 is treated on pages 127-145.

4. For a discussion of the meaning of baptism and an argument for adult immersion, see K. Barth, *The Teaching of the Church Regarding Baptism*.

5. For a discussion of slaves and slavery in New Testament times, see H. Koester, *Introduction to the New Testament;* vol. 1: *History, Culture, and Religion of the Hellenistic Age*, 59-62.

6. For a survey of Paul's understanding of baptism throughout his letters, see excursus 9 in P. Stuhlmacher, *Paul's Letter to the Romans*, 97-101.

CHAPTER NINE

What About the Law?

Romans 7

Twice in Romans 6 Paul asked "Don't you know?" and each time, an illustration followed. Paul begins Romans 7 with another "Don't you know?" and sure enough, an illustration follows. This time the illustration has to do with marriage, and the issue illustrated is the law. In fact, all of Romans 7 has to do with the law. Some of what Paul has said to this point almost makes the law sound like the culprit in the problem of sin and death. Is the law sin? Is it evil? What can we say about the law? In Romans 7 Paul tells us plenty about the law, some of which may even seem contradictory. But if we read and study carefully, we should get a good picture of how Paul viewed the law.

■ Getting Into the Word

Romans 7

Read Romans 7 in at least two different Bible translations, and write out answers to the following questions in your Romans notebook.

1. Take a page from your Romans notebook, and divide it into two columns. In the first, list every statement Paul makes about the law that seems negative. In the second, list every statement about the law that appears positive. Which list is longer? Why? Write a paragraph summarizing what Paul says

about the law in this chapter. What is the function of the law, according to this chapter?

2. There are several statements Paul makes in this chapter that might appear confusing. How do you make sense out of the following:

   a. "You also died to the law through the body of Christ" (vs. 4).

   b. "The sinful passions aroused by the law were at work in our bodies" (vs. 5).

   c. "We have been released from the law" (vs. 6).

   d. "For apart from law, sin is dead" (vs. 8).

   e. "The very commandment that was intended to bring life actually brought death" (vs. 10).

3. What point is Paul trying to make about the law from his marriage illustration in 7:1-6?

4. What does Paul mean by serving in a new way in the Spirit and not in the old way of the written code (vs. 6)?

5. Why does Paul use the tenth commandment about coveting in this chapter? What point is he trying to make?

6. How does verse 12 follow from what has gone before it? Doesn't it seem that what Paul has just said makes the law less than holy, righteous, and good? How can that which brings death be good? What enables Paul to say what he does in this verse?

7. Read verses 14 to 25 again, and note the use of the term *I*. Who is this I? Is it an autobiographical "I" that points to Paul's experience, or is it more general? Does it represent pre-Christian life apart from Christ, or is it the Christian life?

8. How does the latter part of verse 25 serve as a conclusion for this chapter? Doesn't it seem anticlimactic?

9. How does this chapter contribute to Paul's message up to this point in Romans?

■ Exploring the Word

Overview of the Chapter

About this point in our journey through Romans, we seem to be pushing our way through some pretty thick theological undergrowth. It may even be hard to believe that this is a practical, pastoral letter to real people in Rome. But remember, Paul was a pastor who took theology seriously. In other words, he believed that understanding God and what He has done for us makes a difference in daily, Christian life.

Paul knew that only one thing in all the universe had the power to bring both salvation and a spirit of Christian unity to the Romans, the good news that God's grace is poured out to us all. But there were ways that his message could be misunderstood, and in this chapter Paul takes up another potential problem. What about the law? What is its role? But even this question is not merely a theoretical one. We will see in the next chapter, Romans 8, what a difference it makes in practical Christian living when Christians live life in the Spirit. Romans 7 prepares the way by clarifying the role of law.

Paul did what all good pastors do in presenting this topic—he used illustrations. Some of his illustrations are so vivid, however, that it is easy to forget the point he is making and concentrate only on the illustration. Therefore, before we begin looking at each section of the chapter separately, we should note the flow of his argument throughout the chapter. Here is my summary, but be sure that you test it against your own reading of the chapter.

An illustration from marriage (vss. 1-6). Paul argues that the death of one spouse frees the other from the law of marriage. Therefore, as a woman whose husband dies is free to marry again, so we have died to the law in order to be united with Christ to bear fruit for God and serve Him in the new way of the Spirit.

An illustration from the tenth commandment (vss. 7-13). Paul asks if the law is sin and answers with a definite *No.* As the command against coveting shows the law is good, the problem is that sin takes advantage of my weakness and uses the law to increase sin and even bring death.

An illustration from human experience (vss. 14-25). My own experience testifies that the law is good, for I want to live by it even though I don't. That gap between what I do and what I want to do affirms that the problem isn't with the law; it is with me.

These three illustrations taken together show two important truths: that the law is not the culprit in the problem of sin and death and that the law is powerless to overcome the problem of sin and death (indeed, it comes close to being an unwilling co-conspirator in the problem). Paul makes both of these points so strongly that he almost seems contradictory. Sometimes the law sounds a lot like a culprit. It arouses sinful passions (vs. 5), reveals sin (vs. 7), serves as an impetus to sin (vs. 8), and even brings death (vs. 10). Yet at the same time, it is holy, righteous, good (vs. 12), and spiritual (vs. 14). Let's look at the chapter in more detail now and see how Paul puts all of this together.

An Illustration From Marriage (7:1-6)

Paul's point in these verses is that death brings freedom from law. It is true in marriage. A woman is bound to her husband by the law of marriage. To go to another man would be adultery. But if her husband dies, she is no longer bound but is released from the law and is free to marry another. In a similar way (even Paul must have known the analogy wasn't perfect), as we saw in the last chapter, Christians have died with Christ. This death releases us from the law.

What does Paul mean when he says that we are released from the law? Two pieces of evidence should prove that he doesn't mean we can disregard the content of the law and break it as we please. Paul is no antinomian. First, he has laid the groundwork in Romans 6 to confirm that not being under law but under grace hardly means we can go on sinning. Second, he says here that we died to the law through the body of Christ that we might belong to another, "to him who was raised from the dead, in order that we might bear fruit to God" (vs. 4). The experience of belonging to Christ and bearing fruit for God can hardly be one of violating the law. So what does Paul mean?

Paul is contrasting two different kinds of religious experience. For one he uses the term *flesh* and for the other the term *spirit*. Before we explore this contrast, we need to say a bit about these terms. Paul uses the term *flesh* twenty-three times in Romans, three times in this chapter (verses 5, 18, and 25), and ten times in Romans 8. The NIV translates all three occurrences in Romans 7 with the phrase *sinful nature*, and in Romans 8, it uses "sinful nature," "sinful man," and "sinful mind." You might wonder how they get these translations from the simple word *flesh*. The fact is that Paul uses the term in a unique way, quite different from other New Testament writers, such as John. For Paul, "flesh" is not material or bodily existence, nor is it an identifiable part of the whole human. Rather, it is the whole human person subject to the law of sin and death. With this term, Paul points to humans in their mortality and their tendency to respond to sin. The life of slavery to sin is life in the flesh.

On the other hand, the term *spirit* doesn't refer to immaterial existence or life away from the body (a possibility beyond Paul's conception; compare 1 Corinthians 15). We will have to wait until Romans 8 to see the richness of Paul's use of this term, but we can point the way here by saying that life in the Spirit is life oriented toward God and lived under the direction of His Spirit. Now notice the contrast between the two situations Paul presents in these verses (1-6).

In the first situation, when we were controlled by flesh (7:5) the law was an external, written code (vs. 6) to which we belonged. In this situation, the law not only pointed out our sin; it even aroused our sinful passions so that we bore fruit for death (vs. 5). In other words, we acted in ways that led to death. In the new situation, we died to the law so that we might belong to Christ and serve in a new way, no longer with the law as an external code, at once both condemning us and egging us on toward more sin, but now serving by the Spirit so that good fruit for God is produced from our relationship with Him. Being released from the law is being released from this old relationship to the law as a written code. But, as Paul will continue to show us, this doesn't mean the law is bad. As Paul said in 3:31, our faith doesn't nullify it, but establishes it.

An Illustration From the Tenth Commandment (7:7-13)

Paul's charge that the law arouses the sinful passions so that we bear fruit for death could logically lead to the conclusion that the law is sin. But Paul says, "Absolutely not" (vs. 7). What immediately follows, however, doesn't make the "Absolutely not" very convincing. Paul first makes the point that the law reveals sin. He wouldn't have known what sin was without the law (vs. 7). Then he goes further and says that the law not only shows his sin, but also helps produce sin (vs. 8). It makes him sin more.

How can this be so? The tenth commandment shows how. Paul wouldn't have known about coveting if the law hadn't said, "Don't covet!" (vs. 8). Now we might expect that once Paul heard that he shouldn't covet, he would have stopped and lived happily ever after. But that isn't what happened! Instead, the very fact that he wasn't supposed to covet focused his attention on coveting, and he found himself coveting all the more. It is something like being told not to think about a pink elephant. Even though you might not have thought of a pink elephant in years, the very command not to think about it puts it vividly in your mind. The tenth commandment is especially illustrative of this problem, because it involves something in your mind rather than a specific act. One might decide not to kill anyone today, but it is harder to decide not to covet.

Paul therefore finds that "sin, seizing the opportunity afforded by the commandment, deceived me, and through the commandment put me to death" (vs. 11). The very commandment that was supposed to bring life brought death (vs. 10). All this makes it sound as if the law really is sin. If the law becomes an agent of sin and brings death, it must be pretty bad! Yet it is precisely at this point that Paul says, "So then, the law is holy, and the commandment is holy, righteous and good" (vs. 12). Paul's answer to this dilemma is that the problem is not with the law; it is with human beings. The law shows up sin for what it is (vs. 13), but it is good. It is sinful human nature that lets sin utilize the law to make sin even worse.

This view of Paul's is quite different from what we find in rabbinic Judaism. Although the *Mishnah*, the codified teaching of the rabbis, wasn't written down for about 150 years after Paul's time, it represents a long history of oral tradition. In the *Mishnah* the rabbis taught that God had created an evil inclination in humans called the evil *yetzer*. This evil *yetzer* had some similarities with what we would call "ego" and therefore had a good purpose in motivating humans. But it also tempted them to evil. The law was the antidote that held the evil *yetzer* in check. In one passage God says:

> I created within you the evil *yetzer*, but I created the Law as a drug. As long as you occupy yourselves with the Law, the *yetzer* will not rule over you. But if you do not occupy yourselves with the Torah, then you will be delivered into the power of the *yetzer*, and all its activity will be against you (*Kiddushin* 30b, quoted in Barrett, 153).

Paul, on the other hand, saw the whole human as dominated by sin. And the law, rather than an antidote, was drawn into the problem by the combination of sin and the flesh. Therefore, rather than solving the problem, the law only made it worse. To communicate this point, Paul moves to the third and final illustration in this chapter.

An Illustration From Human Experience (7:14-25)

Paul's third illustration is so powerfully poignant that few readers through history have talked about the point he makes; they have concentrated on the illustration itself. Paul uses the first-person "I" to speak of the frustration of not wanting to do the things he does and wanting to do the things he doesn't end up doing. We have all read these verses, and we have all identified with them. They are so true to human nature that we marvel. But Paul isn't simply trying to convey the frustrations of human nature. He trying to say something about the law, just as he did with the marriage illustration.

His point is that the gap between what we do and what we want to do, that all-too-understandable feature of human nature, shows that the problem is not with the law, but with the human person. The very fact that I want to do right is testimony that the law is good. The problem is sin and the flesh that lets sin rule. This tears the human apart so that even though he/she delights in the law (vs. 22) and in the mind is a slave to God's law, in the flesh he/she is slave to the law of sin and death (vs. 25).

For years theologians have debated who the "I" of verses 14 to 25 really is. Many have taken it as autobiographical, referring to Paul's own experience. In a famous essay published in the early sixties titled "Paul and the Introspective Conscience of the West," a Lutheran theologian, Krister Stendahl, challenged this view. He argued that Paul didn't agonize over his ability to keep the law. In Philippians he claims that before his encounter with Christ he was blameless as far as righteousness that comes from the law was concerned (Phil. 3:6). According to Stendahl, the tortured, introspective conscience is a later Western phenomenon that we Westerners read back into Paul's experience.

Most interpreters have taken the "I" as a type, but they disagree as to where the type points. Some have held that this "I" represents the Christian. They point to the fact that this person delights in God's law (7:22) and argue that all Christians can identify with this struggle. The nonreligious person wouldn't care about doing right, so this must refer to the believer.

Others argue that this "I" refers to pre-Christian life, for it seems to be self-oriented (notice all the "I's") and doesn't fit with the picture of life in the Spirit as presented in Romans 8. Others become more specific and see the "I" as the unbeliever who nevertheless takes the law seriously, or as life outside of Christ as seen from the perspective of faith in Christ. (See the "Further Study of the Word" section at the end of this chapter for some representatives of the different positions.)

What should we make of all this? Who is the "I"? My hunch is that interpreters are probably more specific than Paul intended to be. Remember that for Paul, the point is not about the "I" but about the law. Nevertheless, there are some things that can be said about this "I." Certainly Paul is characterizing a kind of experience. Notice some of the characteristics of this experience: it is slavery to sin (vs. 14); sin is living in the flesh (vs. 17); the person is prisoner of the law of sin at work within his/her members (vs. 23); the person is a "wretched" person (vs. 24) and in his/her flesh is a slave to the law of sin (vs. 25). This doesn't sound like Christian experience. On the other hand, the one living this experience delights in God's law in the inner being (vs. 22) and is a slave of God's law in the mind (vs. 25).

When we put all this together, the emphasis falls on the original situation we saw in verses 1 to 6, that of the flesh rather than the Spirit, where the law is an external code and we are still subject to the law of sin and death. It is in that experience of trying to live the right kind of life outside Christ's promise of life in the Spirit that this gap is felt most intently. Yet most of us know from experience that we never seem to live life so totally in the Spirit that we are completely free from that gap between what we do and what we want to do, what we are and what we want to be.

The experience characterized here is not the ideal. But the very fact that we can all identify with it so readily makes the illustration useful. For Paul's point isn't this experience per se, but the way this experience exonerates the law. The very fact that we know this gap shows that the problem is not the law; it is us. Paul's bottom line is that the law is good (vs. 12). But sin is so powerful that it captures the law and makes the law its agent. Because of our sinful nature, the law not only makes us aware of sin; it makes us sin, for when it tells us "No," our human nature responds by doing precisely that "No" (vss. 7, 8). The problem is with the flesh, and there is no way out. The law may promise life, but it doesn't work as long as I am sinful. The problem is me, not the law, but the law is powerless to solve my problem.

In this chapter we have seen Paul use three illustrations, all of them to teach about the law. The illustration concerning marriage (vss. 1-6) has shown us that we died to the law in order to be united with Christ so that we can serve God in a new way through the Spirit. The illustration about the tenth commandment (vss. 7-13) has shown us that the law is good, but that sin can take advantage of our weakness and use the law to increase sin. The final illustration from human experience (vss. 14-25) has shown us that the gap between our expectations for ourselves and the reality of our lives affirms that the problem is not the law; it is us.

If the problem is me, what is the solution? "Who can rescue me from this body of death? Thanks be to God—through Jesus Christ our Lord" (vss. 24, 25). If Romans 7 presents the problem with powerful poignancy, Romans 8 will proclaim the solution with unspeakable joy.

■ Applying the Word

Romans 7

1. Do I continue to experience a gap between what I do and am and what I want to do and be? If so, does that discourage or encourage me? Does it mean that I am a failure, or does it mean that I am a growing Christian who clearly sees my goals?
2. What is the function of law in my Christian experience? Is the law an external written code? If so, is that bad? What would it mean for me to bear fruit for God in the Spirit? How would the law function in that experience?
3. If I were to take a piece of paper and divide it into four parts, labeled self, law, sin, and God, and draw a picture of each, how would these pictures look? How might I draw a diagram that would relate these four to each other in a way faithful to what Paul says in Romans 7?
4. Can I relate to Paul's claim that the law actually serves as an impetus to sin? Has this ever been true for me? If so, in what way?
5. What kinds of feelings do I have after I read this chapter? Do I ever feel "wretched"? If so, what kind of a solution would I hope to have? What would I hope for if I made a list of how God, through Jesus Christ, might rescue me? (Keep this list until we are through studying Romans 8, and see how many of your hoped-for solutions actually appear in that chapter.)

■ Researching the Word

1. Read Exodus 20:1-17 and Deuteronomy 5:1-21. How do the Ten Commandments fit with all that Paul says about the law in Romans 7?
2. Read Psalm 119. Sense the feeling of delight in the law of God that is represented in this psalm. Do you get the same feeling from Romans 7? If you sense a difference, how do you explain it?
3. Use your Bible concordance to look up passages in the New Testament outside the writings of Paul that speak about the law. Some of these might be Matthew 5, John 7, and James 2. What do you find that compares with Paul's teaching in Romans 7?

■ Further Study of the Word

1. For a general discussion of Paul's view of law, sin, and righteousness, see V. P. Furnish, *Theology and Ethics in Paul*, 135-162.
2. For a general study by an Adventist biblical scholar of Paul's attitude to law, see H. Weiss, *Paul of Tarsus*, 84-104. Pages 106 to 108 of the same volume contain a good, brief discussion of Paul's anthropological terms, including *flesh*, *spirit*, *soul*, *heart*, and *body*.
3. For the view that Paul is not speaking autobiographically in Romans 7, see K. Stendahl, "Paul and the Introspective Conscience of the West," in *Paul Among Jews and Gentiles*, 78-96.
4. For the view that the "I" of Romans 7 is autobiographical and refers to Paul's pre-Christian experience, see C. H. Dodd, *The Epistle of Paul to the Romans*, 125-133.
5. For the view that the "I" refers to life before Christ, dominated by sin and death, see K. Barth, *A Shorter Commentary on Romans*, 74-87.
6. For an argument that the "I" of Romans 7 is not autobiographi-

cal but refers to non-Christian life under the law as seen from a Christian perspective, see P. Achtemeier, *Romans*, 118-130.

7. For an argument that Paul was thinking autobiographically of his own history in Adam in 7:7-13 and of his past from his present perspective in 7:14-25, see B. L. Martin, "Some Reflections on the Identity of *ego* in Romans 7:14-25."

8. For a survey of supposed classical parallels to Paul's use of the "I" in Romans 7 and a presentation of the view that Paul is unique *vis à vis* these parallels, see R. V. Huggins, "Alleged Classical Parallels to Paul's 'What I Want to Do I Do Not Do, but What I Hate, That I Do.' "

9. For a brief collection of rabbinic statements about the law, see C. K. Barrett, *The New Testament Background: Selected Documents*, 151-153.

10. For the view that the "I" of Romans 7 is the pre-Christian past seen from eyes of faith, but with an awareness of the continuing temptation, see excursus 10 in Peter Stuhlmacher, *Paul's Letter to the Romans*, 114-116. For a discussion of Paul's doctrine of law throughout his letters, see excursus 11 in the same work, 122-128.

11. For the view that Paul's arguments in Romans concerning the law focus on a misplaced Jewish emphasis on boundary-marking ritual, see J. D. G. Dunn, "The New Perspective on Paul: Paul and the Law," in K. P. Donfried, ed., *The Romans Debate*, 299-308.

CHAPTER TEN

Life in the Spirit

Romans 8

No condemnation! What a promise! Paul has spoken about sin, death, and the weakness of human nature in ways that touch our experience. We have felt the frustration of not doing what we want to do or being what we want to be. We know all too well the weakness of human nature. But now we come to this promise. No condemnation. No chapter in the Bible, nor any human poem or literary passage, expresses the joy and hope of life in Christ more beautifully than Romans 8. Here all the metaphors and symbols for salvation that Paul has used come together to make the matter perfectly clear: "Therefore, there is now no condemnation for those who are in Christ Jesus" (vs. 1).

■ Getting Into the Word

Romans 8

Read this chapter in at least two different translations, and then answer the following questions in your Romans notebook.

1. Take a page in your Romans notebook, and divide it into two columns. Mark the first one "Life in the Flesh" and the second one "Life in the Spirit." Go through the first twelve verses of Romans 8, and put everything you can find that Paul says about life in the flesh in the first column and everything he says about life in the Spirit in the second. (Re-

member that if you are using the NIV, "flesh" may be translated by the terms "sinful nature," "sinful man," or "sinful
mind.") Now write a paragraph contrasting these two different kinds of life.

2. Take another page in your notebook, and make a list of all
the promises you find for the Christian in Romans 8. How
many do you find? Summarize how these promises speak to
your own Christian faith.

3. Work through this chapter, and find every reference that
you can to suffering. According to Romans 8, what role does
suffering play in Christian life? What do you find in this
chapter that would be of most help when you face a time of
personal suffering?

4. How does Paul's metaphor of adoption as children of God
(vss. 12-17) compare with other metaphors for salvation Paul
has used in this letter, such as justification, redemption, reconciliation, and the sacrificial system? What does adoption
offer that is new? Which of these metaphors do you find
most helpful as you picture what God has done for you?

5. How does the Spirit help us in prayer (vss. 26, 27)? Explain
as fully as you can from these two verses what the Spirit
does for us in prayer.

6. How do you understand Paul's reference to predestination
in verse 29? Does what Paul says here seem to be in tension
with the concept of human freedom?

7. Does Paul's message that absolutely nothing can separate
us from the love of Christ open the door to the concept that
once we are saved we are always saved? Why or why not?

■ Exploring the Word

The Flesh and the Spirit

Romans 8 begins with the liberating promise that there is no condemnation for those who are in Christ Jesus. The next several verses
explain the basis for the promise and make the promise real by con-

trasting two kinds of life, life in the flesh and life in the Spirit. We will only understand this promise and the other promises Paul makes in this chapter if we grasp this contrast between flesh and Spirit.

Remember that Paul began making this contrast in Romans 7:5, 6. You might even want to review the paragraphs about those verses in the last chapter. In Romans 8 Paul draws out this distinction with much more detail and vigor. He begins in verse 2 by calling these two different kinds of life "laws." Here "laws" is used in a general sense somewhat synonymous with "principles," "systems," or "methods." He contrasts the "law of the Spirit of life" with the "law of sin and death," which he also calls life in the flesh, and affirms that the former sets a person free from the latter (vs. 2). It is, of course, the latter that he has been talking about with reference to the law in Romans 7. It is because of the principle of sin and death that the law, although good, is powerless to save. What, then, is the difference between these competing systems? Let's look first at what Paul says in chapter 8 about the system of sin and death, or life in the flesh.

In this way of life, the law is powerless to save because of the flesh (vs. 3). The person who lives according to the law of sin and death has the mind set on the things of the flesh (vs. 5), which leads to death (vs. 6). In fact, those who live by the flesh are enemies of God, because of their rebellion against God (vs. 7). They do not obey God's law (vs. 7); indeed, they cannot obey God's law (vs. 8). They are on a collision course with death (vs. 13). In Romans 6 Paul called this hopeless situation slavery to sin, and in Romans 7 he showed us that not even the holy, just, and good law could do anything about it. But now he spells out the alternative, life in the Spirit.

In the last chapter, we promised to say more about the term *spirit* or *Holy Spirit* when we came to Romans 8. The term *spirit* is central to this chapter. Twenty of the thirty-three times it appears in Romans are in chapter 8. At its most basic level, the term simply means a "wind" or "breath." But for Paul it is the life-breathing presence of God. The Holy Spirit is the member of the Godhead who brings God's life-giving presence to the world and to the individual. When this presence is realized in a person, a new kind of life emerges, life in the Spirit.

Several features of the Spirit's work in the life become apparent here. The work of the Spirit is internal, rather than external. Life in the Spirit has to do with the inner self at its deepest level, not merely outward actions. The Spirit has to do with life rather than death, and with the future rather than this age. The Spirit already brings the kind of life that will characterize eternal life. The Spirit is the assurance that the promised future will come. Finally, the Spirit brings community rather than alienation.

In the new system of life in the Spirit, God sends His own Son, in the likeness of sinful flesh, as a sin offering, to condemn sin in the flesh (vs. 3). (We will come back to the meaning of some of these expressions in a bit. But first let's get a complete picture of all that Paul says about life in the Spirit.) As a result, the just requirements of the law are fulfilled in those who live by the Spirit (vs. 4). They have their mind set on the things of the Spirit (vs. 5), which leads to life and peace (vs. 6). God's Spirit (vs. 9), indeed, Christ Himself (vs. 10) dwells in them. Even though their bodies are still mortal, their spirits are alive on account of righteousness (vs. 10), and they will be raised from the dead (vs. 11). They are God's own children (vs. 14). We need to notice two important elements from this list: first, what God has done, and second, the difference that makes for us.

God's central act was sending His Son. Paul reiterated throughout Romans 7 that the problem was not the law; the problem was us, namely, our flesh or sinful nature that inevitably gets stuck in the mud of sin and only spins the wheels in deeper when law comes along. To solve the dilemma, God sent His Son in that culprit flesh to defeat it from within. Through His life, sacrifice, and resurrection, Christ defeated sin from within flesh. In making this point, Paul uses two expressions that demand special attention: Christ came (a) in the likeness of sinful flesh (b) as a sin offering.

Theologians have argued for centuries about the meaning of the word *likeness*. Does this mean that Christ only appeared to come in human flesh, that He came in human flesh but not sinful human flesh, or that He came in sinful human flesh? Obviously Paul didn't set out to solve the fine points about which the theologians argue, or he would have stated the matter more clearly. He uses this term *likeness* only five times, four of them in Romans. The other three occurrences in this letter do not refer to Christ, but to images that are in the *likeness* of humans, birds, animals, and reptiles (1:23); to sins over which death reigned even though they were not in the *likeness* of Adam's sin (5:14); and to Christians being united in the *likeness* of Christ's death (6:5). The other reference in Philippians 2:7 is part of the beautiful hymn about Christ's humility and willingness to sacrifice Himself for us that Paul uses to admonish the Philippians to have the same attitude of humility. This hymn speaks of Christ's being in the *likeness* of a human being.

We should probably not make too much of this term *likeness*, since Paul doesn't take time to explain it and uses it only in passing. He probably hesitated to say simply "in sinful flesh" because of Christ's sinlessness. (If you are reading the NIV, this may be a bit confusing. Since it has used the term "sinful nature" to translate Paul's term *flesh*, it is hard to see that in 8:3 Paul adds the adjective *sinful* to the word *flesh*.) At the same time, Paul affirms in this verse that Christ condemned sin from within the flesh, making it clear that Christ's humanity is real and is not merely a phantom appearance of humanity.

Paul also speaks in verse 3 of Christ's coming as a sin offering, or literally "concerning sin." Bible versions differ over how to translate this phrase. Some translate it literally as "for sin" or "to deal with sin" (see the RSV, NRSV, and REB), while others translate it idiomatically as "a sin offering" (see NIV, NASB, and NEB). The evidence for translating it idiomatically is that the phrase "concerning sin" is used that way in the Greek translation of the Hebrew Old Testament. If Paul is using the phrase idiomatically, the meaning here is much the same as in Romans 3:25. The Old Testament system of sacrifice serves as a metaphor for Christ's act of sacrifice on our behalf.

Not only did Christ come as a sacrifice to condemn sin from within human flesh, however; He also comes through God's Spirit to live within us (8:9, 10) and make Christ's victory over sin and death our victory too. Paul can refer to this experience as the Spirit living in us (vs. 9) or as Christ in us (vs. 10). Here the two are synonymous.

What difference does this make for us? It gives us a new orientation and a new destiny. Our lives are now oriented to God. Our minds are set on what the Spirit desires, not on the desires of the flesh (vs. 5). The entire focus of our lives is different, for the Spirit gives us new values. And this new mind-set means a new destiny. It is a mind-set that leads to life and peace (vs. 6). And even though we continue to live in a world of evil with bodies subject to death (vs. 10; this is what Paul means by "bodies dead because of sin"), we are already connected to the Source of life-giving power, which assures our victory over death and the ultimate resurrection of the body (vs. 11).

Paul also says that when we live life according to the Spirit, the righteous requirements of the law are fully met in us (vs. 4). Does this mean that we now keep the law, which we couldn't keep before? Or does it mean that we are now free from the law and don't have to worry about it anymore? The answer is probably more complex than either of these statements suggests. Important clues to the answer come both earlier and later in Romans. First, remember where Paul started making the contrast between life in the flesh and life in the Spirit in Romans 7:5, 6. In the life of the flesh, he spoke of the law as an external code. In the system of sin and death, the law stands outside and condemns. In the system of life in the Spirit, God's Spirit directs our lives. But certainly the Spirit will direct us in harmony with God's will. If the content of the law is holy, righteous, and good, isn't that how the Spirit will lead? Therefore, when the Spirit leads, we put to death the misdeeds of the body (8:14).

We should also look ahead to Romans 13:8, 9, where Paul says, "[H]e who loves his fellowman has fulfilled the law. The commandments, 'Do not commit adultery,' 'Do not murder,' 'Do not steal,' 'Do not covet,' and whatever other commandments there may be, are summed up in this one rule: 'Love your neighbor as yourself.' " When the Spirit directs our lives, we do not merely live in outward conformity to the law. The Spirit leads according to the heart of the law, which is love. Do we then have to worry about the law when we live according to the Spirit? Yes and no.

We no longer have to worry about the condemnation of the law. Nor is our focus on the law as an external written code. But certainly, reminding ourselves about God's instruction is an important part of keeping our mind set on the things of the Spirit. Later in this letter, we will see Paul remind his readers about matters such as sexual immorality and drunkenness (13:13). The content of the law is still important. Remember that we do not nullify the law through faith; we strengthen it (3:31). But there are two important items to keep in mind. First, when life is lived in the Spirit, the law is always God's gracious instruction that follows our salvation by grace and is never the basis for it. Second, the Christian's primary focus is not on the law per se, for even when Paul reminds his readers about matters of conduct that are included in the law, as he does in Romans 13, he points them to Christ, not the law. He concludes his admonitions about sexual immorality and drunkenness by telling them to clothe themselves with the Lord Jesus Christ (vs. 14), for the righteous requirements of the law can only be fulfilled when Christ is living within.

One important element in the system of life in the Spirit that we all too easily pass over is the communal aspect of this message. Most of us are so much a part of Western, individualistic culture that we pass over important clues that point beyond individual experience. Therefore, it becomes easy for us to see the experience of life in the Spirit as a private matter between ourselves and God. But Paul begins the whole discussion by saying there is no condemnation for those who are *in Christ Jesus* (8:1). This phrase points to the experience of becoming a part of Christ's body, which means being part of a community of believers. The Spirit is sent not only to save individuals, but to form a people that embraces all, both Jew and Gentile. That is an essential part of Paul's thesis and cannot be forgotten when we read this chapter.

In fact, when Paul presents the image of the Spirit living in us and the law no longer serving as an external code, he probably has the new-covenant promises of Ezekiel somewhere in the back of his mind, promises that have to do with God's community. Certainly Paul goes far beyond what we find in Ezekiel, but notice that the promise of a new Spirit that lives within was part of Ezekiel's vision.

> I will give you a new heart and put a new spirit in you; I will remove from you your heart of stone and give you a heart of flesh. And I will put my Spirit in you and move you to follow my decrees and be careful to keep my laws. You will live in the land I gave your forefathers; you will be my people, and I will be your God (Ezek. 36:26-28).

For Paul, too, the indwelling Spirit draws believers into a community, a new inclusive community of both Jew and Gentile.

Before we leave Paul's contrast between life in the flesh and life in the Spirit, we should notice the rich promises that have been included in these verses. There is the promise that there is not condemnation for us (8:1). When we are in Christ, we are justified, and no charges can be brought against us. There is the promise that the Spirit will live in us and give us new orientation and destiny (vs. 5). There is the promise of resurrection (vs. 11). But all this is just the beginning. The rest of Romans 8 continues with more promises that build on the experience of life in the Spirit. There are at least five more major promises for the believer in this chapter. Let's look at each one.

The Promise of Adoption as God's Children

In Romans 8:15 Paul contrasts the spirit of slavery, which leads to fear, and the spirit of being children. The Spirit testifies with our spirit (probably our inner consciousness) that we are God's children (vs. 16). Paul speaks of a unique privilege that comes from being God's children. We can call the God of the universe "*Abba*, Father (vs. 15)."

Abba is an Aramaic word that Paul uses even though he is writing in Greek. (Aramaic was the common, everyday language of Jews in Palestine.) He simply puts it into Greek letters and then gives the translation "father." But the Aramaic expression is not a precise equivalent to the Greek word for father. The term *abba* was a term of endearment that small children used for their fathers. Most languages have words that are easy to pronounce, often simply the repetition of the same syllable, that children use for their parents. This makes it easier for parents to experience the joy of having their toddlers call them by a recognizable name. In English we have words like *Mama, Dada,* and *Papa.* First-century Jews generally considered the term *abba* too familiar to use in addressing God.

However, the Gospel of Mark, also written in Greek, records that in the Garden of Gethsemane, when Jesus fell in agony and asked that the cup He was about to endure might be taken from Him, He used the Aramaic expression *abba* to address God (Mark 14:36). Now Paul proclaims that Christians can use this same intimate, familiar term of endearment that Jesus used to address God. That's how confident we are that we are His children. We can call the God of the universe "Abba."

But being His children not only means intimate fellowship with Him; it also means that we are His heirs. Paul takes a giant leap beyond Romans 6, where he spoke of slavery to God. When we become God's slaves, He adopts us as His children and makes us His heirs, coheirs with Christ (8:17). This means that we suffer with Christ, but also that we share in His glory. Our inheritance is sure because we are God's own children.

C. K. Barrett (*The New Testament Background: Selected Documents,* 152) quotes an interesting rabbinic contrast to Paul's teaching in these verses from *Siphre Numbers, Shelah* 115:35a:

> Why is the Exodus from Egypt mentioned in connection with every single commandment? The matter can be compared to a king, the son of whose friend was taken prisoner. The king ransomed him, not as son, but as slave, so that, if at any time he should disobey the king, the latter could say, "You are my slave." So, when he came back, the king said, "Put on my sandals for me, take my clothes to the

bath house." Then the man protested. The king took out
the bill of sale, and said, "You are my slave." So when God
redeemed the children of Abraham his friend, he redeemed
them, not as children, but as slaves, so that if he imposed
upon them decrees, and they obeyed not, he could say, "Ye
are my slaves."

Although the passage goes on to differentiate between human
slavemasters, who acquire slaves so the slaves may look after them,
and God, who acquires slaves so that He may look after them, the
contrast with Paul's promise that God makes us not slaves, but children and heirs, is striking.

The Promise of Future Glory That Overshadows Present Sufferings

In verse 17 Paul says that part of being God's heir and a coheir
with Christ is sharing in Christ's suffering. Life in the Spirit doesn't
give Christians immunity from suffering, but it does give Christians
a different perspective on suffering: it is overshadowed by hope. "I
consider that our present sufferings are not worth comparing with
the glory that will be revealed in us" (vs. 18).

It is not only Christians, of course, who suffer. Paul says that the
whole creation, all the cultural and natural world, groans and is in
need of liberation from its bondage to decay (vs. 21). He then compares the creation's suffering to labor pains (vs. 22). It was common
in Jewish literature about the end of the world to look for a time of
suffering before the Messiah came that would be known as the labor
pains of the Messiah. Jesus uses this motif when He gives His sermon about the signs of the end (Matt. 24:8). He also uses it to tell
the disciples about their grief over His death and the subsequent joy
that will swallow up that grief:

I tell you the truth, you will weep and mourn while the
world rejoices. You will grieve, but your grief will turn to joy. A
woman giving birth to a child has pain because her time has

come; but when her baby is born she forgets the anguish because of her joy that a child is born into the world. So with you: Now is your time of grief, but I will see you again and you will rejoice and no one will take away your joy (John 16:20-22).

The image of the pains of labor giving way to the joy of a new baby is a vivid one that only mothers can truly appreciate. Labor pain can be the most excruciating pain known to humans, but when you visit a new mother and her baby, how many times does she focus her attention on the pain and tell you all about it? She is usually too excited about the baby. Thanks to Christ's victory, the suffering of the world has been transformed from meaningless despair to labor pains. This doesn't mean less pain; remember that labor can be excruciating. But there is a new meaning in the pain and suffering. We know that we are moving toward a goal that will even overshadow the most excruciating pain. Life in the Spirit doesn't remove suffering, but it does transform the meaning of suffering.

Paul puts Christians in sympathetic solidarity with the whole creation. We are not isolated from it. It groans, and we groan inwardly in eager expectation. But we have already experienced the firstfruits of the Spirit (8:23). The firstfruits of the harvest were devoted to God in the assurance that the full harvest would follow. Living in the Spirit is already the firstfruits. Our present experience makes our hope sure for the future. We don't have the final hope yet, which Paul calls the redemption of our bodies (vs. 23), but what we do already have gives us the assurance to wait patiently (vs. 25). (The Greek word for patience does not have connotations of inactivity that are sometimes associated with our English word. To wait patiently is not to wait passively but is to bear up actively under the strain.) The final salvation comes when our bodies are transformed or resurrected at the last day (vs. 24). Paul knows nothing of bodiless existence. The final hope is not escape from the body but the redemption of the body so that it loses its mortality. This redemption is simultaneous with the end of decay and death in the creation as well. Humans are part of the creation, and only with the complete end of death can their redemption come.

By tying Christians with the creation in this way, Paul shows us our solidarity with the environment in which we live. It is and we are God's creation. This should give Christians a special sense of care for the environment. We are doubly tied to it by creation and redemption. God cares for the creation and will redeem it with us. If God cares for the creation, how can we do less?

Does this promise solve the problem of suffering for Christians? Certainly not. When we face terrible loss in our own lives, and when we see the horrible images of suffering around the world on our TV screens, we are confronted with questions we cannot answer. And the more glib answers we give, the more absurd they appear to be, especially to those in the middle of the pain. Don't try to tell a woman in labor that she isn't really in pain! Suffering is real. And in this world of sin it is also capricious. Many times the good suffer and the wicked prosper. But Christians know the baby is on the way. (In fact, the Baby has already been here and will return as King.) They know where the creation is headed. And this promise, even though it does not answer all the questions about suffering, gives them a perspective that lets them bear up under the strain and look forward in hope. Before we end the chapter, Paul will have even more encouragement for Christians who continue to live in a world of pain.

The Promise of Help in Prayer

In verses 26 and 27, Paul tells us that living in the Spirit includes the promise that the Spirit helps us when we pray. "We do not know what we ought to pray for, but the Spirit himself intercedes for us with groans that words cannot express" (vs. 26). How often have you been in situations in which you wished you knew what to pray for? Here God promises that He doesn't merely listen and respond to our prayers. He answers the prayers we would pray if we really knew what was best and if we really understood our own thoughts, feelings, and needs.

We need to remember that the Spirit interceding for us is not a matter of the Spirit trying to get God to change His mind about us and do something that He might not otherwise do for us. The Spirit that dwells in us is God's own Spirit. There is no split in attitude between God and His Spirit. It is because God is our *Abba* that He dwells in us through His Spirit. And as a good parent He doesn't merely give us what we ask for; He responds to our needs that are even beyond our consciousness.

The Promise of God Working for Good

This promise is merely an extension of the last one. We are most familiar with the King James Version reading of this promise: "All things work together for good" (vs. 28). But the promise is even better than that. This is one of those cases in which the ancient manuscripts of the New Testament differ. The oldest and most reliable manuscripts that have been discovered since the King James Version was finished in 1611 include the word *God* in this promise. It is not just that all things work together for good; it is that in all things God Himself works for the good of those who love Him. No matter how terrible a situation might be, God is there working for our good.

This is another important consideration when we think about the problem of suffering. Even when we don't have answers to our questions, we do have the assurance of God's presence. The cross shows us that God doesn't pull away from our suffering. He Himself endures sufferings. God is present with us even in suffering. And He is not merely present passively; He is working for our good.

The following verses (29 and 30) have been much debated because of Paul's mention of foreknowledge and predestination. We will reserve our discussion of this issue until we study Romans 9, for the issue comes to the fore with even more force at that point.

The Promise That Nothing Can Separate Us From God's Love

Here in verses 31 to 39, we come to the ultimate promise. Nothing can separate us from God's love. These verses are like a work of art. One almost hesitates to comment on them for fear of leaving dirty fingerprints on the canvas of a great painting. Actually, this promise elaborates on the initial promise of the chapter in verse 1: no condemnation. Now we see a vivid picture of what that promise means. As Richard Hays points out (see the "Further Study" section), Paul probably had Isaiah 50:7-9 in mind when he wrote. Isaiah says:

> Because the Sovereign LORD helps me, I will not be disgraced. Therefore have I set my face like flint, and I know I will not be put to shame. He who vindicates me is near. Who then will bring charges against me? Let us face each other! Who is my accuser? Let him confront me! It is the Sovereign LORD who helps me. Who is he that will condemn me?

Paul begins this section in verse 31 by assuring us that if God is for us, who can possibly be against us? Look at all that God has done for us *all* (notice the importance of that little word *again*). Can't we trust Him to give us all things? Then Paul moves to the vivid picture that grows out of the questions in the Isaiah passage.

It is as if we are invited to a criminal courtroom and placed in the defendant's chair, with all the trauma that would involve. Then the question is asked, Who will bring any charge against us? Is there anyone who will condemn us? Are we really safe? Verse 33 tells us that God has chosen us and justified or acquitted us, so He isn't about to condemn us. Verse 34 asks if Christ then will condemn us. The answer: He died for us, was raised for us, and now intercedes for us at God's right hand. It is absurd to think that He would charge us or condemn us. If neither God nor Christ will press charges against us, who could separate us from Christ's love? Hardship, persecution, famine, nakedness, danger, or sword (vs. 35)? At this point (vs. 36), Paul quotes Psalm 44:22 to remind us that such troubles were his lot and the lot of Christ before him.

But the resounding answer is *NO*. Even in the face of all these problems, we are more than conquerors. Absolutely nothing—not death, life, angels, demons (many in Paul's day lived in fear of the effects of demons and other powers in their lives), the present, the future, any powers, height, depth—nor anything else in the whole universe can separate us from the love of God that is in Christ Jesus our Lord (vss. 37-39).

And so we find ourselves no longer the trembling defendant. Instead, we find that the Judge Himself is our *Abba*, we are held tightly in His embrace, and the courtroom is transformed into a loving home where we are ultimately safe from anything and everything that could possibly threaten us. What more could we possibly want? What a transformation! From courtroom to home. In the end, the forensic analogy is answered by the family analogy.

This sounds like a good place to end the story, and it does bring this section of Romans to an end. But it isn't really the end of the story. We still have living to do, and Paul must go on to help us live together as God's children. Some of God's children are Jews, and some are Gentiles. Some are strict, and some are more free. How will they all live together? Don't stop here; we are only halfway through the book. In Romans 9 to 11, Paul will take up the problem of Jew and Gentile. How can God include both in this good news and still be faithful to the promises He made to the Jews? Even though the argument may not be the easiest to follow, we are about to find out.

■ Applying the Word

Romans 8

1. **As I look again at the page of my notebook that contrasts life in the flesh and life in the Spirit, how can I be sure that I am living life in the Spirit? Do I do something to assure that I am living life in the Spirit, or do I simply accept God's promise to send the Spirit to live in me?**
2. **What does it mean for me to set my mind on the things of the Spirit (vs. 5)? What personal, practical suggestions can I make for myself that might aid the Spirit in keeping my mind set on the right kinds of images?**
3. **How does the adoption metaphor speak to me? Is it easy for me to think of God as my parent? How have my own relation-**

ships with my parents affected the way I relate to this metaphor?

4. How might Paul's promise that the Spirit helps us when we pray (vss. 26, 27) affect my own prayer life? When I think about these verses, do they give me any ideas for enhancing my prayer life?

5. Does what Paul says about the whole creation groaning for liberation have any implications for my relationship to and responsibility for the environment? If so, what might they be?

6. How can I internalize the promises of Romans 8? What acts of worship, public or private, or other activities might help me make these promises my own and give me the continual assurance that they are for me?

7. In what creative (such as poetry, music, art, sermon, essay, or drama) ways might I express my joyful appreciation for these promises? Make the list as long as possible, and then pick at least one, and do it.

8. Review the list you made for question 5 of "Applying the Word" in the previous chapter. How many of your hoped-for solutions appeared in Romans 8?

■ Researching the Word

1. Study Galatians 3:26 to 4:7, where Paul contrasts being slaves with being children in much the same way as he does in Romans 8. Compare and contrast the two passages. What is common to both? What unique contributions do each of the passages make?

2. Use a Bible concordance to see how the term *spirit* is used in the prophetic books of Isaiah and Ezekiel. Compare and contrast your findings with Paul's use of the term in Romans 8.

3. Read John 13 to 17. Make a list of what the Spirit does for us according to these chapters. Compare and contrast the work of the Spirit as presented in John with the work of the Spirit in Romans 8.

■ Further Study of the Word

1. For a presentation of the position that "concerning sin" in Romans 8:3 refers to a sin offering, see M. D. Greene, "A Note on Romans 8:3."
2. For Paul's use of echoes from the Old Testament in Romans 8, see R. B. Hays, *Echoes of Scripture in the Letters of Paul*, 57-63.
3. For a study of the role of the Holy Spirit in Romans 8, see G. D. Fee, *God's Empowering Presence*, 515-591.

PART FOUR

Romans 9–11

God's Purpose for
Jew and Gentile

CHAPTER ELEVEN

God
and the Jews

Romans 9

Even a casual reader of Romans can notice that Paul makes a major transition between Romans 8 and Romans 9. However, even the scholars can't agree on how to interpret this shift in focus. Some see Romans 9 to 11 as an appendix, somewhat separate from the flow of Romans. Others see this section as the central core of the book.

If our interpretation to this point is correct, this section is hardly an appendix, for in it Paul takes up the important topic of Jew and Gentile. He raised this question as early as the thesis statement in Romans 1:16, 17. More specifically, in Romans 9 to 11 he tackles the problem of God's faithfulness in relationship to Jewish rejection of Christ. Remember that Paul raised that issue in Romans 3:1. Consider, too, the strong emphasis on the term all that we have seen throughout the first eight chapters of Romans. And if the chapters (12–15) that follow this section speak to the need for unity, a proper understanding of the role of Jew and Gentile in God's plan would be an important basis for that unity. When we put all this together, this section seems much closer to central core than to unrelated appendix.

One thing is certain, however. The three chapters of this section form a cohesive argument that must be understood as a whole. Therefore, this chapter, which is devoted to Romans 9, will take a bit of a departure from our usual format. We begin with brief "Getting Into the Word" and "Exploring the Word" sections that give us an overview of the three chapters as a whole. Then we move to the usual format to study Romans 9. This is necessary because it would be possible to draw terribly unfortunate conclu-

sions from some of the things Paul says in Romans 9 if we didn't under-
stand where he was going and where the argument would eventually lead.
So first an added overview of Romans 9 to 11, then our study of Romans 9.

■ Getting Into the Word

Overview of Romans 9–11

Read Romans 9 to 11 through at least two times, and write answers to the following questions.

1. Outline Paul's flow of argument in these three chapters. What is his basic point?
2. How do these three chapters fit with the rest of the letter? Why would some call them an appendix? Why would others see them as the central core of Romans?
3. How does seeing the "bottom line" in the latter part of Romans 11 change the way you understand the earlier parts of this section?

■ Exploring the Word

Overview of Romans 9–11

In this section we will briefly attempt to follow the progression of Paul's thought throughout chapters 9 to 11. Paul begins with a personal confession of his concern for his people, the Jews (9:1-5). Then from 9:6 to 11:10 he carefully lays the foundation for his main point, which will come in the latter part of chapter 11.

Paul begins this foundation building by taking up the question of God's faithfulness that he had raised in Romans 3. Has God's word failed (9:6)? How can God be faithful to His promises to the Jews if (a) salvation is by faith in Christ, not works of the law, (b) most Jews have rejected Christ, and (c) Gentiles are now included on equal footing? Paul's first answer is that even in Israel's own history there is abundant evidence that belonging to Israel is more than a matter of genes. First of all, Abraham had more than one son, yet it was through Isaac's descendants that the promise came (vss. 7-9). Jacob and Esau provide an even more striking example. They were twins! Same heredity. And Esau was born first. Yet God "hated" Esau and loved Jacob, later called Israel, through whom the promise continued (vss. 10-13).

What is more, Paul argues, God is free to do whatever He wants. He is free to have mercy on whomever He wants (vs. 15). Two analogies make Paul's point. God hardened Pharaoh's heart (vss. 16-18), and God is the potter who can make whatever He wants with the clay (vss. 19-22). In verses 23 to 29, Paul uses several Old Testament texts to make the point that God is free.

Next, Paul points to a stunning irony: Gentiles, who didn't pursue righteousness, have obtained it, whereas Jews, who did pursue it, did not (vss. 30, 31). In Romans 10 Paul explains this irony. True righteousness is based on faith and comes by hearing. Jews sought it in the wrong way, by works, and did not listen.

In 11:1-10 Paul then asks, "Did God reject His people?" His answer is No. After all, Paul himself is a Jew. And as the story of Elijah reminds Paul's readers, it was often the case that only a remnant of Jews were faithful to God. There is still a remnant, chosen by grace (vs. 8).

In verse 11 Paul finally comes to the main point. God has a plan, an amazing plan! His plan is that the Jewish rejection of the gospel will lead to the gospel going to the Gentiles. But that won't be the end of it. The Jews will see the Gentiles' acceptance of the gospel and will become envious or jealous (vs. 11) so that they, too, will accept the gospel. Whatever God has done in hardening hearts and consigning some to disobedience has been done with one, and only one, goal in mind: that God may have mercy on all (vs. 32).

According to Paul, this amazing plan is demonstrated in his own ministry, which opens the gospel to the Gentiles (vss. 13-16). This is no excuse for Gentiles to become arrogant, however. Paul uses the analogy of the olive tree (vss. 17-24) to show that their acceptance doesn't give them privilege over the Jews.

Israel's hardening is only temporary until the full number of Gentiles has accepted the gospel (vs. 25). God's plan is that all Israel will be saved. He will have mercy on all (vs. 32). This wonderful plan is so awesome that Paul can only end this discussion with a doxology of praise to God (vss. 33-36).

Everything we read in Romans 9 to 11 must be read with this bottom line in view. The topic in these three chapters is not individual salvation; it is God's purpose for Jew and Gentile. God's goal is to save all, and whatever He does is for the purpose of reaching that goal. Without this bottom line, some of Paul's remarks could make God sound arbitrary and capricious. He is not. He is working to have mercy on all.

■ Getting Into the Word

Romans 9

Now read Romans 9 again in light of your overview of the three chapters, and answer the following questions.

1. How does Romans 9 fit into the argument of chapters 9 to 11?
2. What does Paul really mean when he says he could wish that he were cursed and cut off from Christ for the sake of his people? Is this realistic, or is it merely rhetorical? What similar expression was made by a leader in the Old Testament?
3. Compare 9:5 in as many different versions as you can. What major difference do you find? How do you explain this?
4. Make a list of all that Paul says was entrusted to Israel. Explain how Israel received each of these blessings.
5. Explain Paul's basic reason for referring to each of the following Old Testament examples:
   a. Isaac
   b. Jacob and Esau
   c. Pharaoh.
6. Explain Paul's analogy of the potter and the clay. Doesn't this make God seem very arbitrary? Does this chapter call

your understanding of human freedom into question? Explain your answer.
7. Explain Paul's reference to Hosea in 9:25.

■ Exploring the Word

Paul's Lament (9:1-5)

Paul begins this section with a poignant, personal lament that flows from the depth of his soul (vss. 1-5). It is a sincere confession of great sorrow and unceasing anguish. The reason for this sorrow (vs. 2) is the condition of his own people, Israel, who for the most part have not accepted the Messiah.

This seems almost unbelievable to Paul, given that Israel has been blessed in so many ways. He produces a whole list of the blessings that have been Israel's possession (vss. 4, 5). The list includes adoption as God's children, divine glory (seen when God revealed Himself on Sinai and in numerous other epiphanies), the covenants (made with Abraham and renewed continuously to Israel), the law (which is still a gracious blessing, even if it cannot save), temple worship, the promises (of which Christ is the ultimate fulfillment), the patriarchs, and finally, according to the flesh (or in terms of human descent), Christ, the Messiah. With all these privileges, how could anyone in Israel not see what Paul saw in Christ?

Paul's attitude, however, is not one of judgment or condemnation. Rather, he would wish that he could be cursed (a word we still use, *anathema*, which meant "eternally damned") and cut off from Christ if it would mean the salvation of his people (vs. 3). This spirit of solidarity with and concern for his people reminds us of Moses, who after Israel worshiped the golden calf said to God, "Oh, what a great sin these people have committed! They have made themselves gods of gold. But now, please forgive their sin—but if not, then blot me out of the book you have written" (Exod. 32:31, 32). There is a difference between these two great pastoral confessions, however. Moses asks to be blotted out with the people; Paul wishes to be shut out for the sake of the people. He can hardly consider the thought that they will not be saved.

Paul's confession gives compelling evidence that his Jewish identity was still very strong. We see it again at the beginning of Romans 11 when he reminds his readers that he is an Israelite, a descendant of Abraham from the tribe of Benjamin (vs. 1). We often have the idea that on the road to Damascus Paul converted from Judaism to Christianity and ceased being a Jew, but this notion is both anachronistic and far from Paul's thinking. Krister Stendahl has shown that what Paul experienced on the road to Damascus was more call than conversion (see the "Further Study" section at the end of this chapter). When Paul accepted a new mission to the Gentiles, he in no way turned his back on Judaism. How could he? Christ was the fulfillment of the law and the prophets. Even though Paul was the apostle to the Gentiles (Gal. 2:9), he was a Jew. True, some of the basic tenets of Judaism, such as the necessity of circumcision, could go by the board once Paul found Christ. But this didn't mean Paul renounced Judaism; it meant he had found true Judaism in Christ. Paul's solidarity with his people, Israel, should make any anti-Semitism absolutely impossible for Christians, as we will see when we study Romans 11.

A translation problem presents itself in Romans 9:5. The NIV reads, "From them is traced the human ancestry of Christ, who is God over all, forever praised!" Here, Paul explicitly calls Christ "God." Other translations, however, such as the RSV, TEV, NEB, and REB, punctuate so that the last part of the verse is a separate doxology to God not connected with the word *Christ*. This difference comes because in the original Greek there were no punctuation marks at all, so modern editors have to supply them. Since either reading is possible, it is best not to force a dogmatic conclusion.

God's Word Has Not Failed (9:6-29)

If the promise belonged to Israel, how could Israel fail? Wouldn't that mean that God's word had failed, and, therefore, that God is not faithful or trustworthy? Paul already uttered a strong "absolutely not" to that idea in Romans 3. Now he gives reasons. First of all, it was never the case that membership in the chosen people was merely a matter of descent. Isaac provides the first example (9:7-9). Abraham had other children, but Jews knew it was only the descendants of Isaac who were heirs of the promise. Verse 7 contains the important word *reckoned* or *considered*, which Paul used in Romans 4. Just as righteousness was "reckoned" to Abraham, according to chapter 4, Isaac's divine inheritance was "reckoned" by God so that he would be a child of promise. Abraham's other children were not "Israel."

Verses 10 to 13 present an even stronger case to illustrate the same point. Abraham's grandchildren, Jacob (later called Israel) and Esau, were twins. Ancestry can't get any closer than that. Yet God loved Jacob and hated Esau. God announced this election before they were even born, predicting that the older would serve the younger. No Jew would want to include Esau's descendants as "Israel." They were the Edomites, who lived south of the Dead Sea (see Genesis 36) and were consistent enemies of Israel. Even in Paul's day, Idumeans were considered Edom's descendants. Herod the Great was an Idumean. No Jew wanted Esau's descendants considered a part of Israel, yet Esau was literally as much a child of Abraham as Jacob. What better proof that being part of Israel is a matter of God's choice rather than simple genetic heritage. If anyone was left unconvinced, Paul quoted God's words to Moses in Exodus 33:19 to show that God can have mercy and compassion on whomever He chooses (9:14, 15).

Paul takes the word *mercy* from this Exodus quotation and makes it an important part of his argument in chapters 9 to 11. He uses it four times here in chapter 9 and another three times at the end of chapter 11, where he reaches his conclusion (and only two times outside this three-chapter section in 12:8 and 15:9). It becomes virtually synonymous with "grace," which Paul only uses in 11:5, 6 within this section. Here Paul shows that God is free to show mercy. At the end of the argument, he will show that it is God's intention to show mercy on all.

This leads Paul to yet another Old Testament example, Pharaoh (9:16-18). According to Exodus, God raised him up and hardened his heart to show his purpose. Therefore, God can show mercy to whom He wishes to show mercy and can harden the heart of whomever He wishes as well.

Paul goes on in the diatribe style to anticipate the obvious objection. If God predetermines it all, how can He blame us? Paul passes this off with a seemingly arbitrary and authoritarian argument. God can do whatever He wants to! Who are you to talk back to Him (vs. 20)? Don't you know that He is the potter, you are the clay, and He can make vessels for noble or common purposes, whichever He chooses (vss. 21, 22)? (The image of God as potter comes from the Old Testament prophets. See Isaiah 64:8 and Jeremiah 18:1-10.)

Paul concludes this phase of the argument with a series of Old Testament quotations that emphasize either the freedom of God to show mercy or the folly of any expectation on Israel's part that she has it made simply because Abraham is her ancestor. The first reference is from the prophet Hosea, who was told to marry a prostitute who gave him children that were not his own. Their very names pointed to the scandal of it all. They were called "Not My People" and "Not Loved." This symbolized Israel's rejection of God in Hosea's day, but God made the promise that these children, representing rebellious Israel, would be called "My People" and "Loved" (Hosea 2:23). Paul quotes this verse and Hosea 1:10 (9:25, 26) but interprets them differently. He sees in these names evidence that God will reach out beyond Israel and embrace those Gentiles who were not His people. In other words, God's ability to include rebellious Israelites justifies His inclusion of Gentiles as well.

Paul then quotes two passages from Isaiah (10:22, 23 and 1:9) to show that even the Old Testament prophets recognized that only a remnant of Israel would be saved and that Israel would have become like Sodom and Gomorrah if God had not intervened (9:27-29).

Is God Arbitrary?

At first sight, it is hard to read this whole argument in Romans 9:6-29 without being put off at least a little bit. Is God really that arbitrary? C. H. Dodd probably expressed the feelings of many readers of Romans when he commented on Paul's potter-and-clay illustration by saying, "It is a well-worn illustration. But the trouble is that a man is not a pot; he *will* ask, '*Why did you make me like this?*' and he will not be bludgeoned into silence. It is the weakest point in the whole epistle" (Dodd, 171). But before we are too hard on Paul, and certainly before we jump to the conclusion that God arbitrarily predestines some to salvation and some to damnation, there are several things we must remember.

1. Remember the context. Paul is not talking about individual salvation. He is exploring God's faithfulness and His purpose for both Jew and Gentile. He never considers individuals being predestined for damnation.

2. Remember Paul's emphasis and the conclusion of his whole line of thought in this section. Even if God consigns some to disobedience or hardens their hearts, it is part of His plan to have *mercy on all* (11:32).

3. Look ahead to the importance Paul places on the human response of faith in Romans 10:15-17. If God is simply arbitrary, that response would be meaningless. In fact, the whole argument is trying to show that righteousness is based on a decision of faith, not on literal kinship to Abraham.

Yes, God is free to do as He chooses. He can do whatever He wants with the clay. But what He chooses to do with the clay is to show mercy, as Paul goes on to show us.

The Irony of Jew and Gentile (9:30-33)

"What shall we say then?" Paul asks in verse 30. Can it really be that the Gentiles, who didn't pursue righteousness, attained it, and the Jews, who did pursue it, didn't attain it? Strange as it seems, the answer is Yes. Paul gives two reasons.

First, Israel pursued it by works, not by faith. Second, they stumbled over the "stumbling stone" (vs. 32). Here Paul puts together two passages from Isaiah that refer to God as a stone (8:14; 28:16), one that points to God's causing the rebellious Israelites to stumble over a stumbling stone and the other that points to God's trustworthiness as the temple cornerstone. In the background, too, is probably the story in Psalm 118:22 of the seemingly worthless stone that became the cornerstone of the temple. The application of this "stone" to Jesus was obviously a popular tradition in early Christianity, for we find it in 1 Peter 2:6-8 (which quotes both passages from Isaiah and Psalm 118) and Mark 12:10, 11; Luke 20:17; and Acts 4:11 (which quote only the Psalms passage).

The Jews' problem is that they have made a stumbling stone of Christ instead of putting their trust in Him. Is there any hope for them? Paul will have lots to say about that in the rest of this section of Romans.

■ Applying the Word

Romans 9

1. Would I be able to say what Paul does in verse 3 and wish myself damned for the sake of someone else's salvation? If Yes, for whom? Would this be a noble act of self-sacrifice or a kind of foolishness? Why?
2. Does the image of clay in God's hands fit my understanding of my relationship with God? Should it?
3. Has God elected me? How do I know? What is the relationship between His election and my freedom?
4. Can I be said to be "pursuing righteousness"? If so, how do I know whether I am pursuing it by works or by faith? Or do I attain it without pursuing it, like the Gentiles Paul spoke of in Romans verse 30?

■ Researching the Word

1. Use your marginal references to make a list of all the Old Testament passages Paul actually quoted in this chapter. Look up each text. Why did Paul quote so many texts in this chapter? Why did he choose these particular texts?
2. Read the articles on Edom and the Edomites in a good Bible dictionary. Look up these terms in a Bible concordance, and

notice how often they occur. Pick a few references (there are too many for you to look up each one), and notice how intense the conflict often is between the Edomites and Israel.

3. Read Exodus 7:1–11:10. List the passages where God hardens Pharaoh's heart in one column and the passages where Pharaoh hardens his own heart in a second. How do you put these together? Do you think Pharaoh was responsible?

4. Read chapters 27 and 33 of Genesis. How does your reading illuminate what Paul says about Jacob and Esau in Romans 9?

5. Read chapters 1 to 3 of Hosea. Why do you think Paul makes use of this prophetic message in Romans 9?

■ Further Study of the Word

1. For a discussion of Romans 9 to 11, see N. A. Dahl, *Studies in Paul*, 137-158.

2. For a brief but very helpful discussion of God's hardening Pharaoh's heart in Exodus, see pages 80 to 82 of J. Dybdahl's excellent volume on Exodus in this same Bible Amplifier series.

3. For a discussion of Paul's use of the Old Testament in Romans 9 to 11, see R. B. Hays, *Echoes of Scripture in the Letters of Paul*, 63-83.

4. For the argument that Paul's experience on the Damascus road should be considered his call rather than a conversion from Judaism, see K. Stendahl, *Paul Among Jews and Gentiles*, 7-23.

5. For a view, opposite the one taken in this volume, which holds that Romans 9 to 11 is an appendix separate from the flow of Romans 1 to 8, see C. H. Dodd, *The Epistle of Paul to the Romans*, 161-164.

6. For a discussion of Paul's relationship to Israel at various stages of his life, see excursus 12 in P. Stuhlmacher, *Paul's Letter to the Romans*, 177-184.

CHAPTER TWELVE

Why Israel Failed

Romans 10:1–11:10

How could Israel possibly go wrong? The people of Israel had received adoption, glory, covenants, the law, temple worship, and the promises (9:4, 5). Not only that, they were zealous for God (10:2). What a combination! How could they lose?

In Romans 10:1 to 11:10, Paul speaks to this enigma as he continues to lay the foundation for the revelation of God's amazing plan, which will come in the last part of Romans 11. Again in this section, Paul's words are saturated with the Old Testament. Paul firmly believed that God's true purpose for Israel could be found there. For when it is correctly understood, the whole law finds its end in Christ (10:4).

■ Getting Into the Word

Romans 10:1–11:10

Read 10:1 to 11:10 in at least two different translations, and answer the following questions in your Romans notebook.

1. How do these verses fit into the flow of Paul's argument in chapters 9 to 11?
2. What does Paul mean when he says that Christ is the "end" of the law in 10:4? Does this mean that the law ceases to have importance for the Christian? Why or why not?
3. Outline the process by which faith comes according to 10:13-

17. What does this suggest about the nature and meaning of saving faith?

4. Why didn't Israel succeed in seeking righteousness? Outline as many reasons as you can from this section of Romans.

5. How does Paul use the term *remnant* (11:5)? How does this usage compare and contrast with the way you ordinarily use the term *remnant* in a religious context?

■ Exploring the Word

Christ, the End of the Law (10:1-4)

Paul begins Romans 10 with another heartfelt expression of his concern for his people, the Jews. His desire and prayer for them is that they will be saved (vs. 1). These words are by no means merely rhetoric. This whole section of Romans from 9 to 11 is permeated with Paul's personal concern for his people and with his affirmation that God has not forgotten them. Yet Paul can't ignore the fact that there is a problem. He has no doubt that the Jews are zealous for God (10:2). And a person would certainly think that their zeal combined with God's promise would be sufficient for their salvation. But Paul sees a problem nevertheless.

The Jews' zeal for God was not based on knowledge. This failure in knowledge wasn't merely ignorance of some theoretical proposition or doctrine. It was a failure to understand the source of righteousness and to focus their efforts and zeal in the right direction. In verse 3 Paul says, "Since they did not know the righteousness that comes from God and sought to establish their own, they did not submit to God's righteousness." This seems like an incredible accusation. If they were zealous for God, how did they fail to see His righteousness and seek their own?

Throughout this section of Romans, Paul seems to see two problems in their understanding that led the Jews to miss God's righteousness. First, they failed to recognize that their election and special position as God's people were gifts of God's grace. Paul makes this clear with his examples of Isaac and Jacob in Romans 9. Israel was tempted to understand her role in terms of a right based on being a descendant of Abraham. But election is always a matter of grace. Second, Israel was tempted to understand its own righteousness in exclusive terms and forget that God was concerned for *all* people. Whenever they forgot the universal nature of God's grace, they were tempted to boast and try to make righteousness their private possession. Paul will elaborate on this temptation in the rest of Romans 10.

So the problem was that Israel did not pursue righteousness on the basis of faith (9:32). Faith is always a response to God's grace. Israel couldn't seek righteousness on the basis of faith unless she understood that her very status as God's people was a gift of grace. And the response of faith is open to all, because God is gracious to all. Therefore, exclusiveness and separatism could only thwart the quest for true righteousness.

This leads Paul to one of the most controversial and debated statements to be found in all of Romans. In 10:4 he says, "Christ is the end of the law so that there may be righteousness for everyone who believes." We will need to spend some time on this short statement because it can be understood in various ways.

The Greek term translated "end" (*telos*), like our English word *end*, can be used in two different ways. It can mean end in the sense of "termination," or it can mean end in the sense of "goal" or "purpose." Is Paul saying that Christ is the termination of the law or the goal of the law? In addition, the latter part of the statement can be understood in different ways as well. Paul literally says that Christ is the end of the law "into [*eis*]righteousness to everyone who believes." The preposition *eis* can be used in different ways to mean "into," "to," "for," "resulting in," "with regard to," "toward," "near," or "for the purpose of." Naturally, this leads to different translations of the last half of the verse. Some translations simply translate "for" and leave the statement ambiguous (see the KJV and NASB). Both the NRSV and the NIV translate "so that there may be righteousness for everyone who believes." This gives the idea that because Christ is the end of the law, righteousness is for everyone who believes. But in his commentary, Dunn (589) translates "as a means to righteousness for all who believe." Here the idea is not that Christ's relationship to the law results in righteousness, but that Christ is the end of the law functioning as a means to righteousness.

With these possible variations in translation and the meanings of words, it is no wonder that commentators come to different conclusions concerning the meaning of Paul's statement. For example, Barth (*Shorter Commentary*, 126) understands *end* in the sense of purpose and concludes that Christ is the meaning and fulfillment of the law so that to believe Jesus Christ is obedience to the law. Best (118) takes *end* to mean "termination," but not termination of the law itself. Rather, it is the end of obedience to the law as a way of being accepted by God. Achtemeier (168-170) understands *end* as both termination and purpose. He says the law was meant to bring righteousness. Christ brings that role of the law to an end so that the law can now function as an aid to understanding our righteousness in Christ. Dunn (589-591; 596-598) also sees *end* as both goal and termination, but he puts the emphasis on the latter and sees Christ as the end of a misunderstanding of law that saw it primarily as a boundary marker to separate Jews from Gentiles by emphasizing distinctives such as circumcision, Sabbath, and food laws.

What are we to make of all this? What does Paul mean when he says that Christ is the end of the law? There are several possibilities. First, Paul could mean that Christ is the end of the law, period. Law comes to an end when Christ appears. Second, he could mean that some function of the law or some misunderstanding of the law comes to an end. Third, he could mean that Christ is the purpose or goal of the law, but that the law continues to have significance.

A study of the way Paul himself uses the terms we find in this verse throughout the rest of Romans, and in his other letters, will help us reach a conclusion about Paul's meaning here. First, let's look at the word *end*, or *telos*. On one occasion in this letter, Paul uses the term in a technical sense common in his day to refer to taxes (13:7; see also Matthew 17:25), but this has no significance for the usage in 10:4. More relevant is the fact that Paul often uses the term to refer to the second coming of Christ as "the end" or "the end of the ages" (1 Cor. 1:8; 10:11; 15:24; 2 Cor. 1:13; 1 Thes. 2:16). Here *end* is not only the termination of the present world, but also the goal toward which it is moving. This sense of a final goal is also seen when Paul talks about death as the *end* of slavery to sin (6:21; see also 2 Cor. 11:15 and Phil. 3:19, where Paul speaks of destruction as the *end* of false teachers) and eternal life as the *end* of slavery to God (6:22). In only one case (1 Tim. 1:5) is the word used purely in the sense of aim or purpose. So, in Paul's usual usage, *end* refers to the final goal, which includes both the ideas of end and purpose.

Such a usage certainly fits the context of 10:4. Christ is the final goal of the law. There is a sense in which this means termination. Any understanding of law as the ultimate solution to the problem of sin and death fades away in the presence of Christ, the true solution. In addition, any understanding of law that leads to an exclusiveness that tries to grasp salvation as its private possession is obliterated by the message that God's grace has come to *all* in Christ.

It is this aspect of the law that Paul emphasizes in the second half of this statement and then goes on to elaborate in the rest of the chapter. The NIV and NRSV translations of the second half of the verse that interpret "into" or *eis* as meaning something like "so that there may be" are undoubtedly correct. Paul uses the term in a similar way in 1:5 and 1:11. The reason that Christ is the final goal of the law, or at least the result of Christ being the final goal of the law, is that now righteousness is available to *all* who believe. Paul will go on in the rest of the chapter to show that such a position is consistent with the law itself by taking us back to the Old Testament and having us see for ourselves.

The fact that Christ is the final goal of the law, however, does not mean that the law is abolished and has no more value for the Christian. Paul already made that clear in 3:31 (we don't abolish the law in Christ; we fulfill it) and in 8:2-4 (the righteous requirements of the law are met in us when we live according to the Spirit). In the last part of Romans, Paul will call Christians to the same kind of moral life to which the law also calls us, for as Paul says in 8:7, 8, the sinful mind that does not submit to God's law cannot please God.

There is no hint in Romans that the law itself is abolished. After all, it is holy, just, and good (7:12). But if Christ is not seen as the final goal to which the law points, it can be misunderstood and mistaken as the solution itself. The law is not abolished, but unless Christ, the only source of righteousness, is the final goal of the law, the search for righteousness can be futile. On the other hand, when Christ is the final goal of the law, then there is righteousness for everyone who believes, both Jew and Gentile. In the next several verses, Paul goes on to elaborate on this truth by taking his readers back to the Old Testament.

A Bible Study on Israel and Righteousness (10:5-21)

What Paul has just said might seem unbelievable. Those zealous for God and seeking righteousness didn't attain it, but those not seeking for it did (9:30, 31). What is more, because Christ is the final goal of the law, now righteousness is available to all who believe (10:4). How can Paul say such a thing? Anticipating this kind of incredulity, Paul resorts to a short Bible study that supports what he has just said and shows in more detail both the true process for attaining righteousness and the reasons why Israel, who sought it, failed.

The following chart shows the passages of the Old Testament Paul uses in the rest of Romans 10. If you have not already completed question 3 at the beginning of this chapter, be sure and look up each Old Testament text so you will be able to follow Paul's discussion more clearly.

Romans	*Old Testament Passage*
10:5	Leviticus 18:5
10:6-8	Deuteronomy 30:12-14
10:11	Isaiah 28:16
10:13	Joel 2:32
10:15	Isaiah 52:7
10:16	Isaiah 53:1
10:18	Psalm 19:4

10:19   Deuteronomy 32:21
10:20   Isaiah 65:1
10:21   Isaiah 65:2

Now let's work our way through the message that Paul presents in this Bible study. Leviticus 18:5 gives the traditional way of understanding the law. If you do them (the commands of the law), you will live by them. But Paul has taken pains in the first three chapters of this letter to show that neither Jew nor Gentile actually does live by them. Therefore, he adds to this traditional understanding in verses 6 to 8 a passage from Deuteronomy (one of the books of the law), which reads, "Now what I am commanding you today is not too difficult for you or beyond your reach. It is not up in heaven, so that you have to ask, 'Who will ascend into heaven to get it and proclaim it to us so we may obey it?' Nor is it beyond the sea, so that you have to ask, 'Who will cross the sea to get it and proclaim it to us so we may obey it?' No, the word is very near you; it is in your mouth and in your heart so you may obey it" (Deut. 30:11-14). A person doesn't have to reach into heaven or across the sea to search for God's message. It is near. It is to be internalized.

Paul affirms that the Christian doesn't have to ascend to heaven or go down to the abyss to find Christ. Rather, there is a message that is near and can be in the reader's heart. It is the very message Paul proclaims, the message of Christ. This is the message to which Moses actually pointed. In other words, when Moses, in his great covenant renewal speech, spoke of God's command as something not beyond the reach of people, he was pointing to the good news of God's grace, the very message Paul now proclaims. Paul sums up this message simply in 10:9: "If you confess with your mouth, 'Jesus is Lord,' and believe in your heart that God raised him from the dead, you will be saved." Notice the words *heart* and *mouth* from the Deuteronomy passage. This confession is certainly more than the outward act of speaking certain words. To acknowledge Christ as Lord is to allow Him to be Lord of your life. To have faith that God raised Christ from the dead is to put your complete trust in Him from the bottom of your heart. When one responds in this way to

God's grace, the command is no longer unattainable. It is near for everyone.

Paul supports this with another Old Testament text in 10:11. Isaiah 28:16 affirms that no one who trusts God will be put to shame. Thus everyone who trusts, whether Jew or Gentile, will be blessed by God, as Paul shows in 10:12. This then leads Paul to the clincher in verse 13, the perfect text for his argument. It comes from Joel 2:32, where Joel talks about the Day of the Lord. Joel says, "Everyone who calls on the name of the Lord will be saved." See, the Old Testament is clear. When understood with eyes of faith, it is clear that God's grace reaches to everyone.

Next, Paul moves to the process of faith. He begins by asking four questions (vss. 14, 15):

(1) How can they call on the one they have not believed in?
(2) How can they believe in the one of whom they have not heard?
(3) How can they hear without someone preaching to them?
(4) How can they preach unless they are sent?

He then quotes Isaiah 52:7, which praises the beauty of the feet of those who bring good news (10:15). Fortunately, there are those who have been sent and now bring this message of good news near. But the very next chapter of Isaiah (53) warns that not all believe the message (10:16). In verse 17 Paul summarizes. Faith comes from hearing the message, and the message is heard through the word of Christ, or the good news about Christ. Thus far, the Bible study has taught us (from the Old Testament) that God's message has come through the preaching of the gospel and is available to everyone who has faith.

Now two questions remain in this Bible study. They both concern Israel, and they are both answered by further reference to the Old Testament. They are: Did Israel hear? and Did Israel understand (and respond with faith)? Paul uses four more texts to answer. First, they did hear, for Psalm 19, which begins by declaring that the heavens declare the glory of God, says in verse 4 that their voice has gone out to all the earth (see 10:18). Second, in verse 19 Paul quotes

Deuteronomy 32:21, a verse from the song of Moses, which speaks of God's jealousy over Israel's idolatry and says that God will bring calamity upon them and "make them envious by those who are not a people" and "angry by a nation that has no understanding." This text serves two purposes for Paul. It points to Israel's disobedience, and it introduces a word that will be central to Paul's conclusion in the latter part of Romans 11. The word is *envious* or *jealous*. We will have to wait until the next chapter to see how Paul uses this clue to reveal God's surprising plan to have mercy on all.

The last two verses Paul quotes in this Bible study are back-to-back verses from Isaiah 65:1 and 2 (10:20, 21). The first affirms the point Paul made in 9:30, 31. God was found by those who did not seek Him. The Gentiles who didn't search have found. The second verse speaks of the disobedience and abstinence of the Jews. Paul now sees their failure to accept the message of good news as continuing evidence of the same disobedience of which Isaiah spoke.

So what is the point of this Bible study? The message of good news is near. It is that whoever trusts Christ and confesses Him can be saved (10:9). The Old Testament testifies to it. But not all the Israelites have accepted the good news. Even though they heard, they did not obey. This is why they have failed. They didn't accept the good news of God's grace for all, but disobediently clung to the old search for righteousness on the basis of the exclusive privilege of ancestry.

From all that Paul has said, it would appear that the promises to Israel have failed. It is over for Israel. But Paul says No. Now that he has taken us to the brink of the cliff, he turns to take us onward toward new vistas.

God Has Not Rejected Israel (11:1-10)

In verse 1 Paul returns to the diatribe style and asks, "Did God reject his people?" Paul answers with another of his "absolutely not's." And he has evidence to support his emphatic No. The first piece of evidence is Paul himself (vs. 1). He is exhibit A. After all, he is an Israelite, from the tribe of Benjamin (Paul also mentions this ancestry in Philippians 3:5). Here we see again how much of Paul's Jewish identity remains with him. He is living proof that God hasn't rejected Israel, for he is an Israelite sent to proclaim the good news of God's grace.

For exhibit B (11:2-4) Paul moves back in Israelite history to Elijah (see 1 Kings 19:10). When Elijah appealed to God against Israel, he was sure that he was the only Israelite left who hadn't bowed the knee to Baal and forsaken God. But God told him there were actually seven thousand! Paul concludes that in his day, as well, God has a remnant. This remnant was chosen by grace (11:5). In other words, this remnant has nothing to boast about. Those who are part of the remnant are not included because of their achievements. It is purely a matter of grace. This is a truth we should keep in mind whenever we think about the concept *remnant*. Being part of the remnant is not a matter of privilege. God always calls a remnant by His grace for a purpose.

In Paul's day, this remnant proved that God had not forsaken Israel. It is true that most of Israel had rejected the message of grace through Christ, but even that was part of God's plan. Paul refers to Deuteronomy 29:4, Isaiah 29:10, and Psalm 69:22, 23 to show that it was God who had blinded Israel (11:7-10). Why would God do such a thing? Does this mean that the rest of Israel (those not part of the remnant) are lost forever? In the rest of Romans 11, which we will study in the next chapter, Paul will answer this question with another "absolutely not" and go on to reveal how even the hardening of Israel is part of an amazing plan God has to show mercy to all.

■ Applying the Word

Romans 10:1–11:10

1. What are the steps by which I "submit to God's righteousness" (10:3)? How does Romans 10 help me outline those steps?
2. When I reflect on my own relationship to the law, how is Christ the end, or final goal, of the law in my life?

3. Have I been "sent" to enable others to "hear" the word of
   Christ? How do I know?
4. Am I part of a remnant, chosen by God? If so, how did I
   become part of the remnant? What difference does it make
   in my life to be part of the remnant? What privileges does it
   add, if any? What responsibilities does it add, if any?
5. Am I ever tempted to think that I am the only faithful person left? What is the best response when it seems that even
   many of God's people have forsaken Him?

■ Researching the Word

1. Use an analytical concordance to look up the passages where
   Paul uses the Greek word *telos*, translated "end." List the
   different ways Paul uses the word, and reflect on how this
   contributes to your understanding of 10:4.
2. Use the margin of your Bible to discover the Old Testament
   passages that Paul uses in 10:6-21. Look up each of these
   passages. How do they contribute to your understanding of
   what Paul is saying in this chapter? Why do you think Paul
   uses all these texts?
3. Use a concordance to look up passages in the Bible where
   the term *remnant* is used. Is it always used in the same way?
   When God has a remnant, is the purpose always the same?
   Compare your findings with those in a Bible dictionary or
   encyclopedia.
4. Read the story of Elijah in 1 Kings 18:1 to 19:18. Why do
   you think Paul used this story? How does it contribute to
   his message?

■ Further Study of the Word

1. For an argument that *end* in Romans 10:4 means end in the
   sense of termination, see W. C. Linss, "Exegesis of *telos* in
   Romans 10:4."
2. For an argument that *end* in verse 4 means end in the sense

of purpose, see J. V. Hills, "Christ Was the Goal of the Law."
3. For a detailed study of the concept of "remnant" in the Old
   Testament, see G. Hasel, *The Remnant: The History and Theology of the Remnant Idea From Genesis to Isaiah*.

CHAPTER THIRTEEN

God's Surprising Plan

Romans 11:11-36

No one can doubt that parts of Romans 9 to 11 are hard to follow. Paul has laid a lot of groundwork, but now he finally comes to the punch line, which brings this section to an end. From all of the seemingly strange twists and turns in the history of God's people, a plan now emerges; an amazing plan. No one would have ever dreamed it up. The plan is for God to have mercy on all. Given the many portraits we have seen of God's grace, that probably shouldn't surprise us. The way the plan winds its way to fulfillment is astounding. Let's turn to the conclusion of this intriguing section.

■ Getting Into the Word

Romans 11:11-36

Read verses 11 to 36 in at least two different translations, and use your Romans notebook to answer the following questions.

1. How do these verses fit with the flow of Paul's argument in Romans 9 to 11? How does this conclusion fit Paul's purpose for this section?
2. What is God's ultimate plan? How is it fulfilled? Who is involved, and how?
3. What is the future of the Jews, according to Paul? What does Paul expect will happen with them? What practical pur-

poses does Paul have in mind when he discusses this issue?
4. What is the relationship between Paul's method of ministry
   (11:13-16) and God's plan?
5. What is the role of "jealousy" in God's plan? Is jealousy an
   appropriate motivation? Why or why not?
6. Explain what Paul is saying by use of the olive-tree illustration in verses 17 to 24. What is the tree? Who are the original branches? Who are the grafted branches?
7. What does the "full number of the Gentiles" (vs. 25) mean?
   Is God waiting for a specific number to be saved?
8. Did Paul really believe and teach that all Israel would be
   saved (vs. 26)? How do you explain his words?
9. Is God's grace truly irrevocable (vs. 29)? What are the implications of this statement?

■ Exploring the Word

God's Plan and Paul's Ministry (11:11-16)

The verses we studied in the previous chapter ended on a bleak
note for Israel. Remember how verses 9 and 10 quoted Psalm 69:22,
23, proclaiming that Israel's eyes would be darkened and their backs
bent forever? It sounds hopeless. Israel is blind and bent forever!
But again Paul has led us to the brink of the cliff, only to make an
abrupt, surprising turn. And so, in the very next verse (11:11), he
asks the question "Did they stumble so as to fall beyond recovery?"
What has preceded would strongly tempt us to say "Yes indeed."
But Paul's answer is "Absolutely not!"

Paul sums up the amazing plan that makes this "absolutely not"
possible in just a few words. He will elaborate on it later in the chapter. The plan is this: the Jews' transgression has opened the door for
salvation to go to the Gentiles. But when Israel sees the experience
of the gospel in the Gentiles, she will become jealous and will come
to God and be restored (vss. 11, 12). So the No of the Jews leads to
the Yes of the Gentiles, which in turn, through jealousy, leads to the
Yes of the Jews as well. That is the plan. Therefore, Paul can rejoice

that if the Jews' transgression means riches for the world, how much greater riches will their fullness bring (vs. 12), and if their rejection of the gospel means the reconciliation of the world, what will their acceptance be but life from the dead (vs. 15)!

In verse 13 Paul specifically addresses the Gentiles. He, after all, is the apostle to the Gentiles. He says that his own ministry follows the pattern of God's plan. Even though he is the apostle to the Gentiles (in addition to this verse, see Galatians 2:7-9), he still has his own people in view. He hopes that the success he has in bringing the gospel to the Gentiles will arouse his own people to envy and save some of them (11:14).

In Acts, Paul's ministry interestingly corresponds to God's plan. When Paul entered a city, he usually began his ministry in the synagogue proclaiming his message to the Jews. Even though he was rejected by the majority of the Jews, a "remnant" would accept the message. With that core, he would take the message to the Gentiles. Notice, for example, Acts 18, where Paul came to Corinth in Greece. Paul started out in the synagogue and had some success. Aquila and Priscilla, who had left Rome under Claudius's decree, joined him (vss. 1-4). Paul continued preaching in the synagogue, but then we read in verse 6, "When the Jews opposed Paul and became abusive, he shook out his clothes in protest and said to them, 'Your blood be on your own heads! I am clear of my responsibility. From now on I will go to the Gentiles.' "

For Paul, the Jewish rejection of the gospel was not merely hypothetical. It was a continuing personal reality in his ministry. Yet he could never forget his own people. He believed that it was God's plan that this very mission to the Gentiles, which grew out of Jewish rejection, would make the Jews envious and bring them to the gospel.

Yet Paul recognized a danger that Gentiles might not perceive their role in God's scheme. Instead of seeing themselves as a part of God's plan to have mercy on all, they might get bigheaded and feel superior to those Jews who had rejected the gospel. They might even scorn them. Perhaps this was more than a potential danger. As we will see later in this letter, there very well may have been tensions between the Gentile Christians in Rome and even those Jews who were Christians. This danger led Paul to an allegorical illustration addressed to the Gentile Christians.

The Allegory of the Olive Tree (11:17-24)

It is not uncommon to find righteous Israel compared to a tree in the Old Testament, although the type of tree can vary. Israel can be an oak (Isa. 61:3), a palm or a cedar (Ps. 92:12), or an olive tree (Jer. 11:16-17). When he wrote verses 17 to 24 of Romans 11, Paul probably had the Jeremiah passage in mind, since it not only uses the olive tree, but also speaks of judgment against Israel in terms of branches being broken. As Jeremiah rebukes Israel for breaking the covenant, he says:

> The LORD called you a thriving olive tree with fruit beautiful in form. But with the roar of a mighty storm he will set it on fire and its branches will be broken. The LORD Almighty, who planted you, has decreed disaster for you, because the house of Israel and the house of Judah have done evil and provoked me to anger by burning incense to Baal (Jer. 11:16, 17).

Paul builds on this analogy of the olive tree and compares his Gentile readers to wild olive shoots that have been grafted into the olive tree after some natural branches (Jews) had been broken off (Rom. 11:17). Now he warns these grafted branches not to boast, but to remember that they don't support the root; the root supports them (vs. 18). True, others were broken off, and they were grafted in. But those broken off were broken off because of their lack of faith, and those grafted in were grafted in because of faith (vs. 20). If natural branches could be broken off, so could wild, grafted branches. And if wild branches could be grafted in, the broken natural branches can be grafted in too. In fact, this is even easier for God than grafting in wild branches (vs. 24).

The point is that Gentiles should not become bigheaded or arrogant (vs. 20). Their place in God's tree may have come as the result of Israel's rejection. But that doesn't mean God has forgotten Israel and has discarded those broken natural branches forever. His plan is to bring them back into His tree as well. Boasting shows a lack of faith (3:27) and would put the grafted branches in danger (11:21-23). Rather than being conceited, the Gentiles should recognize God's plan to bring them and the Jews together in His kingdom. God's mercy can never be a ground for boasting or a private possession. God's mercy is for all. With this warning in mind, Paul goes on to elaborate on God's amazing plan.

Mercy for All (11:25-32)

In verses 25 and 26, Paul repeats the plan he presented in verses 11 and 12, but with some added detail. Israel has experienced a hardening. But this hardening is only temporary. It will continue until the full number of Gentiles has come in (vs. 25). Then all Israel will be saved (vs. 26). Paul seals this promise with a collection of scriptural quotes from Isaiah 59:20, 21; 27:9; and Jeremiah 31:33, 34. God will come as deliverer, turn them from godlessness, restore His covenant, and take away their sins. Then all Israel will be saved. These two verses raise two interesting questions: What does Paul mean by the "full number of Gentiles"? and Will God really save "all Israel"?

There was a tradition that we find in both Jewish and Christian apocalyptic works (books like Revelation that point to the end of the world with the use of symbols) that God was waiting to bring the end until a certain number was completed. This tradition usually addressed the issue of the seeming delay in the promise of the new age. All the works we have that include this tradition are later than Paul, but the tradition may well have preceded him.

Examples of the tradition can be found in the Jewish apocalyptic works (probably written in the latter part of the first century and never taken as canonical by Jews or Christians) of IV Ezra and II Baruch. In IV Ezra 4:36, Ezra wants to know how long until God brings evil to an end. He is told that he must wait until the number of those like him is complete. II Baruch 23:4 teaches that at Adam's sin, a number was set of places that would be prepared, and the end would not come until the number of righteous to fill those places was complete. Even in the book of Revelation, the cry "How long?" from the souls of the martyrs under the altar is answered with the word that they must wait longer "until the number of their fellow servants and brothers who were to be killed as they had been was completed" (Rev. 6:11).

But even though Paul probably knew this tradition and may be playing on it here, he seems to be speaking in a more general way. The motif of waiting for the number to be complete usually answers the question of the delay of the end, and Paul includes no hint of that concern here. He is probably not implying that God has a specific number of Gentiles who must come in before Israel's acceptance, but is more generally referring to God's plan to take the gospel to the Gentiles and show mercy to them in preparation for showing mercy to the Jews as well.

Paul's assertion that "all Israel" will be saved (11:26) is more difficult. Does Paul really mean that all Jews will be saved? Interpreters answer this question in at least three different ways. (1) Paul is referring to spiritual Israel, i.e., those who accept Christ. But this would hardly make "all Israel" different from the remnant that already existed. This amazing plan would really be nothing more than the status quo. Paul doesn't refer to a spiritual Israel that replaces Israel in this chapter. The olive tree, God's community, has now lost some of its branches, and new branches have been grafted in, but God still has a future plan for those old, broken, natural branches that this interpretation ignores.

(2) Others argue that Paul means exactly what he says. C. H. Dodd held that we must draw universalist conclusions from what Paul taught. He wrote:

> If we really believe in one God, and believe that Jesus Christ, in what He was and what He did, truly shows us what God's character and His attitude to men are like, then it is very difficult to think ourselves out of the belief that somehow His love will find a way of bringing all men into unity with Him (Dodd, 194).

But if this is true, how do we fit it together with Paul's emphasis in this same section of Romans that salvation is dependent on human choice (see 10:14, 15, for example) or with warning that a lack of faith does result in being cut off from the tree (11:17-24)?

(3) Others hold that Paul does present God's plan and purpose that all Israel will be saved, but that "all Israel" does not necessarily mean that every individual Israelite will be saved (see the "Further Study" section at the end of the chapter for examples). They often point out that even in Jewish literature the whole of Israel does not include each person. For instance, *Sanhedrin* 10:1 says that all Israel will have a share in the world to come, but then goes on to exclude Sadducees, heretics, magicians, and the licentious. Thus E. Best concludes, "When Paul says that the whole of Israel will be saved he does not necessarily imply that every Jew will be saved; he means that the nation as a whole will be restored" (Best, 131, 132).

Which of these positions represents Paul's teaching? Most of us would probably jump to number three, and it may well be what Paul would agree to if he were pressed. On the other hand, most of us would probably jump to position three too quickly without grasping how radical and assuring Paul's message is. God's plan is to save not only all Israel, but all, period. Paul's conclusion is that "God has bound all men over to disobedience so that he may have mercy on them all" (vs. 32). Paul even proclaims that God's gifts and His call are irrevocable (vs. 29). As I read this, I get the idea that Paul's view of grace was much stronger than ours usually is. It is true that God will not violate human freedom and force us to be saved against our will, but it is also true that His tenacious commitment to have mercy on *all* goes far beyond our wildest imagination.

God's covenant with us is like a marriage that is different from any human marriage we have ever seen, for His commitment is absolutely irrevocable. He gives us the absolute assurance that He will never forsake us. His goal will never change. Even our disobedience is part of His plan to have mercy on all. Only a choice on our part to forsake and reject Him can thwart His plan to save us.

Doxology (11:33-36)

How does a writer like Paul, a mere human, bring such an amazing message of God's irrevocable grace to an end? What words could possibly be adequate? Paul chooses to end the section, not with his own words, but with the words of Scripture. The final words of this section of Romans are based on Isaiah 40:13 and Job 41:11. They are words of doxology, words of praise. Read 11:33-36 again. Read the verses out loud, and if you can read them without vigor and excitement, you haven't grasped how amazing and wonderful God's plan really is. It would be better to say, shout them out loud. An understanding of God's grace erupts into praise. Worship is an inevitable response. "For from him and through him and to him are all things. To him be the glory forever! Amen" (vs. 36).

■ Applying the Word

Romans 11:11-36

1. How should Paul's presentation of God's plan, including the olive-tree illustration, affect my attitude toward Jews and other non-Christians? Am I ever tempted to boast or be arrogant? What are the best antidotes to such a temptation?
2. What is my part in God's overall plan to have mercy on all? Is there a specific part of that "all" on behalf of whom I can play a role?
3. What kind of praise naturally flows from my appreciation of God's grace?

■ Researching the Word

1. Look up references to Israel as a tree in Psalm 92:12-14, Isaiah 61:3, and Jeremiah 11:16-17. Use your concordance to see if you can find additional biblical analogies based on God's people as a tree.

2. Read chapters 13 to 23 of Acts, and see how many times you find the pattern of Jewish rejection and the resulting move to the Gentiles in Paul's ministry.

■ Further Study of the Word

1. For the view that "all Israel" does not include every individual, see E. Best, *The Letter of Paul to the Romans*, 131, 132; C. K. Barrett, *The Epistle to the Romans*, 223, 224; J. R. Edwards, *Romans*, 273-276; and W. L. Osborne, "The Old Testament Background of Paul's 'All Israel' in Romans 11:26a."
2. For the view that "all Israel" should be read literally in a universalist way, see C. H. Dodd, *The Epistle of Paul to the Romans*, 191-196.
3. For a refutation of the view (held by K. Stendahl and F. Mussner) that Romans 11 teaches a special way of salvation for Israel, see R. Hvalik, "A '*Sonderweg*' for Israel: A Critical Examination of a Current Interpretation of Romans 11:25-27."

PART FIVE

Romans 12:1–15:13

The Christian
Life

CHAPTER FOURTEEN

A Living Sacrifice

Romans 12

At places in our study of Romans thus far, we have probably been tempted to doubt that Paul was really writing as a practical pastor. Some of the arguments have been complex and difficult to follow. But remember, Paul was a pastor who believed that the way we understand God makes a difference in life. We now come to an obvious transition in Romans where the practical concerns come to the forefront. Now we can see how Paul's message of God's mercy for all (11:32) affects the way Christians live every day.

When Paul came to the end of the previous section of Romans (9–11), he could only break out in words of praise to God. In this chapter, however, we find that words of praise are still an insufficient response to God's mercy and grace. The appropriate response goes beyond words. God's grace demands a whole life of praise, a living sacrifice of holistic commitment to God. In Romans 12, Paul reveals the shape of this living sacrifice.

■ Getting Into the Word

Romans 12

Take out your Romans notebook, and write out answers to the following questions after you have read Romans 12 in at least two versions.

1. What features do you find at the beginning of chapter 12 that suggest Paul is making a transition at this point? List as

many as you can.

2. How much can you discover about the way Christians should live, or Christian ethics, from the first two verses of this chapter? Again, make a list.

3. How do you understand the term *living sacrifice*? What kind of background does Paul have in mind when he uses it? What meaning would it have had to Paul's first readers? How can we find the concept meaningful for us when we have had no experience with literal animal sacrifice?

4. Explain Paul's use of the analogy of the body in 12:3-8. What is the primary point he makes with this analogy?

5. List the different gifts that Paul mentions in association with his analogy of the body. Are these the only gifts? Are they the most important gifts? Which of these gifts have you received? Are there other gifts not listed here that you have received? How can you utilize these gifts in the best way?

6. What parts of Paul's advice in this chapter focus on life inside the community of believers? Summarize the basic picture Paul gives of how we should live within the community.

7. What parts of Paul's advice in this chapter focus on life outside the community of believers? Summarize the basic picture Paul gives of how we should live with those outside the church.

8. What does Paul mean by his use of the expression "heap burning coals on his head" (vs. 20)? Where does Paul get this expression? How does a person do this, and what is the result?

■ Exploring the Word

Therefore . . . a Living Sacrifice (12:1-2)

Some have argued that Paul's ethical thinking is unrelated to his basic theological message. Morton Scott Enslin, for instance, held that Paul's theology actually militated against ethics. Therefore, the ethical thinking in Paul's letters is merely a remnant of his Jewish past, combined with the commonplace morality of the day, at best tacked on to, and at worst inconsistent with, his theology (Enslin, 63-77). But our study of Romans 12 to 15 will show that this is not true. Paul's practical advice at the end of the letter grows directly out of the message he has shared throughout the first eleven chapters.

In fact, the very first word in this section of the letter is the transitional word *therefore. Therefore* implies a conclusion to something that has gone before. This *therefore* ties the advice about Christian living in the last part of the book with what has gone before. This is the conclusion of the matter. But Paul's *therefore* does more than tie these parts of Romans together. It is not only a literary device. It also transforms the admonition that follows. Without understanding Paul's *therefore*, we misunderstand all that follows.

As the saying goes, advice is cheap (and is often worth the price). Admonitions all by themselves are simply law, and Paul has already waxed eloquent about the powerlessness of law. But these admonitions Paul gives are more than law, and it is the *therefore* that makes the difference. In this whole section, Paul is doing much more than merely saying, "Do this." Rather, he is saying, "Therefore, in the light of God's mercy and grace, here is the appropriate way to respond." He is trying to show us the life that follows from a true understanding of God's grace. The logical, reasonable outgrowth of accepting God's grace "for all" is a holistic response of trust for God and love for others, which Paul calls a "living sacrifice" (12:1).

Paul introduces this concept by using a certain kind of formula that scholars call an appeal formula. It is a statement that was often used in correspondence in Paul's day to introduce a new topic or make a transition in discourse as well as to request a specific behavioral response from the readers. Such a statement followed a form that went "I urge you (a) by (b) to (c)." In blank (a) the author would fill in the person or persons to whom he/she was appealing. In blank (b) would come the basis for the appeal and in (c) the actual response being solicited.

Paul appeals to the "brothers" at Rome (I'm sure if he were writing today he would add the word *sisters*) on the basis of God's mercy (vs. 1). This is precisely where the first eleven chapters of Romans reached their climax—at the point of God's desire to show mercy for all (11:32). Now it is on the basis of that very mercy that Paul appeals to them, although he uses a different term for "mercy" than he has been using throughout chapters 9 to 11. See how Paul's transition again ties his practical admonition with what has gone before. And what is the appeal? It is that Paul's readers will offer their bodies as a living sacrifice to God.

There are only three such appeal statements in Romans. The second is found in Romans 15:30, where Paul asks his readers to pray on his behalf. The third is in Romans 16:17, where Paul asks the Romans to watch out for those who cause divisions among them. These are Paul's three specific requests of the Romans: that they live a life of living sacrifice, that they pray for him, and that they watch out for those who would destroy their unity. We will come to the second and third of these in a few chapters. At this point, we need to explore what Paul means by a living sacrifice.

Much of the language in the first two verses of Romans 12 is technical language associated with the sacrificial system. When animal sacrifices were made to God, they were to be holy and pleasing to Him. In the Pentateuch (the first five books of the Old Testament), this is often presented in an anthropomorphic way. God is viewed as actually smelling the aroma of the sacrifices and being pleased. For example, the following is said about Noah when he came out of the ark, "Noah built an altar to the LORD and, taking some of all the clean animals and clean birds, he sacrificed burnt offerings on it. The LORD smelled the pleasing aroma" (Gen. 8:20, 21; see also Exod. 29:18, 25; Lev. 1:9, 13; 2:9; 4:31; Num. 15:3, 7). Over and over again, sacrifices were pleasing to God because He smelled the pleasing aroma.

The prophets, however, present a somewhat different perspective on sacrifice when they emphasize that outward acts of sacrifice are not pleasing to God apart from a holistic spiritual and ethical response. For example, when Micah (6:6-8) asks what would please the Lord, he concludes that it would not be burnt offerings, thousands of rams, ten thousand rivers of oil, or even one's firstborn, but rather, "to act justly and to love mercy and to walk humbly with your God." Paul continues in this prophetic tradition, emphasizing that the true sacrifice to God is not merely a specific act but a whole life dedicated to God and service for others.

When he uses the term *bodies* (12:1) here, Paul refers to the whole person. The whole person becomes a living sacrifice that pleases God by appreciating His grace and showing love for His children. Paul already introduced this concept in Romans 6 when he spoke of us offering the parts of our bodies to righteousness leading to holiness (6:13, 19). Only a whole life offered to God can be a living sacrifice. According to the NIV, Paul calls this our "spiritual act of worship" (12:1). Other translations speak of "reasonable service."

The Greek word translated either "reasonable" or "spiritual" is one from which we get the English word *logic*. The word could mean logical or reasonable. But it was also used by both Greek and Jewish writers to refer to what was internal or spiritual as opposed to the external act. For example, the Alexandrian Jewish philosopher named Philo (*Special Laws* I:277) used the term this way. It would probably be a mistake to limit Paul's usage to either of these meanings, since they are related. Presenting our bodies as a living sacrifice is the logical, reasonable response to God's grace. Paul's appeal for his request is to the "mercies of God." This is the logical response to the mercy that God has shown us in Christ. Yet it is also a response that is holistic and internal, not merely an external act.

Paul not only ties this response to the past and present revelation of God's mercy and grace, however. He also ties it to the future. We are no longer to be conformed to the pattern of this world (vs. 2), but to be transformed with a new mind-set or way of thinking. The term that the NIV translates as "world" is really the word *age*. Therefore, there are eschatological overtones to what Paul says. Paul uses the term *age* five times in Romans (in addition to this passage, see 1:25; 9:5; 11:36; 16:27), but in the other four it is merely part of a formula to express the idea of "forever." But several passages outside of Romans show us what Paul had in mind when he spoke of "this age." In the introduction to Galatians (Gal. 1:3, 4), Paul says that Jesus "gave himself for our sins to rescue us from the present evil age." In 2 Corinthians 4:4 he speaks of Satan as the "god" of this age who blinded the mind of unbelievers to keep them from seeing the light of the gospel. And the following passage from 1 Corinthians contrasts the wisdom of this age with God's wisdom:

> We do, however, speak a message of wisdom among the mature, but not the wisdom of this age or of the rulers of this age, who are coming to nothing. No, we speak of God's secret wisdom, a wisdom that has been hidden and that God destined for our glory before time began. None of the rulers of this age understood it, for if they had, they would not have crucified the Lord of glory (2:6-8).

All of this makes it clear that for Paul the present age is an evil age ruled by Satan and rulers who oppose God. But Paul calls Christians to begin living even now in a new way. Even though they are in this world, they already live according to the values and goals of a new age, for their minds are already focused on God's kingdom. By responding positively to God's grace, their minds are reshaped according to God's will. Even though the world is still the "present evil age," Christians already experience the new age of God's kingdom because their minds are focused on God's values. This is only possible because the mind is renewed by God's Spirit. Only when the mind is set on the Spirit and what the Spirit desires (8:5) can it be renewed and transformed so that it comes to think in a new way. The renewed mind, in turn, leads to new action.

We must always remember, however, that everything Paul says here follows a "therefore." It is only possible because of the "mercies of God." Most of the rest of Romans will show us the shape of this new, transformed life, the living sacrifice that already anticipates the new age of God's future.

The Body—Self-Awareness and Service (12:3-8)

Paul begins showing his readers the shape of a living sacrifice by pointing them to their life as part of the body of Christ (vs. 5). Although in our individualistic culture some people speak of living a

Christian life apart from the church, such a conception was totally foreign to Paul. To respond to God in faith was to become part of Christ's body and join together with other believers.

Paul gets this section started with a play on words. He uses three words from the same root: *phroneō* ("to think"), *huperphroneō* ("to think too highly of oneself or be haughty"), and *sophroneō* ("to think sensibly"). He urges the Romans to think sensibly, not haughtily (vs. 3). In other words, they are to have an accurate assessment of themselves. We often call this self-awareness. Yet many times when we speak of self-awareness, it is in the context of an individualistic, even self-centered, effort to understand ourselves. For Paul, the goal of self-awareness is service. We need to understand ourselves and our gifts so we will know how to serve. These gifts are not merely natural endowments, but are part of the measure of faith that God gives. He gives diverse gifts so that the body will have different kinds of members for different kinds of service. Yet each member "belongs to all the others" (vs. 5). Even though the members have different functions, they are part of one body. Each one works in harmony with the whole.

The list of specific gifts Paul gives here is hardly exhaustive. It is but a sample. The gifts are prophesying (for Paul, this is not predicting the future, but under the Spirit's inspiration preaching the gospel), serving (we get our word *deacon* from this word), teaching, encouraging, contributing to the needs of others, leading, and showing mercy (vss. 6-8). Paul admonishes the recipients of each of these gifts to use their gifts diligently in accordance with the faith God has given. Notice how strongly these gifts focus on building up both the spiritual life and the sense of community among believers. Notice, too, that these gifts that build up the church are not limited to clergy or super-Christians. They include simple acts like encouraging each other (perhaps with a smile or a note), contributing to the needy, serving, and showing mercy. We have probably put too much emphasis on gifts that belong to a few leaders and not enough on the everyday, practical gifts that do the most to build up the body of Christ. What is unmistakable is that we all have a vital part to play in the functioning of the body.

Love in and Out of the Community (12:9-21)

Within this section, verses 9 to 13 seem to focus primarily on love within the community of believers, whereas verses 14 to 21 apply to the Christian's responsibility to unbelievers. There is some overlap, of course. Here, admonitions tumble out on top of each other so quickly that there seems to be no context or flow of argument. This style is typical of certain kinds of ethical writing by the Hellenistic philosophers of Paul's day.

Yet there is a structure to the language that simply doesn't come across in English. Although Paul's statements appear in English as imperatives or commands, the Greek uses a different form that has the meaning of a command. It allows for a parallelism that ties the various bits of advice together. It is very hard to translate the meaning successfully by keeping the structure. For example, here is a literal translation of verses 10 to 13a that attempts to preserve the structure of the original. It sacrifices too much of the meaning and of English style to be useful, but it does show how Paul uses a repetitious structure to tie these bits of advice together.

In brotherly love for one another, devoting yourselves,
In honor for each other, leading out,
In haste, not being lazy,
In the spirit, boiling,
In the Lord, serving,
In hope, rejoicing,
In affliction, enduring,
In prayer, persisting,
In the needs of the saints, sharing.

But even though this last half of the chapter seems like a catch-all of spiritual and ethical advice, it nevertheless contributes significantly to the shape of the life that is a living sacrifice. Verse 9 begins with the word *love*. The Greek word is *agapē*, the self-giving attitude of concern for and action on behalf of others. Paul frequently uses this word to refer to God's love for us (in Romans, see 5:5, 8; 8:35, 37,

39; 9:25) and to our love for each other (in Romans, see 12:9; 13:8, 9, 10; 14:15). He seldom uses it to refer to our love for God (in Romans, only at 8:28), since he prefers the term *faith* for our response to God. All of the bits of advice in verses 9 to 13 show the shape that love will take in our spiritual and ethical lives within the body of believers. His final admonition in verse 13 is to practice hospitality. This was an important part of Christian responsibility for those such as Paul who frequently traveled and were dependent on the hospitality of others.

In verses 14 to 21, Paul turns to the shape of love vis-à-vis the world of unbelievers outside the church. Much of his advice is reminiscent of Jesus' instruction in the Sermon on the Mount (Matthew 5–7) or the sermon on the plain (Luke 6). Christians are to bless rather than curse those who persecute them (12:14). They are not to be conceited or proud and are to live in harmony with others (vs. 16). Paul recognizes that it is impossible to live always at peace with everyone (he himself had often been arrested), but as far as it is within the power of the Christian, this should be the goal (vs. 18). Christians are also not to repay evil or to take vengeance (vss. 17, 19). This is God's work alone.

One of Paul's emphases in this section is interesting because of the way it contrasts to some of the philosophical thinking current in Paul's day. Paul urges his readers to empathize with others, both rejoicing with them and mourning with them (vs. 15). The Stoics of Paul's day taught that people should keep their emotions in check and not let themselves lose a distanced reserve. For example, Epictetus said that Stoics might mourn with others on the outside, but not in the center of their being (*Encheiridion* 16), and that even when hugging a child, a parent should hold back and remember that the child is mortal (*Encheiridion* 3). Paul's perspective is very different. Christian love genuinely rejoices with others and mourns with them. It is vulnerable and can be touched, either by joy or hurt, in empathy with others.

Love also acts for the good of all, even the enemy. Paul stresses this by quoting from Proverbs 25:21, 22 in Romans 12:20. Christians feed and give drink to the hungry and thirsty enemy. The last part of the Proverbs' quotation is more difficult to understand, however. Paul, quoting Proverbs, says, "In doing this, you will heap burning coals on his head." What does this mean? Most commentators believe that putting coals on the head was a sign of repentance, and therefore the passage means that by being kind to the enemy, you may lead him or her to repentance. This would fit with the final admonition of the chapter, to overcome evil with good.

Stuhlmacher (186) points out that Romans 12 to 13 has certain parallels with 1 Peter (Rom. 12:1ff with 1 Pet 1:14; 2:5; Rom. 12:6ff with 1 Pet. 4:10; Rom. 13:1-7 with 1 Pet. 2:13-17). These similarities may suggest that both Paul and Peter are giving typical instruction that was given to newly baptized Christians in the early church.

As we come to the end of this chapter, we find that three elements stand out. First, Paul is concerned about practical, everyday life. Second, the shape of that life is governed by a "therefore." It is a response to the good news of God's grace that has preceded. Third, the shape of that life is also governed by the promised future. It is not pressed into the mold of this age, but already anticipates the new age of God's kingdom.

In the next chapter, Paul will move from general instruction about how Christians relate with those outside the body to a specific relationship, that of Christians and governmental authorities.

■ Applying the Word

Romans 12

1. If I look at my calendar of activities, what does it reveal about my life as a "living sacrifice"? What if I were to examine my checkbook register with the same question in mind? What are the tangible ways I express the kind of life Paul points to in this chapter? How do I examine these without becoming haughty or conceited?

2. What is my place in the body, and what gifts do I have? Do

any of the gifts Paul mentions in this chapter fit me? If so, how might I use these gifts? If not, what gifts do I have? How might I use them more effectively?

3. Do I have more problems living up to the admonitions Paul gives relating to those within the body or those outside the body? What would it take for me to live peaceably with all?

■ Researching the Word

1. Compare and contrast Romans 12:3-8 with 1 Corinthians 12. What additional information do you learn about the church as the body of Christ in 1 Corinthians that is not in Romans? Notice the lists of gifts included in both chapters. What gifts are included in both lists? What gifts are unique to Romans? To 1 Corinthians? Can you think of any reasons why Paul includes the gifts he does in each letter?

2. Compare Paul's advice in Romans 12 with Jesus' Sermon on the Mount (Matthew 5–7) and sermon on the plain (Luke 6). How many parallels do you see? How do you explain this?

3. Many believe that both 1 Peter and Colossians 3 and 4 contain instruction for newly baptized Christians. Read both, and see if you find evidence to support this view. Now compare these with Romans 12, and see if you think it should be included as possible baptismal instruction as well.

■ Further Study of the Word

1. For the view that Paul's ethical advice is unrelated to his theology, see M. S. Enslin, *The Ethics of Paul*, 63-77.

2. For the view that Paul's ethical advice is closely related to his theology, see V. P. Furnish, *Theology and Ethics in Paul*, *passim*, 212.

3. For a discussion of the significance of the appeal statement

formulas in 12:1 and 15:30, see G. Smiga, "Romans 12:1, 2 and 15:30-32 and the Occasion of the Letter to the Romans."

4. For a discussion of the phrase "reasonable service" or "spiritual worship" in 12:1, see D. Peterson, "Worship and Ethics in Romans 12."

5. For both a discussion and examples of styles of ethical admonition in the Greco-Roman World, see A. J. Malherbe, *Moral Exhortation: A Greco-Roman Sourcebook*, 121-134.

CHAPTER FIFTEEN

Christians and Governments

Romans 13:1-7

These few verses where Paul takes up the Christian's relationship to governments have been the subject of much speculation and even controversy, not only because of what Paul says, but perhaps even more because of what he doesn't say. Paul seems to call for unqualified submission to governing authorities. Yet a Christian can hardly read these words without thinking of the example of Peter standing before the religio-political authorities in Jerusalem saying, "We must obey God rather than men!" (Acts 5:29). Why does Paul say what he does in Romans 13:1-7, and why is that all he says? We will try to find answers to these questions as we open the Word together.

■ Getting Into the Word

Romans 13:1-7

Read verses 1 to 7 in at least two or three different translations, and write out answers to the following questions in your Romans notebook.

1. Outline what Paul says in this section. What is the gist of his advice?
2. How does this section fit the context of Romans? Can you find specific links with Romans 12 and with the remainder of chapter 13? List what you find.

3. Analyze Paul's use of the term *authority* in Romans 13:1-7. Does it mean the same thing each time it is used? Explain your answer.
4. On a page in your Romans notebook, list at least three different ways that Paul says earthly rulers function as God's servants. Explain how each one can be true.
5. List and analyze each of the reasons Paul gives for submitting to the authorities in these verses.

■ Exploring the Word

What Paul Says (13:1-7)

We begin by carefully noting what Paul actually says in these verses. He begins with a command in verse 1 that everyone submit to the governing authorities. The term translated "authorities" can refer to any government official, including the emperor. Although it can also refer to angelic or demonic powers, the context here suggests that Paul is speaking of earthly rulers. (For the opposite view, see the work by Cullmann in the "Further Study" section. I am indebted to the work by Stein, listed in the same section, for some ideas about the structure of this passage.) Following this initial command to submit, we find reasons for the command.

The first reason is found in verses 1b to 2 and is a theological reason. No authority exists except that which God has established. If these authorities are established by God, then to rebel against them is to rebel against God, and to do this is to bring judgment on oneself. Paul is affirming that governments exist by God's authority. He does not say whether this means governments in general or specific governments are ordained by God, but that does not really make a difference in the flow of the argument. The point is that Christians are to submit to them, and to do otherwise is to resist God and violate His will.

The second reason is given in verses 3 and 4. Here the reason is practical and pragmatic. Rulers aren't a terror to those who do good, but to those who do evil. Therefore, if you do good, you don't have to worry about the rulers. You only have to worry if you do evil. Governments don't bear the sword for nothing. They bring God's punishment on the wrongdoer to keep order. By doing this, they actually serve God. In fact, Paul calls them God's "servants" or "deacons" (vs. 4). No one would want to live in a situation of anarchy. Therefore, Christians have a practical reason as well for submitting to civil governments and rulers.

Verse 5 begins with a *therefore* and summarizes Paul's argument to here. Christians should submit to avoid punishment (the pragmatic reason Paul has just given) but also for an additional reason—because of conscience. This goes back to the first reason Paul gave. If governments are instituted by God, then submission is more than a practical matter; it is a matter of Christian principle as well. Internal commitment to God should motivate the Roman Christians to submit to the governing authorities.

In verse 6, Paul gives a specific example of such submission. Christians are to pay taxes, because the authorities are God's servants who give their full time to governing. In other words, they deserve to be paid for their work, and this comes through taxes. The word for "authorities" here is a different word than is found in verse 1. This word was generally used for lower-level government functionaries, including tax collectors. Finally, Paul summarizes in verse 7 with a general command, followed by four specifics. The Roman Christians are to pay everyone they owe, whether that debt be taxes, revenue, respect, or honor. In verse 8, which we will study in the next chapter, Paul goes on to say that the only debt his readers should have outstanding to anyone is the debt of love.

What Paul Doesn't Say

These verses are probably discussed more because of what Paul doesn't say than what he does. There are some surprising omissions. First, he says nothing in this section that is explicitly Christian. Although he ties this advice with God's will, he doesn't link it with Christian motivations. It was standard teaching in Judaism that God ordained civil governments. For example, the following passage from the Wisdom of Solomon affirms this, even though it makes a different point from the one Paul makes. Whereas Paul uses the idea that God ordains rulers to argue for submission to them, Wisdom uses the same idea to address the rulers regarding their responsibility. The passage reads:

> Listen therefore, O kings, and understand; learn O judges of the ends of the earth, Give ear, you that rule over multitudes, and boast of many nations. For your dominion was given you from the Lord, and your sovereignty from the Most High; he will search out your works and inquire into your plans. Because as servants of his kingdom you did not rule rightly, or keep the law, or walk according to the purpose of God, he will come upon you terrible and swiftly, because severe judgment falls on those in high places. For the lowliest may be pardoned in mercy, but the mighty will be mightily tested (6:1-6, NRSV).

Second, Paul gives no qualifications or hints that there might be circumstances where Christians have to stand up to civil rulers. He doesn't consider the possibility that governments might terrorize those who do good, perhaps persecuting them precisely because they try to follow God's will. This seems especially surprising in light of Paul's own experience. Even though Paul was a Roman citizen (see Acts 16:37 and 22:25) and according to the book of Acts often came out better when he appeared before Roman rulers than he did at the hands of his Jewish brothers, he certainly knew what it was to be persecuted by both the Jews and by Rome, as his autobiographical statement in 2 Corinthians makes evident:

> Five times I received from the Jews the forty lashes minus one. Three times I was beaten with rods, once I was stoned, three times I was shipwrecked, I spent a night and a day in the open sea. I have been constantly on the move. I have been in danger from rivers, in danger from bandits, in danger from my own countrymen, in danger from Gentiles; in danger in the city, in danger in the country, in danger at sea; and in danger

from false brothers (11:24-26).

Yet in spite of this personal experience, Paul gives not a hint that civil rulers could ever be a problem for those who do good in this passage. Obviously if Paul doesn't mention the possibility that these civil governments can be problematic even though they are ordained by God, neither does he give any advice for the Christian about what to do when responsibilities to God come in conflict with the demands of the civil government.

Finally, Paul does almost nothing in this passage to apply the advice he gives to specific situations. He comes close only when he admonishes that Christians should pay taxes. But he doesn't address such questions as whether Christians can legitimately carry the sword for the civil rulers. How, for instance, does Paul's advice translate into specific action when Christians are drafted as soldiers? Paul makes no such applications to difficult situations. He simply leaves us with the basic advice in its simplicity with no apparent recognition of the complexity of the actual decisions that Christians often face.

Why Paul Says What He Does

How are we to understand Paul's admonition about civil governments? Why does he say what he does and fail to say other things that we might expect to be part of the discussion? We can point to two possible explanations.

First, Paul may be repeating typical, general advice that was presented to new Christians at baptism. Such admonition might not be expected to include a discussion of exceptions and applications. It would be limited to the basic issue of respect for civil governments to let new converts know that their newfound faith didn't absolve them from earthly responsibilities. In favor of this explanation is the parallel advice in 1 Peter 2:13-17:

> Submit yourselves for the Lord's sake to every authority instituted among men: whether to the king, as the supreme authority, or to governors, who are sent by him to punish those

who do wrong and to commend those who do right. For it is
God's will that by doing good you should silence the ignorant
talk of foolish men. Live as free men, but do not use your
freedom as a cover-up for evil; live as servants of God. Show
proper respect to everyone: Love the brotherhood of believers,
fear God, honor the king.

Although there are obvious differences between Peter and Paul
(Peter, for instance, does not emphasize that civil governments are
ordained by God), it is the similarities of both thought and vocabulary that stand out. These similarities may well suggest that this was
common instruction that Paul repeated without entering into discussion of exceptions and applications.

In the previous chapter, we noted that there are parallels between
Romans 12 and 1 Peter, suggesting that in Romans 12 Paul may have
been giving instruction that was typically given to newly baptized converts. Now we find similar instruction about civil governments in both
Peter and Romans. Later on in chapter 13, Paul will also use language
about putting on clothes that was typical of baptismal language in early
Christianity. All of these factors suggest the possibility that Paul may be
thinking about newly baptized converts as he gives this advice, and that
may have influenced what he chose to say and not to say.

A second explanation is that Paul was addressing a specific situation in Rome and because of the particularities of that situation
wanted to present only one side. As we saw in the introductory chapter, Christians in Rome had already been part of a dispute with Jews
that attracted so much attention that Emperor Claudius had expelled
the Jews from Rome. Presumably, Jewish Christians also had to leave,
but the presence of Pricilla and Aquila in Rome (16:3; compare with
Acts 18:1-3) shows that they had returned. Perhaps Paul was concerned that the Roman Christians not repeat this kind of affront to
the Roman authorities.

Various scholars have suggested other possible situations in Rome
that might have been in Paul's mind, such as unrest about taxes (see
Tacitus, *Annals* 13:50-51) at the time or Jewish sympathy with Zealot
activity in Judea. But there is no evidence that would connect either

of these directly with Roman Christians.

Paul doesn't give us enough information to allow us to conclude with certainty why he says what he does in Romans 13. I think there is good evidence that he is repeating typical instruction that was probably included in the advice given to new converts. It is also not hard to imagine that the past difficulty involving Roman Jews and Christians with the emperor would have been in Paul's mind when he gave this advice about civil governments. What, then, should we make of this advice for us today?

Paul, Civil Governments, and Us

There are several things we should keep in mind as we think about the relevance of this passage for us today. First, this is not all the Bible says about how God's people should relate to civil authorities. The Bible is filled with examples of faithful followers of God, from Daniel in the lions' den to John exiled on the Island of Patmos, who had to say No to the demands of the state for the sake of conscience. If tradition is correct, Paul himself was beheaded by the very Roman authorities he speaks about in this passage. In fact, this is not even all that Paul says on the topic of civil governments. For example, in 1 Corinthians 6 he advises that Christians not participate in the civil courts by initiating lawsuits against other Christians. When we think about our relationship to civil governments, we need to look at many different biblical passages.

Second, we should take what Paul does say here seriously. Even though there are exceptions that Paul doesn't mention, that in no way detract from the basic point that Christians should be responsible citizens who respect governments and recognize that God orders the world and keeps it from anarchy through the work of governments. Too many commentators on this passage spend all their time saying what Paul should have said, rather than recognizing that what he has said is important for us. In fact, what Paul has said here is the most important consideration for most of us on a daily basis.

Most days don't confront us with major dilemmas where conscience and duty to God come into conflict with the demands of government, but all days confront us with many decisions that call our commitment to be responsible citizens into question. Do we, for example, obey speed limits when we drive, and do we report untraceable incidental income when we fill out our tax forms? And do we take advantage of many opportunities for good citizenship that were not open to Paul but are open to us in a democracy, to influence our community to act with justice and compassion? Our world is very different from Paul's. We live in a democracy, where we have much more opportunity for participatory citizenship than Paul had. We will not all agree on what good citizenship and responsibility to God demand in every situation, but if we take Paul seriously, we cannot deny that it is part of our responsibility to God to respect, but never to worship, the authority of government.

■ Applying the Word

Romans 13:1-7

1. In what specific ways do I have the opportunity to show my respect for government? How many can I list?
2. Have I ever had situations that demanded resistance to governments for the sake of conscience? What did I decide, and how was the situation resolved? How do I relate Paul's advice with these situations?
3. Is it possible that Paul's advice could tempt me to give too much honor and respect to my country so that I give it honor that is due only to God? Why or why not?
4. If governments are ordained by God and do not bear the sword in vain, is it permissible for me to assist my government by bearing the sword as a soldier or police officer?

■ Researching the Word

1. Make three columns in your Romans notebook, and compare and contrast 13:1-7 with 1 Peter 2:13-17. Which elements are unique to Paul, which ones are unique to Peter,

and which are common to both? What conclusions do you draw from this comparison?

2. Make a list of all the passages in the Bible that you think should be included in a study of the Christian's relationship to the state. Try to include both instructions and stories, both the Old and New Testaments, and both incidents from Jesus' life and stories that He told.

■ Further Study of the Word

1. For a detailed treatment of the structure of this passage, see R. H. Stein, "The Argument of Romans 13:1-7."
2. For an opposite view of the one taken in this chapter, which holds that the authorities are demonic powers that stand behind earthly rulers, see O. Cullmann, *The State in the New Testament.*
3. For the view that in this passage Paul was addressing a specific situation relating to Jewish revolutionary activity in Palestine and the sympathy of Roman Jews for this activity, see M. Borg, "A New Context for Romans 13."
4. For a discussion of Christian life and the power of the state in Paul and other New Testament writers, see excursus 13 in P. Stuhlmacher, *Paul's Letter to the Romans*, 205-208.

CHAPTER SIXTEEN

Love
and the Law

Romans 13:8-14

Hasn't Paul already said enough about the law? We heard about it way back in Romans 3. We focused on it in Romans 7 and came back to it in chapter 8. And here we are in chapter 13, still talking about the law. But now Paul comes to the heart of the matter. He has spoken eloquently about the powerlessness and insufficiency of the law. He has affirmed the law as holy, just, and good. Now he shows us the root of the law. We see what it is really all about.

In these verses, Paul also brings to an end the short pieces of advice about the Christian life that began in 12:1. This two-chapter section in 12 and 13 comes to end as it began, with a reference to eschatology and its significance for Christian living.

■ Getting Into the Word

Romans 13:8-14

Read these verses in at least two different translations, and answer the following questions in your Romans notebook.

1. Why does Paul sum the whole law up in just one command, when Jesus used two commandments (see Matt. 22:35-40) for the same purpose? Why doesn't Paul include the greatest command: to love God with all the heart, mind, and soul?
2. Can all God's commands be summed up in the one com-

mand to love the neighbor? Can you think of any that cannot? If so, why didn't Paul think of them as well?
3. Explain Paul's analogy of light and darkness. What do light and darkness symbolize?
4. What does Paul mean when he tells Christians to "put on" or "clothe" themselves with Christ (vs. 14)? Does a comparison with Galatians 3:27 help in understanding this passage?

■ Exploring the Word

The Law of Love (13:8-10)

In verse 7, which we studied in the previous chapter, Paul admonished Christians to pay whatever they owed, whether taxes or respect. Once a Christian has followed this advice, he or she should be paid up and have no debts. But in verse 8 Paul says that there is one debt Christians will still have, even after they have paid everyone what they owe; that is the debt of love. Christians are indebted to love one another. Paul goes on to add that Christians who do love each other have fulfilled the whole law. He then mentions four specific commands from among the last six of the Ten Commandments, those prohibiting adultery, murder, stealing, and coveting, and asserts that these four commands, as well as any other commands, can be summed up in just one command: "Love your neighbor as yourself" (13:9).

This, of course, is a quotation of Leviticus 19:18, although it is more familiar to us through Jesus' use of it than in its original setting. But it is precisely Jesus' use of this text that makes Paul's use somewhat problematic. When Jesus was asked by one of the teachers of the law about the greatest commandment, He answered with two Old Testament commands. The first was from Deuteronomy 6:4-5, emphasizing love for God (see Mark 12:28-31; Matthew 22:34-40). Love for the neighbor, even though it placed in the top two, came in second. Why does Paul seem to omit the first, greatest commandment?

One thing is clear; this was not merely an oversight, for Paul does the same thing twice, both here and in Galatians 5:14, 15, where he says: "The entire law is summed up in a single command: 'Love your neighbor as yourself.' " (The word translated "summed up" in Galatians is the same word translated "fulfilled" in Romans 13:8 and should be translated "fulfilled" in Galatians as well. In Romans 13:9, where he does say that the law is "summed up" in the one command to love the neighbor, he uses the same word as in Ephesians 1:10, where the promise is made that Christ will "sum up" all things.)

How, then, do we explain the fact that Paul sums up the law in one command, whereas Jesus uses two? Since Paul doesn't tell us, we can't say for sure, but two reasons seem plausible. First, we already noted when studying Romans 12 that Paul only rarely speaks about loving God. He seems to prefer the term *faith* for the appropriate human response to God and love for the appropriate Christian attitude and action toward other humans. Second, it is Paul's view that an appropriate attitude toward God inevitably results in love for others. Therefore, he only needs to mention our relationship to others as evidence for a holistic response that includes responsibility to both God and other humans. He certainly doesn't ignore our relationship to God, as our study of the first two-thirds of the letter demonstrated. But now Paul emphasizes that the real evidence of our relationship with God is our love for others.

The term for love that Paul uses here is *agapē*. It is not the romantic notion or the emotional feeling that we often think of when we use the English word *love*. Rather, it is both concern and action for other people that puts their interests on a par with our own. We can see what Paul means by love when we read passages such as 1 Corinthians 13:4-7 or Philippians 2:1-4. The person who loves is the person who follows Paul's counsel in the latter passage: "Do nothing out of selfish ambition or vain conceit, but in humility consider others better than yourselves. Each of you should look not only to your own interests, but also to the interests of others" (Phil. 2:3, 4).

When we love in this way, can we then disregard the law? No, for law is an important part of God's instruction that gives specific shape to love. True love will hardly find itself stealing, murdering, or committing adultery. The person who loves will therefore fulfill the law. And even though love will never break the law, when the law is properly understood, love might appear to be violating the law to those who understand the law only in a legalistic or literalistic way. The way the religious leaders of the day viewed Jesus' actions on the Sabbath proved this (see Mark 2:23–3:6, for example). They thought He was breaking the law when He was actually acting in love to show the true meaning of the law.

Night and Day (13:11-13)

In verse 11, Paul returns to the topic of eschatology, which he had introduced in 12:2. In the earlier passage, he only alluded to the topic with a reference to the present, passing age and the implication that Christian life should be transformed by the coming age. Now he goes into more detail with the use of the metaphor of day and light as opposed to night and darkness. The Romans are to understand the significance of the time in which they live. Salvation is nearer than when they first believed (13:11). The present age is symbolized by night and darkness. The works of darkness are evil. The metaphor gains part of its power from the fact that evil works are often done in shame and, therefore, also in secret—shrouded in darkness. The new world to come, by contrast, is a world of light, where good works, light, and openness prevail. Therefore, it is appropriately symbolized by the light of the day. Paul calls his readers, in light of the approaching second coming, to begin to live already in its light.

This means avoiding the works of darkness, which Paul lists in a vice list much like the one we saw in 1:29-31, although this one is shorter. This list includes orgies, drunkenness, sexual immorality, debauchery, dissensions, and jealousy (13:13). Rather, it means letting life be governed by the light of the day that is about to dawn. Paul speaks of this as putting on the armor of light (vs. 12). The term translated "armor" is not the general term for armor that is used in Ephesians 6:11, but means "tools," "instruments," or "weapons." It is the word Paul used in 6:13 to speak of not offering the parts of the body as "instruments" of sin. In this context, it probably means weapons. The Christian's weapon is to be light, the light of the dawning day.

Paul is fond of this metaphor. He also uses it in 1 Thessalonians 5:1-11. There, too, it is tied to both eschatology and proper Christian living. There are always those who argue that the belief in Christ's soon coming is a negative motivator for ethical behavior. If Christ is coming soon, why bother about trying to help others by making the world better? Why bother with working for the good of others? Paul's view is exactly the opposite of this. Knowing that Christ is coming soon should motivate Christians to begin living now according to the values of justice, compassion, and love that characterize God's coming kingdom. J. C. Beker is right when he says: "Apocalyptic hope, then *compels ethical seriousness*, because it is existentially impossible to believe in God's coming triumph and to claim his Holy Spirit without a lifestyle that conforms to that faith" (110).

Can this ethical seriousness still be motivated by the belief that Jesus is coming soon when over nineteen centuries have passed since Paul wrote about the second coming? If we truly understand Paul's perspective, the answer is Yes. For Paul, eschatology was not merely a matter of the future. Christ's resurrection was already the beginning of the end. It already transformed the world, for it assured God's final triumph and the ultimate defeat of evil. Thus there is "an already" and a "not yet" to Christian existence. Even though the final triumph has not come as soon as anyone expected, we still live in a special time that, although it is characterized by evil and darkness, is enlightened by the coming dawn. And our lives can be transformed by the coming light. Our present experience with Christ assures us that the dawn is coming in spite of the years, for our hope is based not on chronology, but on Christology.

Putting on Christ (13:14)

Paul's final word of the chapter in verse 14 is the imperative: "Clothe yourselves with the Lord Jesus Christ." This kind of language appears to be associated with Christian baptism. We see it in

Galatians 3:27, where Paul says, "[A]ll of you who were baptized into Christ have clothed yourselves with Christ." He then goes on to express the oneness of all in Christ. In Colossians 3:10-12, we find the same expression of oneness tied with the language of clothing. Apparently, when Christians were baptized, they thought of themselves as clothing themselves with a new life, that of Christ Himself. All of this strengthens the possibility that the instructions in Romans 12 and 13 are typical of the kind of instruction given to new Christians. To put on Christ is another metaphor for accepting Christ's values and living according to His love and compassion. Paul contrasts this with gratifying the desires of the flesh (13:14), which reminds us of what he said in 7:5 and 8:5-8.

This final metaphor of putting on Christ reminds us again that Paul is doing much more than giving us isolated rules to live by. All that he has said falls under the initial *therefore* and culminates in clothing ourselves with Christ. He is not merely calling on us to keep a list of rules. He is inviting us to respond to God's amazing grace in the only manner that is logical, by committing ourselves to God in a holistic way that is nothing short of being transformed into the values of Christ's coming kingdom. God's grace for all serves as the basis for our faith in God as well as for our own love for all.

■ Applying the Word

Romans 13:8-14

1. Which of the metaphors of new life (transformation by the renewing of the mind, putting on the weapons of light, clothing myself with Christ, etc.) resonates the most closely with my own spiritual understanding? How can I make that metaphor live as I go through the daily routine of life?
2. How might I picture the metaphor of light and darkness with a drawing that includes me in the picture?
3. Is it ever necessary for me to break the letter of the law to act in love? Illustrate and explain.

■ Researching the Word

1. Compare 13:11-14 with 1 Thessalonians 5:1-11. What elements are unique to each, and which are common to both?
2. Through the use of a concordance, compare Paul's usage of *light* and *darkness* in this passage with John's usage in his Gospel and epistles. Compare your findings with the articles on those words in a Bible dictionary or encyclopedia.

■ Further Study of the Word

1. For a discussion of the nature of Paul's exhortation to the church, see excursus 14 in P. Stuhlmacher, *Paul's Letter to the Romans*, 214-219.
2. For a study of the significance of eschatology in Paul's thought, see J. C. Beker, *Paul's Apocalyptic Gospel: The Coming Triumph of God.*

CHAPTER SEVENTEEN

The Weak
and the Strong

Romans 14:1–15:13

When confronted with differences and debates in the contemporary church, we are sometimes tempted to idolize and to idealize the early Christians, whom we perceive to have lived in unity and to have had it all together. This section of Romans reminds us that the early Christians had their differences and debates too. In fact, they were probably a lot like us. But perhaps that makes Paul's advice to them especially useful for us as well. Even though the issues may have been different, see if these verses don't scratch places that continue to itch in the church.

■ Getting Into the Word

Romans 14:1–15:13

Read 14:1 to 15:13 in at least two different versions, and use your Romans notebook to answer the following questions.

1. Explain Paul's use of the terms *weak* and *strong*. What can you say about each group? List all you can about them.
2. What are the two issues introduced in the first five verses that seem to have been controversial? What possible historical circumstances might have led to such a controversy?
3. Do you think these issues were actually dividing the Roman Christians, or is Paul giving general advice? What elements do you find in the text to support your answer?

4. Divide a page of your Romans notebook into three columns. In the first, list all the advice that Paul gives to the weak. In the second, list all that he says specifically to the strong. In the third, list advice that seems to apply equally to both groups. Then compare and contrast the advice in the three lists. What conclusions do you reach about Paul's purposes for the Romans? What relevance do you see for the church today?

5. Does Paul identify himself with one group or the other? Why or why not?

6. How do verses 7 to 13 serve as a summary to this section? What is Paul's conclusion?

7. How do you explain Paul's words in 14:14 that nothing (or in the NIV, "no food") is unclean? What does Paul mean?

■ Exploring the Word

Overview

Paul begins this section with a command, apparently addressed to the "strong" (a term he will not mention until Rom. 15:1), that they should accept the "weak in faith," but not merely for disputing and quarreling (14:1). He goes on to mention two areas of debate. The first involves those who eat only vegetables as opposed to those who eat anything (vs. 2). The second involves those who consider one day more important than another, as opposed to those who consider every day alike (vs. 5). It is clear from the discussion that the weak were the more scrupulous Christians who abstained from eating meat and who "considered" certain days.

Paul identifies with the "strong" (15:1) but has advice for both groups. The strong are not to scorn the weak, and the weak are not to judge the strong (14:3). In addition, the strong are to be willing to bend on behalf of the weak rather than destroy them (vss. 15-21). The conclusion of the matter is that both groups should accept each other (15:7).

There has been considerable debate over this section of Romans.

Is Paul addressing a specific situation in Rome, or is he giving general advice by using a hypothetical situation? If there is a specific situation, what is it? Who were those with dietary prohibitions? What kind of "days" were involved?

We will begin our discussion of 14:1 to 15:13 by looking at the situation in Rome. We will then analyze the advice Paul gives to both groups and will conclude by exploring the significance of this important advice for the Romans and for us.

The Situation in Rome

General advice or specific situation?

Many scholars hold that Paul is using food and days as hypothetical examples of the kinds of situations that might divide Christians in order to give general instruction about unity among believers. They point to the similarities between this passage and Paul's instruction regarding food offered to idols in 1 Corinthians 8 to 10 and conclude that since Paul is much more specific in the Corinthian passage, which all agree was written first, Romans 14 to 15 is a generalized rewrite of his specific advice to the Corinthians about food offered to idols. (This was a question that the Corinthians had raised to Paul in a letter they had written to him; see 1 Corinthians 7:1 and 8:1.) These scholars also argue that since Paul had never been to Rome, he would hardly know what specific problems the Romans might have had, and therefore he gave general advice based on the specific problems he had faced in churches that he knew well.

Two basic clusters of evidence speak against this position, however. The first is the comparison between 1 Corinthians 8 to 10 and Romans 14 to 15. It is true that there are many similarities, including the use of weak-strong terminology. But when we carefully compare and contrast the two passages, we find that the similarities have to do with the kind of advice Paul gives and the principles with which he backs up the advice. The differences come with the specifics.

For example, there can be no question that in both passages Paul is more concerned with how Christians relate to each other than he is with the specific dietary question, and the concerns in both passages are often very similar. In 1 Corinthians 8:8 and Romans 14:17, Paul uses different language to express the same conviction that dietary matters are not of ultimate significance. Also, in both passages Paul refers to the motif of offering thanks for food as a legitimation for why it may be eaten (Rom. 14:6 and 1 Cor. 10:30). In both passages, Paul sets forth the theme of concern for others and of putting their interests above one's own (1 Cor. 10:24, 33 and Rom. 15:1-3). The explication of this broad general theme includes many of the same specific motifs and concerns: one is not to put a stumbling block in the way of another (1 Cor. 8:9; 9:12 and Rom. 14:13, 21); there is danger of destroying the weak, on whose behalf Christ died (1 Cor. 8:11 and Rom. 14:15, 20); concern is expressed for the "edification" of the community (1 Cor. 8:1; 10:23 and Rom. 14:19; 15:2). In addition, both passages connect this principle of concern for the other person specifically to dietary matters and emphasize that it is better to give up legitimate dietary practices than to cause harm to another (1 Cor. 8:13 and Rom. 14:21). Finally, there are other similarities of terminology, such as *weak* (1 Cor. 8:7, 8, 10, 12 and Rom. 14:1, 2; 15:1), *blaspheme* (1 Cor. 10:30 and Rom. 14:16), and *glory* (1 Cor. 10:31 and Rom. 15:6, 7, 9).

All this makes it quite clear that Paul had 1 Corinthians 8 to 10 in mind when he wrote our passage. And it is not hard to understand why this might lead to the conclusion that our passage is a generalized rewrite of the earlier one to the Corinthians. But the differences, and the nature of those differences, must be noted as well.

First, there are a number of elements in 1 Corinthians that are not repeated in Romans. These include all references to the problem of idolatry and food offered to idols. The terms for "idol meat" (1 Cor. 8:1, 4, 7, 10, 11; 10:19, 38) and "meat market" (1 Cor. 10:24) are not used. Even more striking, however, are the specific elements introduced in our passage that have no counterparts in 1 Corinthians. One of these is the reference to "vegetables" in 14:2. Paul never uses this term elsewhere. A second is the mention of "days" in verse 5. There is nothing even remotely similar in 1 Corinthians. Finally, there is no mention of the words *clean* or *unclean* (14:14, 20) in all of 1 Corinthians.

If Paul is rewriting 1 Corinthians in a generalized way, why would he introduce specific terminology that neither is in 1 Corinthians nor is a part of his standard vocabulary? It seems more logical that he introduces this terminology because it has to do with specific issues disputed in the Christian community at Rome. We have already argued in the introduction that Paul had sufficient contact with Rome, even though he had never been there, to know people in Rome. If he had contact with people in Rome, he would have had access to information regarding the situation there as well.

A second cluster of evidence against the idea that the advice in our passage is a generalized rewrite of 1 Corinthians 8 to 10 has to do with echoes of earlier passages in Romans that reverberate in this section. It seems that Paul has been preparing the way for this section throughout the book. If that is true, it might suggest that Paul recognized this material in Romans 14 and 15 would be sensitive and began getting his readers ready for it earlier in the letter. Here are some examples of these echoes.

The analogy of Abraham in Romans 4 is echoed in several ways in chapter 14. In 4:19-21, readers are told that Abraham, who is presented as the spiritual father of all Christians, both Jews and Gentiles, was not "weak in faith" and did not "doubt," but rather was "strong" and was "fully convinced" that God could do what He had promised. All of these elements appear in our passage as well. Paul, who identifies himself with the "strong" (15:1), admonishes those who share his perspective that they are to bear with the failings of the weak (vs. 1) and welcome the "weak in faith" (14:1). Those who "doubt" are condemned if they eat (vs. 23), and all are to be "fully convinced" in their own minds (vs. 5). These echoes link Paul's advice about unity on matters of food and days with the key figure in his earlier discussion of the basis for unity between Jew and Gentile in Christ.

Another example comes from Romans 2:1, where Paul proclaims that the person who judges another is without excuse, for in judging another, one condemns oneself. God alone is judge, and His role should not be usurped (see 2:16 and 3:6). Romans 14:4, 10, and 13 echo Paul's earlier discussion in Romans 2 and 3. The recognition that God is a faithful and just judge leads to a willingness to let Him be judge. This links God's moral integrity with the Christian's moral responsibility toward others. The advice that Christians should refrain from judging others in matters of food and days is not merely general advice tacked on the end of the letter for the sake of convention. It is linked with Paul's basic message through these echoes.

Although Romans 14:7-9 might appear as a mere digression, the theme of belonging to Christ, who is Lord of the living and the dead, echoes the language of living and dying in Romans 6, especially verses 10 to 13. This links the present advice with the context of moral responsibility in Romans 6, where Paul argues that Christians should not use God's grace as an excuse for continued sinning. To be alive to God (vs. 11) means to be dead to sin. To live to the Lord (14:8) means recognizing that Christ is Lord of all and letting Him be judge. Judging and scorning others are subtly linked with the sin that Christians leave behind if they are alive to God.

Finally, in Romans 5:6 Paul proclaims that Christ died for the ungodly. He died for us when we were still "weak" (the NIV uses the word *powerless*, but it is the same word used in Romans 14 for the weak). In 14:15 Paul reminds the strong that the weak brother is one for whom Christ died.

If Romans 14 and 15 is a generalized rewriting of 1 Corinthians 8 to 10, why does it contain so many connecting links with the rest of the letter? A better conclusion is that Paul is addressing a specific and sensitive concern in the Roman church. He begins early in the letter to prepare the way for this discussion. By laying the theological groundwork beforehand, he makes the specific advice easier to swallow. This makes it more likely that he will be able to accomplish his goal and bring the two sides together rather than stir up the waters of controversy and push them farther apart. And although he repeats the same basic principles of Christian conduct already found in 1 Corinthians, he uses new terminology that is uncommon to him to apply these principles to a new situation in the Roman congregation. Paul doesn't tell us enough about the situation for us to understand it in detail, but those scholars who believe that Paul is addressing a specific situation present various possibilities.

Those who eat only vegetables

Who might these people have been who ate only vegetables (14:2)? Many suggestions have been made. Some see them as Jews who would not eat any meat because they were concerned about the problem of eating meat offered to idols. Thus the situation would be the same as in 1 Corinthians 8 to 10. But we have already seen evidence against this view. If Paul were addressing the same situation in 1 Corinthians and Romans, why would his terminology change so strikingly? Paul's dropping of any language relating specifically to the problem of food offered to idols speaks against that being the issue here.

Others see the issue in Romans 14 as a Jewish Christian versus Gentile Christian issue involving kosher foods. This is supported by the reference to clean and unclean in verses 14 and 20. However, kosher food laws did not involve vegetarianism, and Paul is quite specific about this dispute involving those who eat only vegetables.

Some hold that the Roman vegetarians were Gentile Christians who were influenced by various strands of asceticism that attempted to deny the body for the sake of the spiritual life. For example, Seneca was influenced by Neo-Pythagoreans to become a vegetarian in his younger life, although he did not remain one (*Moral Epistles to Lucius*, 108:17). Plutarch's *Moralia* includes an essay titled "On the Eating of Flesh" in which he argues for vegetarianism. Gentile writers give various reasons for vegetarianism (Plutarch mentions most of them), including cultic ritual, denial of pleasure, antiluxury, health, belief in the transmigration of souls, and avoidance of cruelty to animals. It is possible, although there is no specific evidence to support it, that some Roman Christians had been influenced by this ascetic tradition in the Greco-Roman world.

Still others hold that although kosher food laws did not involve vegetarianism, such a practice cannot be ruled out among Jewish Christians. Although it is true that the kind of Judaism represented in rabbinic sources definitely had no trace of a tendency toward vegetarianism, rabbinic Judaism was not the sum total of first-century Judaism, and there are some hints of vegetarianism in Jewish sources. Philo says that the Therapeutae, a sect of Egyptian Jews, kept their table clear of all flesh animals (Philo, "On the Contemplative Life").

They would have had no influence in Rome, but it is possible that such practices might have arisen in other parts of the Jewish disper-sion from Palestine as well. It was also not uncommon for Jewish sources to refer to abstinence from meat on a temporary basis for special occasions, such as preparation for a revelation or as penance for some sin (4 Ezra 9:23-25; Testament of Reuben 1:9-10; Testa-ment of Judah 15:4).

What shall we make of all this? It is impossible to say for certain who the Roman Christians were who ate only vegetables. It is a fairly safe assumption that their reasons did not have to do with health, but with the various kinds of ritualistic asceticism that popped up in both the Jewish and Gentile worlds of the first century.

The matter of days

The NIV translation begins 14:5 by saying, "One man considers one day more sacred than another." The word *sacred*, however, is an interpretation not in the original text. Paul simply says that one judges or considers day from day while another judges or considers every day. To what is Paul referring? There are three main views: the Sab-bath, Jewish feast days, and fast days. Some time ago, a German scholar by the name of Rauer gave several convincing reasons why Paul was speaking about fast days, a possibility that would hardly occur to us, since such days have ceased to have much significance in our culture. But in the first century we find plenty of evidence for the importance of fast days in the Jewish, Gentile, and early Chris-tian worlds.

The first reason Rauer gives is that it is hardly possible that some Christians in Rome observed either all days alike or no days at all. All would have had a day of worship when they came to-gether. If they worshiped together, they had to observe days. Sec-ond, the terminology here is different from that of Galatians 4:10 or Colossians 2:16, where the observance of days does seem to come to play. (Here Paul speaks only of "days," whereas in Galatians he speaks of "days, months, seasons, and years" and in Colossians of "feasts, new moons, and Sabbaths.") Third, the phrase "to judge every day" is a curious expression for "to keep no day holy." Finally, the reference to days is most logically seen in the context of the same overall problem referred to in verse 2, that of dietary practice. All of this makes it probable that the "days" of 14:5 has to do not with worship days, but with fast days. In other words, the debate in Rome was not only about what to eat, but when to eat it as well.

The *weak* and *strong* terminology

Paul had already used this terminology in 1 Corinthians 8 to 10, although there he only spoke of the weak, not of the strong, and there he only expressed concern for the weak, but never addressed them directly. But why does he use the term *weak* for the more careful, scrupulous Christians? Isn't this pejorative, to begin with? There is some evidence in the Greco-Roman world that the term *weak* was used to mean "scrupulous" (see Horace, *Sermons*, 1:9:60-78). Paul may have been using the term in that way. The term *weak in faith* does seem to have some negative connotations in Romans. Yet Paul never argues that the weak should become strong, as we will see later. All we know for sure is that the weak are the more scrupulous Christians who hold to the dietary restrictions and to the consideration of days, which Paul identifies with the strong (15:1), and that rather than urge uniformity of practice, Paul points to a deeper unity in Christ.

Clean and unclean

Paul makes two references to the language of clean and unclean in this section (14:14, 20). This adds even more intrigue to the situation at Rome, since Jewish regulations of clean and unclean had to do with abstinence from pork and other foods specified as unclean in Leviticus 11 and not with vegetarianism. Again, Paul doesn't give us enough information to allow us to say with certainty why he raises this issue, but there are several items we should keep in mind.

First, in both verses, the NIV translation makes reference to food that is clean or unclean, but the term *food* is added by the translators and is not in the original text. Paul simply says that he is convinced nothing is unclean (vs. 14) and everything is clean (vs. 20) unless one thinks it unclean. Since the context of the chapter does involve food, that may be what Paul has in mind, but that is an assumption.

Paul may have known that issues regarding clean and unclean were causing tensions between Jewish and Gentile Christians. It is easy to see that such issues could produce tension when we realize that one of the ways ancient Jews interpreted their laws about clean and unclean foods was to see them as a symbol to remind them not to associate with unclean people, namely, Gentiles (see Letter of Aristeas 139-142, for example). Such an understanding would crash head-on with Paul's emphasis of God's grace and mercy for all. This may account for at least part of the reason Paul raised the issue of clean and unclean in Romans 14.

Conclusion

Although Paul doesn't give us enough information to allow us to understand the situation in Rome fully, the best evidence points to the idea that he is addressing a specific situation or situations in Rome in this passage. It involved disputes about dietary practice and days, specifically vegetarianism and fast days. In other words, Roman Christians were arguing about what to eat and when to eat it. We don't know exactly what led some Christians to hold these views or whether they were Jewish or Gentile Christians. The situation may have been complex, involving several groups. Somehow, tensions between Jewish and Gentile Christians were probably part of the mix in Rome as well. What is most important for us, however, is what Paul had to say to Roman Christians about these differences, and it is to this advice that we now turn.

Paul's Advice to the Weak and the Strong

Throughout this passage, Paul mixes advice to the weak and the strong. We will review this instruction by looking first at that which is for all, then at instruction specifically for the weak, and finally to advice directed to the strong.

Advice to all the Christians

Paul brackets this section with the command to accept each other. Romans 14:1 admonishes the strong to accept the weak; verse 3 reminds both that God has accepted all of them; and 15:7 admonishes both to accept each other as Christ accepted them. To accept means to welcome fully and have fellowship with someone. The only other time Paul uses it is in Philemon 17 when he pleads with Philemon to accept the runaway slave Onesimus even as he would accept Paul. The Greek version of the Old Testament uses this term in Psalm 65:4 to portray God accepting His people into His courts for worship. If the first part of Romans makes any point at all, it is that all of us have been accepted by God's grace. Accepted Christians are to become accepting Christians, even accepting of those who may hold different practices and opinions. This is Paul's most fundamental point. Even in this situation in which not all Christians agree, they are to accept each other.

Paul's second point to both groups seems a bit strange. In 14:5 he tells them that each one should be fully convinced in his or her own mind. Wasn't that already the problem? Isn't that how the dispute got started? They were all fully convinced in their own minds and didn't agree with each other. But Paul makes no attempt to get all the Christians to agree. He doesn't try to convince the weak they should believe like the strong, nor does he admonish the strong to take on the convictions of the weak. Rather, both are to be fully convinced in their own minds.

Paul was willing to leave room for a good bit of Christian freedom when it came to matters such as this, but this was never freedom to sin. Had Paul felt that the issue or issues under dispute in Rome were crucial matters of a person's relationship to God or others, he would not have spoken in this way. For example, when he wrote to the Corinthians about matters of sexual immorality in the church in 1 Corinthians 5, he didn't say that each should be fully convinced in his or her own mind. He gave clear and definite instructions about what had to be done. Nor did he tell the Galatians, who were being tempted to return to salvation by works of law, that each should be fully convinced in his or her own mind. Freedom is not the freedom to sin. But there are legitimate differences among Christians with regard to both practice and opinion. And on such matters Christians must be willing to respect each other, not merely tolerating each other but fully accepting each other. In 14:6 Paul reminds both that those who disagree with them are acting sincerely in relationship to the Lord.

This is hard advice. To hold convictions strongly but fully accept those who don't share those convictions is never easy. Only the gratitude that comes when we know God has accepted us can make us that accepting.

Paul's next piece of advice to both groups addresses the matter of priorities. In verses 17, 18 he says, "The kingdom of God is not a matter of eating and drinking, but of righteousness, peace, and joy in the Holy Spirit, because anyone who serves Christ in this way is pleasing to God and approved by men." We have already seen in Romans 12 that Christian behavior is important. Standards are important. But righteousness, peace, and joy are more important. Christians need prioritizing wisdom to separate the important from the most important and the essential from the nonessential. People are more important than standards, and fellowship is more important than winning debates.

It is in this context that we should probably understand Paul's statements about everything being clean and nothing being unclean (vss. 14, 20). This doesn't mean that behavior is unimportant. Paul has spent too much time in Romans 6, 12, and 13 arguing that it is. Nor does it mean that everything you eat is good for you or everything you do is beneficial. What it does mean is that external matters, such as ritual purity and standards of dietary practice, can never be the essentials of the kingdom. There will be legitimate differences in these areas. But the kingdom is a matter of righteousness, peace, and joy, and whenever external standards get in the way of these fundamentals, our priorities are wrong (14:17).

Finally, Paul gives a very important piece of advice that should apply to both weak and strong in verse 22. Within the context of this dispute, he tells them to keep their beliefs on these matters between themselves and God. Stirring up trouble on such matters of behavioral standards is not what builds up the church. Think what a difference it would make if everyone in the church followed this advice today.

These admonitions to accept each other, to be fully convinced in one's own mind, and to keep the fundamental values of the kingdom of God in proper perspective apply to both weak and strong. But there are specific needs and problems that are part of each group, and we now turn to Paul's specific advice to the individual groups.

Advice to the weak Christians

Paul never tells the weak to take on the opinions or practices of the strong. Nor does he criticize them for being weak (although the statement about Abraham being strong and not weak in 4:19 could be seen as an implicit criticism). His primary advice to them concerns their special temptation. Because they hold strong convictions that lead to scrupulous action, they are faced with the temptation to judge those who don't hold these convictions. But Paul is relentless in his admonition that they refrain from judging. The one who doesn't eat everything must not condemn the one who does (14:3). Paul's justification for this advice is the fact that God alone is judge. Why should a person judge someone else's servant (vs. 4)? Whenever we judge, we are judging one of God's servants. Christ is the Lord of the living and the dead (vs. 9). Everyone will stand before God's judgment seat to give an account (vss. 10-12). To judge another is to usurp God's role as judge, and that is a form of blasphemy. It denies God. The strong or less scrupulous don't have the same tendency to judge, although they have their own temptation, as we shall see later. But the special temptation of the weak is to judge, and it is a serious temptation indeed. Paul concludes, "Therefore let us stop passing judgment on one another" (vs. 13).

But there is another important piece of advice for the weak that comes at the end of Romans 14. Paul speaks of those who doubt or waver concerning their convictions. It is wrong for them to go ahead and eat if they have convictions against it, for then their action doesn't spring from faith, and whatever doesn't spring from faith is sin (vs.

23). In other words, it is wrong for a person to violate convictions. Christian action should spring from faith. Violating one's conviction is not an act of faith. Therefore, it is sin to go against conviction, even mistaken conviction, for it is an act of disobedience to God to act in ways that a person believes to be wrong. The weak then should follow their convictions.

Here Paul gives one of the most profound statements about sin to be found in the Bible. Sin is not merely breaking a law. It is any act that doesn't spring from faith. If our entire life is to be a living sacrifice to God (12:1), then everything we do should grow out of our faith. Violating what we believe to be right doesn't meet this criterion.

The advice to the weak has implications for the strong. If the weak sin by violating their convictions, then to try to get a scrupulous person to violate his or her convictions is to lead that person into sin. It is acceptable to try to convince a person that his or her convictions are mistaken with evidence, but it is never permissible to try to lead anyone to violate conviction. So the weak are to follow their convictions, but they are to do it without judging those who fail to share their convictions. In other words, even if I encounter someone who holds convictions that I find absurd (perhaps they say it is wrong to eat celery or wear blue), I lead them into sin if I merely talk them into doing what they believe is wrong. It is only legitimate for me to convince them that their convictions are misplaced.

Advice to the strong Christians

Strong Christians, those who are more free and less scrupulous, don't have the same tendency as the weak to point the finger of judgment and condemnation. But they cannot take comfort in that, because they have their own temptation. Paul mentions it twice in this chapter (14:3, 10). The temptation of the strong is to "look down on" or scorn the weak. With an air of superiority, they roll their eyes and shake their heads at those poor, misguided legalists who are neither as enlightened nor as liberated as they are. This way of writing people off is no less offensive to God than judging. It, too, fails to recognize that God has accepted both the weak and the strong. It doesn't please the neighbor and work to build him or her up (15:2). The strong fail to accept the weak by their scorn just as much as the weak fail to accept the strong by their judging.

Paul has some hard advice for the strong too. They are to bear with the failings of the weak (vs. 1). Specifically, this means that they must be willing to give up their legitimate rights for the sake of the weak. If their action, even perfectly acceptable action, would be a stumbling block or obstacle to a brother or sister, they must be willing to give it up (14:13). It is wrong to do anything that causes someone else to stumble (vs. 20).

Paul has important theological undergirding for this advice. The key is found in verse 15: "If your brother is distressed because of what you eat, you are no longer acting in love. Do not by your eating destroy your brother for whom Christ died." The grace of Christ transforms every brother and sister into one for whom Christ died. If we understand God's grace, we will never see another Christian merely as one who disagrees with us on this or that opinion or one who eats what we don't or one who won't participate in activities we know are wholesome. Rather, we will see every person as one for whom Christ died. Only that new way of viewing other people will get rid of the scorn that the strong are tempted to show to the weak or the condemnation that the weak heap on the strong.

Paul's conclusion

Paul concludes this discussion of Christian unity and mutual acceptance with a beautiful statement that returns to the theme of God's inclusion of the Gentiles in salvation. It is impossible to know for sure whether this means that the disputes over food and days in Rome involved tensions between Jews and Gentiles, for in some ways, this passage seems to reach back and summarize more than just the previous two chapters. Paul again, in chapter 15, repeats that Christians are to welcome or accept each other as Christ accepted them (vs. 7). Then in verse 8 he reiterates that Christ has become a servant of the Jews on behalf of God's truth, to confirm the promises made to the patriarchs, so that the Gentiles may glorify God for His mercy. Following this, he quotes from four Old Testament passages that speak of the Gentiles rejoicing and finding hope in God (Psalm 18:49, paralleled in 2 Samuel 22:50; Deuteronomy 32:43; Psalm 117:1; and Isaiah 11:10). The last of these speaks of the Root of Jesse, who will spring up to rule over the nations (or Gentiles) and proclaims that the Gentiles will hope in Him. This leads Paul to his concluding prayer in verse 13: "May the God of hope fill you with all joy and peace as you trust in him so that you may overflow with hope by the power of the Holy Spirit."

Paul's desire was that the squabbles and debates would give way to a mutual acceptance, based on God's mercy, that would fill them all with joy, peace, and hope.

The Significance of Paul's Advice

For the Romans, this section of Paul's letter brought the exalted theological message of God's grace for all right down to the nitty-gritty surface of life where it was lived day by day. Unfortunately, we don't have any report on how the Romans responded to the message. But Paul's goal for them was clear. He didn't try to create a uniformity of opinion or practice. He was willing to let them be fully convinced in their own minds. He did try to create a unity in Christ that transcended their differences and made the peace of Christ a reality in their community.

It is hard to imagine how any advice in the Bible could be more relevant for Christians today than that which Paul gives in this section of Romans. So many beliefs and standards divide the church. Not only do the scrupulous (today we would probably call them conservatives or right-wingers) point fingers of judgment; they blanket the world with broadsides of condemnation from their computers and duplicating machines. And the "strong" (today we would probably call them liberals) have continued to hone their skills of arrogant derision. And as the world continuously becomes more of a global village so that Christians come into contact with greater cultural diversity, all hopes of uniformity go by the boards, leading many to despair that the church can ever find unity.

There is no need for despair, however. Even though as sinful humans we will always fall short of the ideal, Paul shows us the basis for unity. It is the realization that Christ has accepted us. If Christ would die for us when we were still sinners, how can we refuse to accept other Christians just because we don't see eye to eye on every point or follow every standard in the same way? Paul is not just talking about tolerating each other. He is pointing us to true mutual acceptance that leads us to embrace each other even though some of us are conservative and some of us are liberal (although those terms have been used for so many different things that they should be banished from our language). The grace of Christ can lead us not only to tolerate but to appreciate those who are different from ourselves.

Paul's message of God's grace for all is simply incomplete until it finds reality in a community of mutual caring, edification, and nurturing. Romans not only calls us to trust God; it also calls us to loving acceptance and mutual nurturing of each other that will demonstrate the meaning of this message in everyday life. Such a demonstration will be a powerful evangelistic witness as well. Which of our churches would not do well to keep Paul's prayer in 15:5, 6 before us continually: "May the God who gives endurance and encouragement give you a spirit of unity among yourselves as you follow Christ Jesus, so that with one heart and mouth you may glorify the God and Father of our Lord Jesus Christ."

■ Applying the Word

Romans 14:1–15:13

1. As I think about my own local church, what issues would be the modern equivalent of the disputes about dietary matters and fast days that divided the Romans? Are there specific strategies that I can take from Paul's letter to the Romans that might help me make a difference with regard to these issues? What are those strategies?
2. How would my response to question 1 be different if I

thought about my denomination as a whole? If I thought about the whole Christian world?

3. Which is the greater temptation for me, to scorn others or to condemn others? What does this say about me? How does Paul's advice help me avoid this temptation?

4. How would I represent the present unity of my church in a drawing or other work of art? How would I represent the unity I would like to see in my church with a drawing or piece of art? How can I help move my church from the present to the ideal?

5. What convictions that I hold are essential and which ones, though important, should be matters of personal freedom within the church? How can I know the difference?

6. Are there specific actions in my life that I could alter for the sake of others who might be hurt by what I do? Where would I have to draw the line and recognize that I can't please everyone?

■ Researching the Word

1. Carefully compare and contrast 14:1–15:13 with 1 Corinthians 8 to 10. In one column of your Romans notebook, list the similarities, and in another list the differences. How do you explain what you find? What do you learn about Paul's manner of ethical teaching from this comparison?

2. In 14:19 and 15:2, Paul uses the term *edification* or *building up* to refer to the mutual nurturing that strengthens the church. Look at Paul's other uses of this term, and write a paragraph about what you believe Paul means by "building up." (Since this word is translated in various ways, the use of an English concordance is difficult. Other Pauline occurrences of the word are found in: Rom. 15:20; 1 Cor. 3:9; 8:1, 10; 10:23; 14:3, 4, 5, 12, 17, 26; 2 Cor. 5:1; 10:8; 12:19; 13:10; Gal. 2:18; Eph. 2:21; 4:12, 16, 29; 1 Thess. 5:11.)

■ Further Study of the Word

1. For the argument that 14:1 to 15:13 was general advice that did not directly speak to any situation in Rome, see R. J. Karris, "Romans 14:1–15:13 and the Occasion of Romans," in K. P. Donfried, ed., *The Romans Debate*, 65-84.

2. For the argument that these chapters did speak to the actual situation in Rome, see "False Presuppositions in the Study of Romans," in K. P. Donfried, ed., *The Romans Debate*, 102-124.

3. For the argument that the weak of Romans 14 and 15 are Jewish Christian remnants of the original Roman congregation and the strong are Paulinist Christians, see F. Watson, "The Two Roman Congregations," in K. P. Donfried, ed., *The Romans Debate*, 203-215.

4. For the present author's attempt to examine Paul's advice that all things are clean from both a historical and Adventist perspective, see J. Brunt, "Unclean or Unhealthful: An Adventist Perspective."

PART SIX

Romans 15:14–16:27

Plans
and Greetings

CHAPTER EIGHTEEN

Paul's Plans for Ministry

Romans 15:14-33

Throughout Romans, Paul has said very little about himself. Rather, he has focused one eye on God and the good news of His grace and the other eye on the Roman believers and their needs. But the last part of Romans 15 gives us one of those rare chances to understand Paul better as a person. We have a chance to understand something of his identity as a minister, as well as something of his hopes, dreams, plans, and fears. This is our chance for an "up close and personal" view of the messenger who has conveyed the good news to us so powerfully. We get this view because Paul wanted the Romans to understand how much he wanted to come and see them and why he wouldn't be coming immediately. But Paul couldn't talk about those plans without revealing a good bit about himself. That is fortunate for us. So let's take advantage of this opportunity to meet Paul "up close and personal."

■ Getting Into the Word

Romans 15:14-33

Read verses 14 to 33 in at least two different versions, and answer the following questions:

1. Make a list in your Romans notebook of all that you learn about Paul's ministry in this section. What terms does Paul use to describe his ministry? To whom was his ministry addressed? What was his favorite mode of ministry? What

257

analogies did he use to describe his ministry?
2. Make a list of all the references to sacrifice that you find in this chapter. What is Paul trying to say with this analogy?
3. List Paul's plans for the future. What three places does he intend to go? In what order does he plan to reach them? Look on a map of the first-century world, and trace these plans. How far would Paul be traveling? Why does Paul plan his itinerary in this way?
4. Using your concordance and a Bible dictionary, find out all you can about the collection that Paul was making for the poor in Jerusalem. When did Paul first begin this task? Why did he begin it?
5. What fears does Paul express in these verses? Were they realistic fears? What previous events in Paul's life might have led him to these fears?
6. Read Acts 21:17 to 22:30. How do these verses relate to Paul's request for the Romans' prayers in 15:31? Read about the plan of Herod's temple in Jerusalem in the *Seventh-day Adventist Bible Dictionary*, 1076-1080. How does this aid in your understanding of Acts 21?

■ Exploring the Word

Paul's Ministry

Already in the introduction of this letter, Paul told us that he had received grace and apostleship from God to call the Gentiles to the obedience of faith (1:5). Here, at the end of Romans, Paul amplifies the meaning of this ministry by using the analogy of a priest in the temple offering sacrifices to God for the people (15:16). Most of us have never watched a priest slaughtering an animal as a sacrifice to God, but most of Paul's readers in Rome had. Paul puts a new twist on this familiar picture. His priesthood isn't carried out in a temple, but in marketplaces, synagogues, and homes in cities throughout the Mediterranean world. And his sacrifice or offering to God isn't animals, but people, Gentiles (vs. 16). And, thankfully, he doesn't slaughter them; he tells them the good news of God's grace and makes them part of God's covenant people. This is Paul's offering to God, and he prays that it will be an acceptable offering.

Paul always saw his ministry as a ministry to Gentiles. Peter was an apostle to the Jews, Paul to the Gentiles (Gal. 2:8). Paul says that he led the Gentiles to obey God (15:18) and was even given signs and miracles through the power of the Spirit to accomplish this task (vs. 19). He adds that what God had done through him for the Gentiles was his only conversation, and his glory was only in Christ (vss. 17, 18).

All of this made Paul a unique blend of pastor and evangelist. He was clearly an evangelist who liked to plow new ground and build new foundations. Verses 19 and 20 make that clear. He wanted to go where no one else had been. Yet the fact that he stayed with congregations to build them up (three years in Ephesus and a year and a half in Corinth, for example) as well as his letter-writing activity and his method of sending co-workers back to check up on his congregations shows that he had a pastor's heart too. In fact, that dual focus on plowing new ground but wanting to make sure the old was properly cultivated created a constant tension for Paul. He was always wishing he could be in at least two places at once. Even as he wrote Romans, his hopes and dreams led in opposite directions. Therefore, he told the Romans about his ultimate, intermediate, and immediate plans.

Paul's Hopes and Dreams

Spain, the ultimate goal

Paul's goal was to get to Spain. He mentions it twice, in verses 24 and 28. He even tells us why he wants to go to Spain. That strong drive to take the gospel, not only to Gentiles but to Gentiles in new areas where the gospel had never been heard, pushed Paul toward Spain. He didn't want to build on someone else's foundation (vs. 20). Paul, by his own account, had already preached from Jerusalem to Illyricum. Jerusalem, of course, is in Palestine, inland from the eastern end of the Mediterranean Sea. Illyricum was the area of

Dalmatia on the eastern coast of the Adriatic Sea northwest of Macedonia. It is the area of the former Yugoslavia that is constantly in the news as I write this. Acts reports Paul's brief stint of preaching in Jerusalem (Acts 9:28-30) but doesn't tell us of Paul's travels to Illyricum.

There is no doubt that Paul was anxious to get to Spain. The challenge of taking the gospel far beyond where it had ever been before was exciting. Spain was more than two thousand miles west of Greece, where Paul was when he wrote his letter to the Romans. But even though the challenge excited Paul, he knew he had other work to do before his trip to Spain. He would need support for such an ambitious endeavor, and the Christians at Rome would be the ideal base for such support. Rome was not only a prominent church at the capital of the empire; it was also already an influential congregation. In addition, it was probably the westernmost Christian congregation at the time. This leads us to Paul's intermediate plans and dreams.

Rome, the intermediate goal

Paul was not bashful about letting the Romans know that he needed their help for his trip to Spain. In 15:24 he says he hopes to have the Romans assist him on his journey to Spain. But that wasn't the only reason Paul was looking toward Rome. He was genuinely interested in getting to know the Romans and enjoying fellowship with them (vs. 23). After all, he had friends there, like Priscilla and Aquila, who were especially dear to him. He was also interested in their spiritual growth. He was the apostle to the Gentiles, and he had to know that the Roman congregation, with its location at the seat of the empire, would become one the most influential congregations. His statement at the beginning of the letter that he wanted to enjoy mutually encouraging fellowship with them (1:11, 12) was certainly true.

This desire for fellowship and mutual encouragement with the Roman Christians is what led Paul, by his own admission, to write to them "quite boldly on some points" (15:15). Wouldn't it be fun to know what parts of Romans Paul was thinking of when he said this?

What parts of Romans would you consider "bold"? My guess would be that his instruction on the specific issues that divided them in Romans 14 and 15 might lead the list. But in spite of this boldness, Paul had confidence in the Romans. He was convinced that they were "full of goodness" (15:14). He wanted to enjoy their company before he went to Spain (vs. 24). He even expected this fellowship to refresh him (vs. 32). In other words, as he thought of his mission to Spain, he looked for both financial and personal, moral support from the Romans.

Yet he hoped for more too. He also hoped for their prayers. In verse 30 he uses the same kind of appeal formula he had used at 12:1, a formula by which the writer pleads with his or her readers for a specific, behavioral response. Paul urges the Romans to pray for him. He isn't only concerned with his trip to Spain here. He seems more concerned with his immediate trip to come, before Spain or Rome. As much as he wanted to go west to Rome (more than seven hundred miles) and on to Spain (more than two thousand miles), he had immediate business that would take him in exactly the opposite direction, about eight hundred miles east to Jerusalem.

Jerusalem, the immediate goal

In verse 25 Paul tells the Romans that even though he is anxious to come see them, he must first go to Jerusalem. In verse 26 we find out why. Paul has been collecting money from the Christian believers in Macedonia and Achaia (Corinth was in Achaia) for the poor among the believers in Jerusalem. Obviously, this collection had to be very important for it to take Paul so far in the opposite direction of his hopes and dreams. We can only understand the collection's importance when we understand both its history and the theological significance it held for Paul.

In Galatians 2 Paul tells us of a meeting that he had with the apostles and leaders of the church in Jerusalem almost a decade before he wrote Romans. At stake was the issue of accepting Gentiles into the church without circumcision, a vital issue for Paul as the apostle to the Gentiles. At the conference, Paul's ministry to the Gentiles was affirmed. Luke's account of the same meeting in Acts 15 affirms this basic point and reports other matters, such as the "apostolic decree," which Paul doesn't mention. But there is one issue Paul mentions that Luke omits. Paul says that the leaders asked him to remember the poor (in Jerusalem), which he was eager to do (Gal. 2:10). Thus he had taken on this task as part of the agreement about the legitimacy of his ministry to the Gentiles that was so crucial to his life and identity. He even devoted two chapters of 2 Corinthians (8, 9) to this collection for the poor in Jerusalem.

This collection not only had historical significance for Paul, however; it also had a serious theological meaning, which Paul explains in 15:27 when he says that the believers in Macedonia and Achaia were pleased to give to the collection and indeed owed it to the poor in Jerusalem, "for if the Gentiles have shared in the Jews' spiritual blessings, they owe it to the Jews to share with them their material blessings." In other words, this financial gift from Gentile Christians to the Jewish Christians in Jerusalem was a symbol of the unity of Jew and Gentile in Christ. It was a tangible sign of the *all* that Paul emphasized again and again throughout Romans.

There were Christians in Jerusalem who were poor. The area around Jerusalem had suffered economically for decades. Yet the gospel had originated with them. On the other hand, some of the Gentile Christians throughout the Mediterranean world where Paul preached had means. By sharing their financial blessings with the poor Jewish Christians in appreciation for the spiritual blessing they had received from these same Christians, Gentile believers not only helped their brothers and sisters, but symbolized the unity between the two. Paul's whole Christian ministry had been devoted to the gospel that *all*, both Jew and Gentile, were embraced by the same good news of God's grace. Therefore, this collection was vital, so vital it would take him in the opposite direction of his hopes and dreams. It would take him to Jerusalem.

Yet as anxious as Paul was to take the collection to Jerusalem, the trip was not without its dangers and fears, and Paul shared these fears with the Romans.

Paul's Fears

Paul expressed his fears to the Roman believers in the form of a serious request for their prayers on his behalf in verse 31: "Pray that I may be rescued from the unbelievers in Judea and that my service in Jerusalem may be acceptable to the saints there." Both of these fears had to do with his trip to Jerusalem. He feared the unbelieving Jews in Jerusalem who opposed his ministry, and he even feared that the Jewish Christians in Jerusalem might not accept his gift, which symbolized their unity with the Gentile believers.

The unbelievers in Jerusalem

Unfortunately, Paul's first fear was well-founded. We read about it in Acts 21:17 and following. Luke tells us that Paul returned to Jerusalem as he planned to do. He was greeted by James, the Lord's brother, and all the elders in Jerusalem. They listened to the details of his ministry among the Gentiles and praised God, but, as is clear from Acts 21:20-22, they nevertheless considered Paul to be a problem, for they told him: "You see, brother, how many thousands of Jews have believed, and all of them are zealous for the law. They have been informed that you teach all the Jews who live among the Gentiles to turn away from Moses, telling them not to circumcise their children or live according to our customs. What shall we do?"

The leaders in Jerusalem decided that in order for Paul to prove his loyalty to Jewish customs, he should sponsor a seven-day ritualistic vow that some men were making in the temple area. Paul agreed (Acts 21:23, 24, 26). In order to understand what happened next, we need to understand something about the temple complex in Jerusalem in Paul's day.

Herod had rebuilt the Jewish temple into a spectacular sight. When we think of a temple, we usually think of a building, but the actual building on the temple site was only a small part of the gigantic complex. Only Jewish priests could approach the temple proper (remember that it was not a place of meeting but a place of sacrifice), but the complex as a whole was the center of community activity. (Look at the diagram of the temple area on page

1102 of the *SDA Bible Dictionary* if you have it available.) The inner court of the temple was a rectangle over five hundred feet long and about three hundred feet wide. It was divided into three parts. The western part was the court of the priests, which contained the temple building itself. As the name implies, only Jewish priests could enter this area. The middle part was the court of the men, which any Jewish man could enter. The eastern part was the court of the women, which all Jews could enter. Surrounding this inner court on the north, east, and south sides was a complex system of courtyards known as the court of the Gentiles. This area was open to all.

There were several entrances from the court of the Gentiles into the inner court, and at each was an inscription engraved in stone warning all Gentiles that they would be killed if they entered. Archaeologists have unearthed some of these stones. You can see a picture of one on page 1104 of the *SDA Bible Dictionary*. Finally, at the northwest corner of the court of the Gentiles was a Roman fortress called Antonia, where Roman guards kept watch over the activities of the temple.

According to Acts 21:27-36, when the seven days of the vow Paul sponsored were about over, some Jews from Asia falsely accused Paul of taking a Gentile co-worker named Trophimus into the inner court of the temple. An angry crowd seized Paul and tried to kill him, but Roman soldiers rescued him by arresting him. We cannot go into the details of Paul's arrest and imprisonment here, but you can read about it in the final seven chapters of Acts. Suffice it to say that from the moment of this arrest, Paul spent about the next five years of his life as a prisoner, two awaiting trial in Judea, where he appeared before Felix, Festus, and Agrippa and finally appealed to Rome; one year traveling to Rome; and two awaiting trial in Rome.

Paul's intermediate goal of reaching Rome was thus met, but not in the way he had planned. It took him over three years to get there, and he arrived as a prisoner. He probably never realized his dream to preach the gospel in Spain. Given the tensions against him in Jerusalem, the church leaders there put Paul on very dangerous ground when they suggested that he sponsor this vow in the temple. The results were devastating, although Acts shows how God continued to use Paul and how Paul continued in his faithfulness to God, even in the face of adversity that brought his fears, rather than his dream of Spain, to reality.

The acceptability of his gift

The second fear Paul asked the Roman believers to pray about was the fear that the saints in Jerusalem might not be willing to accept the gift he had collected from the Gentiles (15:31). Even earlier, when Paul wrote to the Corinthians, he expressed his desire to avoid criticism of the way he carried out the collection (2 Cor. 8:20). We don't know whether this fear came to reality or not. Our only biblical account of Paul's trip to Jerusalem is Luke's account in Acts, and Luke makes absolutely no mention of the collection. This seems like a strange omission, given the fact that it was Paul's purpose for going to Jerusalem and that it played such an important role in both his theology and his ministry. But Luke is silent, and we simply don't know what happened with the collection.

What we do know is that Paul sacrificed his own hopes and dreams to remain faithful to God and to do what he thought would further the cause of unity between Jew and Gentile. The message of God's grace for all wasn't just something Paul preached; it was something he lived. We see it clearly in the following statement Paul made to the believers in Ephesus when he was on his way from Corinth, where he had just written Romans, to Jerusalem:

> You know how I lived the whole time I was with you from the first day I came into the province of Asia. I served the Lord with great humility and with tears, although I was severely tested by the plots of the Jews. You know that I have not hesitated to preach anything that would be helpful to you but have taught you publicly and from house to house. I have declared to both Jews and Greeks that they must turn to God in repentance and have faith in our Lord Jesus.
>
> And now, compelled by the Spirit I am going to Jerusalem,

not knowing what will happen to me there. I only know that in every city the Holy Spirit warns me that prison and hardships are facing me. However, I consider my life worth nothing to me, if only I may finish the race and complete the task the Lord Jesus has given me—the task of testifying to the gospel of God's grace (Acts 20:17-24).

■ Applying the Word

Romans 15:14-33

1. What ministry has God given to me? Am I as committed to it as Paul was to his? Can I be as sure about my calling as Paul was about his?
2. What are my hopes and dreams, and what are my fears? Can I be confident that prayer will keep my fears from becoming reality? If not, what confidence can I have?
3. Is there a "Spain" in my life? If so, what is it? Does Paul's experience give me any help in handling my "Spain"?

■ Researching the Word

1. Study Paul's instruction to the Corinthians about the collection in 2 Corinthians 8 and 9. What principles about giving do you find?
2. Read Luke's account of the Jerusalem conference in Acts 15 and Paul's account in Galatians 2. What is the basic result of the conference that both accounts affirm? Why do you think the two accounts either add or omit other details?

■ Further Study of the Word

1. For a treatment of Paul's Gentile mission, see H. Weiss, *Paul of Tarsus*, 30-36.
2. For the story of Paul's trip to Jerusalem, see E. G. White, *The Acts of the Apostles*, 399-418.

CHAPTER NINETEEN

Real People

Romans 16:1-23

It has to be just a little hard to get excited about a long list of names. At first glance, Romans 16 might seem a little like reading the telephone directory. Although no one would try to argue that chapter 16 is the theological summit of this letter, it is interesting for at least two reasons. First, it tells us quite a bit about the early church. Second, it helps us grasp the reality of this letter by reminding us that it was a real letter written to real people. And some of these real people are intriguing. So let's take a look at this list of real people.

■ Getting Into the Word

Romans 16:1-23

Read verses 1 to 23 in at least two versions of the New Testament, and write your answers to the following questions in your Romans notebook.

1. What does Paul say about Phoebe? What do you think her role was? Why was Paul concerned about her?
2. List the names of people in Rome whom Paul greeted in verses 3 to 16. How much can you say about each one? Make a list of any whom you know from other parts of the Bible.
3. Why did Paul add the warning found in verses 17 to 20? What did he warn against?

4. List the names of people who were with Paul in Corinth when he wrote and whose greetings Paul sent to Rome. Use a Bible concordance to find out all you can about each one.
5. Make a list of all the information you can learn about the church at Rome from this chapter. Where did the Christians meet? What kind of people led out?
6. Notice the number of women included in this list and what is said about each one. What does this suggest about the role of women in ministry in the early church?

■ Exploring the Word

Was This Chapter Part of Paul's Original Letter?

As we saw in the Introduction, many scholars question whether Romans 16 was part of the letter Paul wrote to the Romans, although no one questions that Paul wrote it. There are various theories, but the most popular is that Paul sent a copy of his letter to Rome to the Ephesian church as well, and this list of greetings was attached to that copy. Those who argue for this position point to the number of names, twenty-six in all, and question whether Paul could have known so many people in a church he had never visited. They also point out that many of the names were commonly used for slaves or former slaves, and they doubt that these people would have been sufficiently mobile for Paul to have known them in the east and then for them to have moved to Rome. They look specifically at names like Priscilla and Aquila, who, according to Acts 18, Paul had last met in Corinth, and Epenetus, who was the first convert in Asia (perhaps Ephesus), and conclude that these people would probably not have been in Rome.

Another line of evidence has to do with the various early manuscripts of the New Testament. Although most of the early manuscripts look like our versions with 16:25-27 as the conclusion to the letter, there are some manuscripts that place this final benediction at the end of chapter 14 as well, and the very oldest we have places it at the end of chapter 15, suggesting that perhaps the letter ended there, although it does go on to include chapter 16 as well.

But none of this evidence is conclusive, and it is still most probable that Romans 16 was originally addressed to the Romans as the conclusion of this letter. The manuscript evidence proves nothing, and it is not at all difficult to suppose that Priscilla and Aquila would be in Rome when Paul wrote, since Acts 18:2 tells us that they were among those forced to leave Rome by Claudius's decree. It is altogether probable that they would have returned to Rome when Nero lifted the ban. And it certainly would have been to Paul's advantage to mention every contact he might have had in Rome. In addition, Paul himself is evidence of the mobility of the population in the first century. All of the evidence against this chapter being a part of Paul's original letter is speculative. We will avoid the speculation and assume that this chapter is addressed to Rome.

Paul Recommends Phoebe

The first two verses of the chapter contain Paul's recommendation on behalf of Phoebe. Since she was from Cenchrea, a suburb of Corinth, and Paul probably wrote Romans during his three-month stay there (see Acts 20:2, 3), she was likely the one who carried the letter to Rome. Paul wanted the Romans to accept her and give her hospitality.

Paul tells us some interesting things about Phoebe. First, he calls her a "servant" or "deacon" of the church at Cenchrea. Although the King James Version calls her a deaconess, the Greek word Paul uses has no feminine ending, so the translation "deaconess" is wrong. But there are two possible correct translations. In some cases, Paul uses this word for an office in the church, which is translated "deacon" (Phil. 1:1), but in other cases, it simply means "servant," as when he calls himself a servant of the new covenant (2 Cor. 3:6) or of the gospel (Col. 1:23). It is impossible to say for sure which meaning he intends here, although the words "of the church at Cenchrea" seem to suggest she was an actual church official or deacon.

Paul also says she had been a "great help" (NIV) to many people.

The word he used may suggest she was a patroness who offered financial support to many people. She was probably an influential woman of means who could not only carry this letter for Paul, but who would begin to make preparations for his expected arrival there.

Greetings to Those in Rome

Paul greets a total of twenty-six people in Rome. We know nothing about most of these people, but we do learn some interesting things about the church at Rome from some of them. We will comment on only a few of the names.

Priscilla and Aquila (vss. 3-5)

As we have seen from Acts 18, Paul met up with them in Corinth after they had been expelled from Rome. By the time Paul wrote Romans, some years had passed, and they had now returned to Rome. Paul calls them fellow workers. He also sends greetings to the church that met in their house. In the first century, Christians didn't have their own church buildings but usually met in homes. It was apparently only part of the Roman believers who met in their house. They must have been well-to-do in order to have a house big enough to be used for worship. A nice home might have held from fifty to seventy-five people. We have no idea how many Christians there were in Rome, but probably enough to necessitate meeting in several homes.

Paul says one thing about Priscilla and Aquila that might indicate that they, like himself, were Roman citizens. In verse 4 he says that they risked their "necks" for him. Since only Roman citizens were beheaded as punishment, Paul may have been speaking of the way they would have been punished as citizens. Of course, he could have simply used this as a figurative expression as well.

Andronicus and Junias (vs. 7)

These are the names of a male and female respectively, perhaps a married couple. Paul tells three interesting things abut them. They were his relatives, although Paul may have used this term figuratively. They had been in prison with Paul at some point in his ministry, but we don't know where. Finally, they had been apostles before Paul was an apostle. This is the only passage in the New Testament that speaks of a woman apostle, just as the first verse of the chapter is the only passage that speaks of a woman deacon. This chapter speaks loudly of the important role of women in the ministry of the early church. In addition to Phoebe, Priscilla, and Junias, whom we have already mentioned, Paul tells us that Mary worked very hard for the Romans (vs. 6) and that Tryphena, Tryphosa, and Persis worked hard in the Lord (vs. 12).

Those of the household of Aristobulus (vs. 10) and the household of Narcissus (vs. 11)

Paul is probably speaking of slaves and free servants who worked in the households of these two people. Aristobulus, a man, had a name that usually signified an aristocratic Jewish background. Narcissus was a woman's name often used by former slaves. Probably neither of these heads of households or estates were Christians, but a number of their slaves and former slaves were. Each of these groups probably made up a separate house church that met with the permission of their masters.

Rufus (vs. 13)

This name presents an intriguing possibility, although it involves a lot of speculation and must be seen only as a possibility. We find the name Rufus at another point in the New Testament. Mark 15:21, telling the story of Jesus' crucifixion, reads: "A certain man from Cyrene, Simon, the father of Alexander and Rufus, was passing by on his way from the country, and they forced him to carry the cross." Mark seems to write as if his readers would know who Rufus and Alexander were. Tradition has it that Mark's Gospel was written for Christians in Rome about a decade after Paul wrote his letter. Could it be that this Rufus, whose mother had been a mother to Paul, was the son of the man who carried Jesus' cross? It is an intriguing possibility.

The brothers (vs. 14) and saints (vs. 15) and those with them

In these two verses, Paul greets a list of people and then adds a reference to those "with them." Although we can't say for sure, it may be that in each case Paul is greeting the leaders of a house church and the words *with them* refer to the members of each group. If so, Paul may refer to as many as five different house churches meeting in Rome: One in Priscilla and Aquila's house, one each in the households of Narcissus and Aristobulus, and these two mentioned in verses 14 and 15 by the words *with them*. And there may have been even more separate groups meeting in various homes in Rome. We don't know how these separate house churches were organized, but they seem to have had sufficient contact with each other that Paul could address the Christians there as a whole.

Paul concludes these greetings to those in Rome with the command that they greet each other with a holy kiss. He does the same in 1 Corinthians 16:20. It is interesting that both of these letters treat problems that threatened Christian unity.

A Warning

Paul interrupts the flow of greetings in verses 17 to 20 to offer a warning for those who cause division and teach false doctrines. He makes it clear that he knows the Roman believers are obedient but simply wishes to make sure they are aware of the presence of false teachers and how they work. The command is accompanied by the promise that the God of peace will soon crush Satan under their feet.

Greetings From Those at Corinth

In verses 21 to 23, Paul sends greetings from those who are with him in Corinth. There are some interesting names here as well.

Timothy (vs. 21)

Timothy was one of Paul's closest associates and chief troubleshooters. He is listed as the coauthor of 2 Corinthians, Philippians, Colossians, 1 and 2 Thessalonians, and Philemon, and is, of course, the recipient of 1 and 2 Timothy. Paul sent him to Corinth when that church was divided (1 Cor. 4:17) and extolled Timothy's faithfulness in Philippians 2:19-22.

Lucius (vs. 21)

This is another form of the name Luke. It is impossible to know whether this is Luke, the author of Luke and Acts. But in Acts the section of the story where Paul travels from Corinth to Jerusalem (Acts 20, 21) is one of those where Luke used the first-person term *we*, suggesting that he may have been with Paul at the time.

Jason (vs. 21)

Acts 17:5-8 tells the story of a Jason in Thessalonica who welcomed Paul into his house and was persecuted as a result, but there is no way of knowing if this is the same Jason.

Tertius (vs. 22)

His name meant "third," which may indicate that he was born a slave. (Compare the name Quartus or "fourth" in the next verse.) Tertius was the scribe who actually wrote down this letter as Paul dictated it to him. This shows us that Paul didn't do the actual writing of his letter. Here Tertius adds his own greeting.

Gaius (vs. 23)

Acts 20:4 says that Paul was accompanied by Gaius when he set out for Jerusalem, and 1 Corinthians 1:14 informs us that Paul had baptized Gaius at Corinth.

Erastus (vs. 23)

The final name we will mention is one of special interest. Paul sends greetings from a man of some prominence, Corinth's director of public works. Archaeologists have discovered an inscription mentioning an Erastus who was director of streets in Corinth in the middle of the first century. This inscription states that he secured his position by constructing a street at his own expense. This almost certainly refers to the same person whose greetings Paul sent to Rome. (For a picture of the inscription, see the *SDA Bible Dictionary*, 338.)

Wouldn't it be interesting to know more about all these people whom Paul greeted in Rome, as well as those who were with Paul in Corinth? Even though we don't know much about most of them, they do remind us that Paul was writing to real people.

■ Applying the Word

Romans 16:1-23

1. If Paul were greeting the members of my congregation, what might he say about them? What might he say about me?
2. What would it be like for me to meet for church in someone's living room? Would there be advantages for me to worship in a house church? Would there be disadvantages? What are they?
3. Do I need to hear the warning Paul gives in 16:17-20? How do I correlate this warning with Paul's advice in 14:5 that each should be fully convinced in his or her own mind? How do I draw the line between those I should accept and those I should watch out for?

■ Researching the Word

Use a Bible concordance to look up all references to Timothy. How would you characterize Paul's special co-worker?

■ Further Study of the Word

1. For the argument that Romans 16 was not addressed to the Romans (but to the Ephesians), see T. W. Manson, "St. Paul's Letter to the Romans—and Others," in K. P. Donfried, ed., *The Romans Debate*, 3-15. For a recent, novel, and speculative view that Romans, 1 Corinthians, 2 Corinthians, and

Galatians in their present form were edited by Paul as a literary unit for friends in the Ephesian church, see D. Trobisch, *Paul's Letter Collection: Tracing the Origins*.

2. For the argument that Romans 16 was originally addressed to the Romans, see K. P. Donfried, "A Short Note on Romans 16," in K. P. Donfried, ed., *The Romans Debate*, 44-52.

3. For an additional argument that Romans 16 was addressed to the Romans, see excursus 15 in P. Stuhlmacher, *Paul's Letter to the Romans*, 244-246.

4. For a study of the names of Roman Christians in Romans 16 that reaches the conclusion that there were several different groups of Christians meeting separately at Rome, see P. Lampe, "The Roman Christians of Romans 16," in K. P. Donfried, ed., *The Romans Debate*, 216-230.

5. For a survey of the name Junia in 16:7 and the argument that it is feminine, see R. S. Cervin, "A Note Regarding the Name 'Junia(s)' in Romans 16:7."

CHAPTER TWENTY

The Obedience
of Faith

Romans 16:25-27

*By now we should have all guessed how Paul would end this letter. In it
Paul has proclaimed the gospel of God's grace. He has pointed his readers to
the life of living, loving sacrifice that is the appropriate response to God's
grace. He has revealed his hopes and fears. He has greeted the believers in
Rome and has passed along greetings to them from his co-workers in Corinth.
What is left to say?*

*There is only one way to end such a letter. It is the same way Paul ended
the theological message of the letter at the end of Romans 11. How could
the letter possibly end with anything but an expression of praise and glory
to God? Let's see what we can learn from this final doxology.*

■ Getting Into the Word

Romans 16:25-27

Instead of merely reading, why not memorize these final three
verses of Romans, and then use your Romans notebook to answer these questions.

1. Compare the last three verses of Romans with the first half
   of Romans 1. How many similarities can you list? What is
   the significance of these points of contact between the beginning and ending of Romans?
2. What does Paul mean when he uses the term *mystery* in

verse 25? What was the mystery? How was it revealed?
3. What were the prophetic writings Paul mentions in verse 26? How was the mystery made known through them?
4. When you have finished this chapter, either read or listen to (if you have an audio tape) the letter as a whole in one sitting again, and keep two pages of your Romans notebook with you. On one page, make notes of everything that surprises you or that you seem to hear in a new way. On the other page, make a note of every text or idea you want to keep in mind for your own future spiritual growth.

■ Exploring the Word

Glory to God

Many of the late manuscripts of the New Testament include a verse 24 in Romans 16 that says, "May the grace of our Lord Jesus Christ be with all of you, Amen." Although this is the kind of benediction Paul often includes at the end of his letters, it was probably a later scribe who added those words to Romans. Some have even wondered if verses 25 to 27 were part of Paul's original letter. We already saw that it is placed in different spots in the various manuscripts. But the close link between this concluding doxology and the beginning of Romans, and the fact that these words are always present in the manuscripts, even if in different places, make it unlikely that verses 25 to 27 were a later addition.

This concluding doxology, in typical Pauline fashion, is expanded to remind readers, yet once more, of Paul's purpose. Paul could have left out the entire middle section and simply said, "Now to him who is able to establish you by my gospel . . . to the only wise God be glory forever through Jesus Christ! Amen." But by now you should know Paul well enough to know he won't do what he could have done. He will take advantage of his last opportunity and within the ellipsis will add a final reminder of what his gospel is all about.

With this addition within the doxology, Paul brings us full circle, back to where he began the letter. In Romans 1:5, right at the beginning, Paul said that his task was "to call people from among all the Gentiles to the obedience that comes from faith." Paul uses almost the exact wording again in 16:26, although the NIV translators render them quite differently ("so that all the nations might believe and obey him"). Remember that *nation* and *Gentile* are the same word in Greek. In both passages Paul is speaking of Gentiles coming to obedience to God, obedience that is characterized by faith. Paul's whole letter is bracketed by this expression, which conveyed his goal. He ministered so that Gentiles might come to the obedience of faith.

He carried out this goal by proclaiming the gospel. That word that played such a prominent role in the first chapter of the letter occurs again here at the end. This "good news" is the "revelation" of a mystery that was hidden through the ages but was made known in Paul's day. In Greek a mystery was always a secret that hadn't been revealed rather than something inherently unfathomable. But in Jesus Christ, the secret was out. Paul began Romans by announcing that the righteousness and the wrath of God were being "revealed." He ends by proclaiming that the mystery has been "revealed."

Paul says the mystery was made known through the prophetic writings (vs. 26). Here again, we have a contact with the beginning of the book. In just the second verse of the letter, Paul spoke of "the gospel he promised beforehand through his prophets in the Holy Scriptures." At the beginning and at the end, Paul shows that the Scriptures, which were for him the Old Testament, played an important role in revealing the gospel. It is therefore quite understandable that every page of Romans includes both quotations from and allusions to the Old Testament.

This final reminder of the revelation of the mystery of the gospel comes like a parentheses inside a doxology giving glory to God. Paul begins this doxology in verse 25 by pointing to God as the one able to strengthen the Romans. He uses the same word he had used in 1:11 when he spoke of the mutual strengthening that would come when he visited Rome and enjoyed fellowship with his readers. But the ultimate strengthener is God. Paul gives the Romans the promise that God is able to strengthen them. Their future is in His hands. So what is left to do but give Him glory—"to the only wise God be glory forever through Jesus Christ! Amen." That is how the letter ends. How else could it end? How could we possibly respond to such a message but by giving glory to God with our words and lives!

Concluding Summary

It isn't easy to find a way to summarize a letter as rich and complex as Romans. Perhaps it might be helpful to review some of the contrasts Paul has made in the course of announcing the good news. Romans is a letter of contrasts. Paul seems to enjoy confronting us with contrasting images and metaphors. By reminding ourselves of a few of them, we might find a way to help us do a better job of remembering what he has said.

In the first chapter, Paul contrasted the revelation of God's righteousness with the revelation of God's wrath. Even though we have all sinned and deserve wrath, God breaks in with His righteousness to save everyone who believes, whether Jew or Gentile. In Romans 2 he contrasted hearers and doers of the law and reminded us that only the doers would be saved. The same chapter made a distinction between physical circumcision and circumcision of the heart. In chapter 3 he juxtaposed the method of works of law to attain righteousness with the righteousness that comes through faith.

Romans 5 offers us the vivid distinction between the death that came to all people through Adam and the life that comes through Jesus. An equally vivid metaphor in chapter 6 contrasts slavery to sin (which ends in death) with slavery to God (which ends in eternal life). In the seventh chapter, Paul differentiates the old way of the written code with the new way of the Spirit. Romans 8 is rich in metaphors of contrast. The condemnation of the law is distinguished from the "no condemnation" we find in Christ. Life in the flesh is contrasted with life in the Spirit. And in the same chapter, Paul shows the vast distance between the spirit of slavery and the spirit of sonship, or being an heir.

In chapter 12 Paul contrasts letting the world squeeze us into its mold with the transforming life of a living sacrifice. At the end of chapter 13, he differentiates between the deeds of darkness and the armor or weapons of light. Finally, Romans 14 and 15 contrast judging and scorning with loving acceptance.

So many contrasts. I'm sure you could come up with a lot more. What shall we make of all this? With each one of these contrasts, Paul confronts us with a choice. But he does more. He encourages us with the good news that God can strengthen us (16:25) and make us stand (14:4). The way of righteousness by faith, of freedom from wrath, of circumcision of the heart, of life in identity with Christ, of slavery to God, of life in the Spirit, of life with no condemnation, of life as an heir, of light, of accepting love that welcomes even those with whom we disagree, and of becoming transformed into a living sacrifice, pleasing to God, can be ours.

Continue to reflect on each of these metaphors, images, and promises, and renew your commitment to the way of Christ. God's grace is the freest of gifts. But we must accept the gift by responding in faith. And this gift is for every one of us. No one is excluded. Mercy for all! What good news! Every one of these metaphors lets us anticipate the consequences of accepting this good news. We envision a new relationship with God in which we experience Him as the loving Father He has always been, rather than the condemning judge we thought He was. We envision a new relationship with others in which we recognize every person as a brother or sister, rather than a threat or an enemy. But perhaps the best news of all is that through the Spirit these visions become reality. We find peace with God (5:1). We live, as far as possible, at peace with others (12:18). And this newness of life lifts our vision to an even greater eternal future and gives us hope. My prayer for each reader is simply Paul's prayer in Romans 15:13: "May the God of hope fill you with all joy and peace as you trust in him, so that you may overflow with hope by the power of the Holy Spirit."

■ Applying the Word

Romans 16:25-27

1. **Were I to make some final work of art to sum up my experience with Romans, and my experience with God through this letter, what would it be? (Give it a try.)**

2. If one of my friends or family members noticed that I had been studying Romans and that I was now finishing the last chapter, and asked, "What did you get out of your study?" what would I say?
3. Are there any tangible ways my life will be different because I have completed this study of Romans?

■ Researching the Word

1. A student once told me, "Once you've read one of Paul's letters, you've read them all. They're all the same." Pick one of Paul's other letters, read it, compare and contrast it with Romans, and decide whether my student was right or not. Include your comparisons, contrasts, and conclusions in your Romans notebook.
2. Read the concluding benedictions or doxologies in each of Paul's letters. How does the ending of Romans compare and contrast with the rest? Do you see any significance in your findings?

■ Further Study of the Word

1. For a rhetorical analysis of Romans, see R. Jewett, "Following the Argument of Romans," in K. P. Donfried, ed., *The Romans Debate*, 265-277.

NOTES

NOTES

NOTES

NOTES

NOTES

NOTES